Politics
& Structure

Essentials of American National Government
4th Edition

Politics & Structure

Essentials of American National Government
4th Edition

Thomas G. Ingersoll
U.S. Environmental Protection Agency

Robert E. O'Connor
The Pennsylvania State University

Brooks/Cole Publishing Company
Monterey, California

Brooks/Cole Publishing Company
A Division of Wadsworth, Inc.

©1986, 1983, 1979, 1975 by Wadsworth, Inc., Belmont, California 94002. All rights reserved. No part of this book may be reproduced, stored in a retrieval system, or transcribed, in any form or by any means—electronic, mechanical, photocopying, recording, or otherwise—without the prior written permission of the publisher, Brooks/Cole Publishing Company, Monterey, California 93940, a division of Wadsworth, Inc.

Printed in the United States of America
10 9 8 7 6 5 4 3 2 1

Library of Congress Cataloging-in-Publication Data

Ingersoll, Thomas G.
   Politics and structure.

   Rev. ed. of: Politics and structure / Robert E. O'Connor. 3rd ed. c1983.
   Includes bibliographies and index.
   1. United States—Politics and government.
I. O'Connor, Robert E., [date]   II. O'Connor, Robert E., [date]   Politics and structure.
III. Title.
JK274.I43   1985   320.973   85-20939
ISBN 0-534-05844-2

Sponsoring Editor: *Marie Kent*
Editorial Assistant: *Amy Mayfield*
Production Editor: *Michael G. Oates*
Manuscript Editor: *Betty Seaver*
Permissions Editor: *Mary Kay Hancharick*
Interior and Cover Design: *Sharon L. Kinghan*
Art Coordinators: *Judith Macdonald, Suzi Shepherd*
Interior Illustration: *John Foster, Cool, California*
Typesetting: *Instant Type, Monterey, California*
Cover Printing and Binding: *Malloy Lithographing, Inc., Ann Arbor, Michigan*

To Betty and Charley O'Connor and Ed and Jane Ingersoll. They taught us a long time ago the value of understanding, which we hope is reflected in this treatment of the politics and structure of the American national government.

Preface

Politics and Structure provides

- a description of how politics combines with the structures of government to produce public policy;
- an in-depth description of the four essential institutions—the Presidency, Congress, Federal Courts, and the Federal Bureaucracy;
- a demonstration of the interactions of the four institutions through a single case study—the multibillion dollar "Superfund" hazardous waste cleanup program;
- a case study, cross-referenced to the text, that illustrates for students by a specific example that the text's core material applies to how issues are resolved and policies made;
- marginal notations throughout to assist students in following main arguments and in review; and
- an authoritative reference with a complete index.

This book arose, more than a decade ago, with our dissatisfaction with the large, expensive hardbound texts. We found that our students shared this dissatisfaction (particularly with the expense). From a pedagogical angle, we each preferred to use one of the popular point-of-view texts or a series of topical paperbacks. New texts appeared every year, and we liked the idea of being able to use those that contained new insights or viewed the problems of American politics from challenging, indeed unorthodox, perspectives. When one discards the use of the large hardbound text, however, one also discards the treatment of the essentials of the operations of American political institutions. The point-of-view texts (and we are not faulting them for this) simply cannot give adequate coverage to the essential operating functions of government and remain relatively concise points of view.

We were dissatisfied as well with the few short paperback texts on the market that purported to give the student the "essentials" while trying to cover everything from the Constitutional Convention to political parties to civil/military relations. The result was very superficial treatment of the many topics covered. Finding no adequate description of this basic material to supplement our other assigned readings, we were forced to spend considerable lecture time simply presenting the essentials—time we (and our students) would have preferred to spend on more interesting topics and discussion. One afternoon, around a pitcher of beer, we discovered that others shared our conviction that a true "essentials" text was needed but unavailable. We determined then to undertake the first edition of the project you hold in your hands.

In the ensuing years, our colleagues around the country encouraged us to improve and expand our first effort and reinforced our perception that this text not only was helpful from a pedagogical standpoint but served as a useful reference tool as well for faculty and students alike. The detailed index, the marginal notations, and the use of a single case study throughout to demonstrate the otherwise "theoretical" treatment of American politics combined to produce a book that has proven to be consistent and yet flexible enough to be adapted to many different teaching styles. Even the order in which the chapters are placed—Presidency, Congress, the Courts, Bureaucracy—does not hinder this adaptability. Each chapter, while referencing the others, is designed to "stand on its own," and, therefore, can be assigned in any order (adaptive to the teaching style of the instructor).

The text provides a straightforward description of the operation of the four essential institutions of the American national government: the presidency, Congress, the courts, and the bureaucracy. Because of our awareness that the policy decisions made in Washington affect the lives of all of us, we feel that it is important that all of us understand *how* these decisions are made. Gaining such an understanding entails learning about two interrelated elements of the American national government: politics and structure—neither of which can be understood in isolation.

Our national institutions cannot be understood apart from the *political* context in which they exist and have their purpose. These institutions are more than mere organization charts and lists of authority. They are an intricate network of interconnected bargaining points in the political process, and the personnel who staff these institutions act "politically." Therefore, we have sought to describe the *politics* of the institutional structures under consideration—the personal interactions, the human elements, the personal and organizational influences, and the leadership potentials involved in the actual operation of those otherwise "static" structures. We continually emphasize that none of these structures operates in a vacuum, and we accordingly have attempted to delineate the milieu in which they actually function—the decidedly political atmosphere in which decisions are made.

Because of the nature of our original assumption—that political decisions affect our lives—we have adopted a political-policy criterion of selection by which policy-relevant elements have been included in the text and others have been omitted. This criterion arises from our understanding that politics is, in essence, about public policy—the choice of one policy instead of others. It is our judgment that certain elements have a bearing on the nature of policy, and we have attempted to delineate those elements within the scope of the American national government.

In keeping with our original intent to produce a "corollary" text—one that could be used with virtually any instructor's selection of point-of-view texts or annotated collection of readings—we have consistently resisted the temptation to expand the book by adding chapters on additional topics in American national government. Our intransigence in this regard is not meant to imply that these other topics are unimportant—quite the contrary. We do not deal, for example, with levels of government other than the national level; nor do we treat the crucial element of federalism—the complex set of relationships between the national level and state and local levels of government. Our reason for noninclusion is twofold. In the first place, each instructor of American politics chooses different subjects to cover beyond the essentials. Even instructors who agree on what should be covered treat those subjects in quite different ways. Indeed, the decision to adopt a particular point-of-view text is influenced by both the selection of subjects and how they are treated. It would have been inconsistent with the purpose of *Politics and Structure* if we had selected topics beyond the generally agreed-upon essentials and then provided our own point of view on those topics.

The second reason for our refusal to further expand the topical coverage of this book rests with our original intent in writing it: we wanted to offer a basis for a thorough appreciation of the American national government, which is the first step toward an understanding of these other topics. By presenting here the essential features of the national governmental structure, it is our hope that students will be better able to understand the context in which policies are formulated and executed at the national level. Such an understanding ultimately entails the realization that (1) similar influences operate at other governmental levels and (2) each level, in turn, influences the others. Thus, *Politics and Structure* is the prelude, rather than the conclusion, to related topics such as American federalism.

In order to emphasize the interrelatedness of political reality, we have chosen to demonstrate politics and structure with a single case study, presented in four sections, as a conclusion to each chapter. Because of the importance of the hazardous waste disposal problem in the United States in the 1980s, we have selected a new case for this edition: the Comprehensive Environmental Response, Compensation, and Liability Act of 1980 (popularly known as the Superfund Law). We use this case to demonstrate the pervasive nature of politics and to delineate the separate structures within which politics operates. All too often, authors of introductory texts illustrate their points with a variety of case studies. This method ignores the opportunity for integrating material that the single-topic case study provides. We hope that by employing the Superfund Law as a means of illustrating the activities of the presidency, Congress, the courts, and the bureaucracy, we have offered our readers the opportunity to better understand the interactions of those four institutions. To assist the student in relating the case study to the substantive material, we have also included marginal references to those pages in the text in which the relevant powers or interactions are discussed in detail.

Finally, a few personal notes. This book is truly a shared endeavor in every sense. The order of our names on the cover is not meant to imply that a disproportionate portion of credit (or blame) for the book should go to either author. We have, in fact, reversed that order with each edition just to emphasize the shared nature of our responsibilities—not to confuse Library of Congress catalogers.

We remain, of course, deeply indebted to many people who assisted us in this and earlier editions. Particularly helpful were the reviews of Justin Green, Virginia Polytechnic Institute and State University; James Knauer, Lock Haven University; Robert Locander, North Harris County College; Gary London, Everett Community College; and Bradley Rice, Clayton Junior College.

We benefited from the editorship of Marie Kent and the sharp copy editing of Betty Seaver. Student assistant Lisa Rowley resourcefully provided accurate documentation of obscure or questionable information. Bob appreciates the warm support of—in alphabetical order—Mon Petit Baby, Molly MaGuire, and Janice Hensyl O'Connor. Tom continues to be grateful for all that Barbara has done. Yet, with all of this assistance, all errors and weaknesses that remain in the book are solely our own.

Thomas G. Ingersoll
Robert E. O'Connor

Contents

1 The Presidency 1

Constitutional Prerogatives 1
Presidential Leadership 16
Electoral Procedures 23
Term of Office and Succession 28
The Institutionalized Presidency 34
Conclusion 43
Selected Additional Readings 44
Case History: "Superfund" 1980, 1985 45
    Part I: The President 45

2 The Congress 51

Constitutional Prerogatives 51
Congressional Leadership 57
Electoral Procedures 62
Senators and Representatives 64
The Leaders of Congress 67
Congressional Committees 77
How a Bill Becomes a Law 84
The Budgetary Process 90
Conclusion 93
Selected Additional Readings 94
Case History: "Superfund" 1980, 1985 94
    Part II: The Congress 94

3 The Federal Judiciary — 105

Constitutional Prerogatives   105
Judicial Leadership   111
Judicial Activism versus Judicial Restraint   119
Judicial Recruitment   122
The Judges   124
The Operation of the Court System   130
Conclusion   134
Selected Additional Readings   134
Case History: "Superfund" 1980, 1985   135
    Part III: The Courts   135

4 The Federal Bureaucracy — 142

Characteristics of Bureaucratization   142
The Organization of the Federal Bureaucracy   143
The Bureaucrats   159
Leadership and Limitations   163
Conclusion   170
Selected Additional Readings   171
Case History: "Superfund" 1980, 1985   172
    Part IV: The Bureaucracy   172

The Constitution of the United States — 179

Index — 191

Politics & Structure

Essentials of American National Government

4th Edition

Chapter 1

The Presidency

The Constitutional Convention of 1787 created political institutions that have evolved so dramatically that there is little current resemblance to the institutions as they existed in the 1790s. For example, the early presidents scheduled a weekly open house in the White House; today, citizens touring the White House very rarely even glimpse a government official. The early Congresses met for only a couple of months; today, Congress is almost constantly in session. And in 1802 the federal bureaucracy numbered only 2,875 nonmilitary employees; at last count just under three million nonmilitary employees received paychecks from the national government. However, all three institutions—the presidency, Congress, and the bureaucracy—have evolved within a framework of stability provided by the Constitution.

Article II, Section 1 of the Constitution reads the same today as it did in 1789; it simply states that "the executive Power shall be vested in a President of the United States." What has changed since 1789 is not the Constitution but accepted definitions of what Article II, Section 1 entails as proper presidential behavior. For nearly 200 years lawyers, justices, members of Congress, presidents, journalists, and ordinary citizens have debated the nature and extent of the "executive power" granted in that short sentence. Similarly, the thirteen other powers granted to the President in Article II have been discussed, often heatedly, as presidents have attempted to act in the "best interest" of their country. Thus, the prerogatives provided to the president by the Constitution are a logical starting point for a description of the modern presidency.

Constitutional Prerogatives

The president's constitutional prerogatives can be conveniently grouped under five presidential roles: commander in chief of the armed forces, director of foreign relations, executor of the nation's laws, administrator of domestic affairs, and head of state (table 1-1).

The President as Commander in Chief

The president's power as head of the armed forces. Article II, Section 2 of the Constitution declares that the president "shall be Commander in Chief

Table 1-1
The President: Constitutional Prerogatives and Powers

1. Commander in Chief
 	
    Power as head of armed forces (Art. II, Sec. 2)
 	
2. Director of U.S. Foreign Relations
 	
    Power to negotiate treaties and executive agreements (Art. II, Sec. 2)
 	
    Power to nominate ambassadors (Art. II, Sec. 2)
 	
    Power to receive ambassadors (Art. II, Sec. 3)
 	
3. Chief Executor
 	
    Power to execute the nation's laws (Art. II, Sec. 3)
	4. Administrator of Domestic Affairs
	
	    Power to convene and adjourn Congress (Art. II, Sec. 3)
	
	    Power to address Congress on the state of the Union (Art. II, Sec. 3)
	
	    Power to recommend legislation (Art. II, Sec. 3)
	
	    Power to veto legislation (Art. 1, Sec. 7)
	
	    Power to nominate judges (Art. II, Sec. 2)
	
	    Power to command the executive branch (Art. II, Sec. 2)
	
	    Power to appoint top administrators (Art. II, Sec. 2)
	
	5. Head of State
	
	    Power to grant reprieves and pardons (Art. II, Sec. 2)
	
	    Power to commission officers (Art. II, Sec. 3)

of the Army and Navy of the United States, and of the Militia of the several States, when called into the actual service of the United States." The Constitution makes no attempt to define his duties as commander in chief or to establish any sort of guidelines. Ordinarily presidents have delegated their authority in this area to career military officials while retaining the ultimate responsibility for all military actions to ensure civilian control over the military. There are no constitutional provisions, however, that require a president to delegate this or any other executive authority. For example, George Washington personally commanded the forces that crushed the Whiskey Rebellion in 1794.

The president is not required to delegate any of his powers. He may exercise them himself, even when he has no previous experience.

Succeeding presidents, some with little or no previous military experience, have assumed the role of ultimate military strategist, in addition to peforming their function of assuring civilian control over the military. During the war between the states, for example, Lincoln, who had no previous military experience at all, often visited the Army of the Potomac to instruct the generals on military strategy. Similarly, Jimmy Carter, whose experience had been in the U.S. Navy, took personal command of the ill-fated attempt to rescue the American hostages in Iran in 1980.

As this power has evolved, the president can never forget the enormity of the responsibility entailed. He is constantly shadowed by a military aide who carries the "black box" that contains the cryptographic orders the president would have to issue to initiate a nuclear attack. Although U.S. nuclear-strike capability has been used only once (during World War II), the threat of its use was made by Dwight D. Eisenhower in 1953 and by John F. Kennedy in 1962.

The undefined constitutional provision for presidential authority in the area of military affairs has placed few limitations on presidents. In contrast, the constitutional provision for congressional authority in this area is quite specific. Congress has constitutional authority to tax for the common defense, declare war, make rules concerning capture on land and water, raise and support armies, provide and maintain a navy, make rules governing the armed forces, and call out the state militia and provide for its training and discipline. Congress cannot send an army anywhere, however, and its decision *not* to declare war has not inhibited presidents from engaging U.S. troops in armed conflicts.

> *Presidential authority in military affairs is less specific, and therefore broader, than congressional powers.*

Extensions and limitations of commander-in-chief powers.

By using his power as commander in chief, the president is able to authorize the mobilization and use of United States forces anywhere in the world. Although only Congress can declare war and has done so five times—the War of 1812 against Britain, the Mexican War, the Spanish-American War, and the two world wars—the president has always requested such declarations. In the absence of such a request, presidents have initiated military conflicts on more occasions than those authorized by Congress. For instance, no declaration of war accompanied United States involvement in the naval war with France (1798–1800), the first and second Barbary wars (1801–1805 and 1815), the Mexican-American disputes (1914–1917), the Korean War (1949–1953), or the Indochina War (1960–1973).

> *Caution must be exercised in "interpreting" the meaning of constitutionally granted powers because their scope has changed considerably over time.*

The Founding Fathers did not intend that the power to wage war should reside with the president, but the evolution of the meaning ascribed to the term *commander in chief* has resulted in this acquired constitutional power. This is a particularly good example of the caution one must exercise in attempting to interpret phrases of the Constitution. The title *commander in chief* was initially intended to confer upon the president the authority to act as the military commander in the event of an internal insurrection or a congressionally declared war with a foreign power. Over the past 200 years, however, *commander in chief* has come to mean that the president of the United States can order troops into combat in any area of the world. This is far from the original intent of the Constitutional Convention, and it underscores the point that in order to understand the manner in which any political system operates, we must look beyond the title of public officials to the meaning those titles have acquired over the years. The British monarch, for example, is also the

> *Although the declaration of war is a congressional prerogative, the president may dispatch troops anywhere in the world without the consent of Congress.*

commander in chief of the United Kingdom's armed forces, but the queen holds that title for ceremonial reasons only—it carries with it no actual military power. Clearly, it would be unwarranted to apply a uniform meaning of the term *commander in chief* to the British monarch and the American president. The title may be employed in both political systems, but the powers it confers are dramatically different.

We do not mean to imply that the president's power as commander in chief is unlimited. Although he certainly has the power to commit troops to combat anywhere in the world, his actions are more likely to go unchallenged if the conflict is over quickly. No one challenged Ronald Reagan's authority to send troops into Granada in 1983, for example, but that military excursion was clearly of limited duration. If the conflict to which troops are committed promises to become prolonged, the political tenor of the times influences the extent to which Congress tolerates the use of military power. In 1973, after the unpopular Indochina War, Congress passed the War Powers Act, which forbade the president to commit troops for an extended period without congressional consent. This accounted for Reagan's close consultation with Congress when he committed troops to Lebanon in 1983; he acted only after passage of a joint resolution by Congress permitting commitment of troops for no more than eighteen months.

The extent to which Congress scrutinizes presidential actions in the area of military affairs often varies, even within a single presidential term of office. In 1981, for example, Congress offered little resistance to President Reagan's plans for massive increases in military spending. The takeover of the U.S. embassy in Iran combined with Soviet interference in Afghanistan and Poland produced both popular and congressional support for an enormous military buildup. By 1985, the pendulum had swung back and Congress treated Reagan's requests for additional military spending with skepticism and, in some cases, outright rejection.

The President as Director of U.S. Foreign Relations

A second crucial area of presidential authority relates to foreign policy. The Constitution gives the president three specific powers in this area: (1) "He shall have Power, by and with the Advice and Consent of the Senate, to make Treaties, provided two-thirds of the Senators present concur"; (2) "he shall nominate, and by and with the Advice and Consent of the Senate, shall appoint Ambassadors, other public Ministers and Consuls"; and (3) "he shall receive Ambassadors and other public Ministers." As with his power as commander in chief, the importance of this area of his authority rests *not* with the specificity of the grant but rather with its evolution, by which the president has become the nation's principal spokesman in foreign affairs. George Washington set the tone for this evolution of power as early as 1793, when, in the face of heated congressional and popular criticism, he declared American neutrality during a war between France and England.

The president speaks for the nation in foreign affairs.

The Presidency

Power to negotiate treaties and executive agreements. Although the Constitution requires senatorial consent to treaties, the initiative in treaty making is the president's. Only the president or his representatives are entitled by law to negotiate with other nations. The president decides the kinds of treaties he wants to negotiate.

Once approved by the Senate and ratified by the president, treaties have the force of law. If a treaty conflicts with a state law, the latter is null and void; if the conflict is with a federal law, whichever was enacted or ratified last prevails.

Treaties have the force of law, even overriding previously passed legislation.

The Senate's deference to presidential initiative in foreign affairs is suggested by the Senate's having rejected only about 1 percent of all treaties proposed. Another 15 percent have been conditioned or passed with specific reservations, and the rest have been consented to without alteration. The most notable exception to this generalization was the Senate's refusal in 1920 to follow Woodrow Wilson's lead by its rejection of the Treaty of Versailles and U.S. participation in the League of Nations. With this in mind, Franklin D. Roosevelt was careful to include key members of the Senate Foreign Relations Committee in crucial negotiations during World War II. The inclusion of senators in those negotiations was not dictated by constitutional or legal necessity but by political wisdom. Although Presidents Nixon, Ford, and Carter did not directly involve senators in the negotiations concerning the Panama Canal, all three kept key senators well informed and sought their advice to ensure future Senate approval. When Reagan sent negotiators to Geneva in March 1985 to resume arms control talks with the Soviet Union, an official delegation from both houses of Congress accompanied them. Again, the president is not required to involve Congress in this manner, but political expediency indicates that its inclusion early in the process makes Congress more receptive to the outcomes of negotiations.

Presidents keep the Senate informed of important treaty negotiations to build support for approval.

Congressional-executive international agreements. In addition to formal treaties, the United States has entered into numerous compacts with foreign governments that have never been presented to the Senate for ratification. Known popularly as *executive agreements,* these compacts are referred to by the State Department as *international agreements other than treaties* and are really of two distinct types. The first type, which is known as a *congressional-executive international agreement,* concerns matters over which Congress has been granted specific powers by the Constitution. An example of such powers, which will be discussed in chapter 2, is Congress's constitutional responsibility "to regulate Commerce with foreign Nations" (Article I, Section 8). As a result of this constitutional stipulation, any matter dealing with the regulation of foreign trade falls under the power of Congress, not the president. However, the power to *negotiate* with foreign nations lies with the president alone. Therefore, in matters of trade with foreign governments, both the president and Congress have constitutional powers, and

Congressional-executive international agreements require the approval of Congress as well as the president.

agreements dealing with such matters constitute congressional-executive international agreements.

A specific grant of power to Congress by the Constitution is the basis of congressional involvement in these agreements.

Such agreements must be ratified by a simple majority vote of *both* houses of Congress, even though this ratification may sometimes precede the actual negotiation. In 1934, for example, Congress gave advance ratification when it passed the Reciprocal Trade Agreements Act, which *authorized* the president to conclude certain types of trade agreements with foreign nations. Under this act, presidents have negotiated many such agreements, which have the same force of law as treaties. It is also possible, of course, to invert the procedure, so that the president negotiates first and then presents the agreement to Congress for its ratification. Such was the case with the congressional-executive international agreements by which Texas (in 1845) and Hawaii (in 1889) were annexed to the Union. The case of the annexation of Texas is interesting because it illustrates that a president may use the congressional-executive international agreement as a means of avoiding the two-thirds vote of the Senate that would be necessary to ratify a treaty. During the presidency of John Tyler, the United States negotiated a treaty with Texas for its annexation as a state, but the Senate, on January 8, 1844, refused to ratify the treaty by the necessary two-thirds vote. Yet, barely one year later, when President James Polk presented the annexation of Texas to both houses as a congressional-executive international agreement (requiring only a simple majority vote in each house), it was approved in the Senate by a vote of twenty-seven to twenty-five. By presenting the proposal in this way, Polk accomplished what Tyler had been unable to do.

Congressional-executive international agreements are "easier" to move through Congress because they do not require a two-thirds majority in the Senate.

The decision to present a proposed agreement as a treaty (thereby requiring two-thirds consent of the Senate) or as a congressional-executive international agreement (necessitating only majority concurrence in each house) is, with one exception, merely a matter of political receptivity and is determined by the number of votes the president expects to have in the Senate.

Treaties may cover matters that are reserved to the states by the Constitution; international agreements other than treaties may not.

The one exception to this general rule is that certain matters can be dealt with *only* by treaty. The Tenth Amendment stipulates that powers that have not been granted by the Constitution to the federal government are "reserved to the States respectively or to the people." Under this amendment, certain matters (although none is specifically mentioned) are not within the jurisdiction of the federal government. If a proposed compact with a foreign government includes such matters, the act of ratifying the compact as a congressional-executive international agreement would be unconstitutional because neither the president nor Congress has been granted constitutional authority in those matters. The same proposed compact could be ratified, however, as a treaty, because the treaty power has been specifically granted, without limitations of any kind, by Article II, Section 2 of the Constitution. For example, the very first treaty negotiated by the United States after ratification of the Constitution (the Jay Treaty of 1794 with Great Britain) contained provisions that dealt with the ownership of private property by

British subjects in the United States, even though the Constitution does not give either Congress or the president the power to deal with matters of private property. This agreement with Great Britain was presented to the Senate and was ratified as a treaty with the necessary two-thirds vote. It could not have been presented to both houses for a simple majority vote because although treaties may deal with matters that are reserved to the states, congressional-executive international agreements may not (table 1-2). Thus, any matter that might be handled as a congressional-executive international agreement could also be handled as a treaty, but the opposite is not true.

"Pure" executive agreements. We noted that there are two types of international agreements other than treaties, and the second of these is known as the *pure "executive* (or presidential) *agreement*. Whereas the congressional-executive international agreement relies on powers granted to both Congress and the president, the pure executive agreement stems from constitutional powers that have been granted solely to the president. We have seen, for example, that the president is the commander in chief of the armed forces. In his role as commander in chief he may, therefore, negotiate with foreign governments on military matters without submitting the results of these negotiations to Congress for ratification. It was a pure executive agreement that ended both world wars, even though Congress had declared those wars. The president, in these instances, was acting as commander in chief, and Congress was powerless to intervene.

Executive agreements rely for their authority on powers granted exclusively to the president.

Table 1-2
Differences between Treaties and International Agreements Other Than Treaties

| Treaties | International Agreements Other Than Treaties ||
	Congressional-Executive International Agreements	"Pure" or True Executive Agreements
Specified in the Constitution (Art. II, Sec. 2)	Not specified in the Constitution but based on congressional and presidential powers	Not specified in the Constitution but based on presidential powers
Two-thirds Senate approval required	Simple majority vote of each house required	No congressional action required
Binding on succeeding presidents	Binding on succeeding presidents	Not binding on succeeding presidents
May include matters reserved to the states	May not include matters reserved to the states	May not include matters reserved to the states
May include congressional, presidential, and judicial prerogatives	May include congressional and presidential prerogatives	May include only presidential prerogatives
Used extensively before 1900	Used extensively since 1900	Used extensively since 1900

Executive agreements are another example of the evolution of presidential powers, but Congress has acted to eliminate the secrecy that often shrouded these agreements in the past.

In recent years presidents have increasingly relied on these pure, or "true," executive agreements in the realm of foreign policy (table 1-3). Although not specifically granted by the Constitution, presidential authority to conclude such agreements has been upheld by the Supreme Court as a "modest implied power" deriving from the president's authority to conduct the nation's foreign relations. As a result, hundreds of such agreements are now negotiated each year by executive-branch officials acting in the president's name and under his authority, and none of these agreements has to be approved by Congress. Congress has, however, attempted to curb the president's powers in this area. In 1972 it passed legislation requiring the secretary of state to submit to Congress within sixty days the final text of any pure executive agreements negotiated by the administration. The purpose of the law is to assure that Congress has knowledge of the content of these agreements. In 1974 Congress tried to go even further. A bill was passed by the Senate that would have permitted Congress to veto any such agreement within sixty days by a majority vote of both houses. The House of Representatives refused to follow the Senate's lead, thereby leaving the president's powers unaffected.

Power to appoint ambassadors. Even less disputed by Congress has been the president's prerogative to nominate ambassadors. The more popular ambassadorial posts often go to wealthy campaign contributors whose experience in diplomacy is nonexistent, but the Senate usually concurs with the president's wishes. There was a trend toward using more Foreign Service officers as ambassadors, but the Reagan administration halted this trend. President Jimmy Carter appointed a committee of distinguished leaders to identify for him the best-qualified individual for each position. The committee was to consider "campaign activities" only if two candidates were equally qualified. When Reagan replaced Carter in the White House, wealthy campaign contributors were again relied on to form the pool from which ambassadorial nominees were selected. Although half of Reagan's nominees have been

The more popular ambassadorial nominations often go to wealthy campaign contributors who have little or no experience in diplomacy.

Table 1-3
Number of Treaties and International Agreements Other Than Treaties Negotiated by the United States (1789-1984)

Period	Treaties	International Agreements Other Than Treaties
1789-1839	60	27
1840-1889	215	238
1890-1939	524	917
1940-1984	554	9,987

Source: U.S. Department of State.

Foreign Service officers, they have generally been excluded from ambassadorial posts in the more significant nations.

Power to receive ambassadors. The president's power to receive ambassadors carries the implied authority to recognize or refuse to recognize foreign governments, and this implied authority rests with the president alone. Historically, the president received an ambassador if that ambassador's government had de facto (actual) control over the territory that it claimed to govern. This criterion was being applied to all governments in the late eighteenth century when the Constitution was drafted.

American presidents have used this authority (as have other heads of state) as a political tool in the conduct of foreign policy. For example, the USSR was not recognized until November 1933, although the Soviet government had been in power for more than sixteen years. From the end of World War II through 1978, the United States withheld recognition of China. The process of normalizing relations with that country included its "partial recognition," beginning with Richard Nixon's 1972 trip to China. From then until January 1, 1979, the United States exchanged cultural programs, diplomatic missions, and even Ping-Pong teams—but not ambassadors. Only with the exchange of ambassadors does one country "officially recognize" the existence of the other. At this writing, the United States is withholding official recognition of Cuba, Vietnam, and Iran. The decision to recognize any one of these countries by receiving its ambassador has become completely political. It rests with the president alone, and neither Congress nor the courts can legally force or forestall his decision.

Of course, as a part of his power to receive ambassadors, the president also has the authority to demand their recall as well as the recall of other diplomatic personnel. In recent years diplomats have been expelled primarily for suspected espionage activities. When a country expels a diplomat, the "offended" nation often retaliates by expelling one of the first country's diplomats.

The President as Chief Executor

Power to execute the nation's laws. The president's constitutional power and duty to "take Care that the Laws be faithfully executed" provides a convenient link between the president's powers in foreign and domestic affairs. This clause provides the president with authority to carry out congressional legislation—that is, because there are no constitutional provisions permitting Congress to enforce its own legislation, Congress must rely on presidential action. The president, therefore, has tremendous latitude to decide how vigorously he will enforce a law.

Presidents have always expressed their intention to enforce all the laws—

Presidents used to recognize the ambassador sent by whichever faction actually controlled the territory.

Today, the power to receive ambassadors is a political tool used by presidents to grant or withhold official recognition of other governments.

"Partial recognition" has been applied during the process of "normalizing relations" with another country—another evolution of presidential powers.

Congress has no authority to enforce its legislation; it must rely on the president to enforce any law it passes.

to "take care that the laws be faithfully executed." In reality, however, all presidents emphasize certain laws and almost ignore others. The strong antipollution laws passed by Congress at the turn of the century are a case in point. It has been illegal to dump industrial waste into the nation's rivers and streams for over seventy years, but the law has been enforced only sporadically and selectively.

Laws may be selectively and sporadically enforced by the president.

One kind of law that presidents generally execute involves the expenditure of funds appropriated by Congress. Yet, at least since the time of Thomas Jefferson, presidents have withheld, or "impounded," funds from programs or projects authorized by Congress. These impoundments have occurred primarily for two reasons: the president wished to promote efficient management, or he had statutory or constitutional authority to withhold money. In 1803, for example, Jefferson impounded $50,000 that had been appropriated by Congress for the purchase of gunboats to be used on the Mississippi River as a protection against the French. After Congress had appropriated the money, however, Jefferson completed negotiations for purchase of the Louisiana Territory; this removed the French from the river, and eliminated the immediate necessity for gunboats. Within a year, however, when gunboats of improved design were available, Jefferson released the funds. He had, therefore, impounded appropriate money in the interest of more efficient management and ultimately expended the money for the purpose that Congress had intended. In this case, Jefferson withheld money on his own initiative, but a president might also act with statutory direction. Congress may direct the president to impound funds by passing legislation that imposes spending ceilings or unspecified budget cuts. Thus, in 1950 Congress passed an "omnibus" appropriations bill ordering President Harry Truman to cut the budget by not less than $550 million "without impairing national defense," whereupon Truman impounded $572 million of nonmilitary funds.

Presidents have usually impounded funds in order to promote efficient management of programs or in response to congressional directives.

Presidents have also impounded funds in order to eliminate programs for which Congress has appropriated money but with which the president was not pleased. This has been applied especially to domestic programs—often to programs that enjoyed considerable congressional support. To counter this type of impoundment, Congress passed the Budget Impoundment and Control Act of 1974 to require the president to report all impoundments to Congress. However, the act was so ambiguously worded that the administration was able to interpret it as legislative permission to impound, at least to a limited extent. In general, since passage of the act in 1974, presidents have deferred expenditures but have eventually been willing to spend whatever Congress has appropriated with little argument that permanent impoundment is a presidential privilege.

Funds have been impounded as a means of penalizing programs with which the president disagrees.

Chief executor, commander in chief, and foreign relations roles combined. The president's power to execute laws, his primacy in the conduct of the nation's foreign relations, and his role as commander in chief of the nation's armed forces have, in concert, contributed to the evolution of presidential power. One stage of this evolution occurred during the outset of the Civil War with Lincoln's reliance on the constitutional mandate that the president faithfully execute the nation's laws. Within ten weeks after the firing on Fort Sumter, he had spent $2 million not appropriated by Congress, called out the militia, ordered a naval blockade of the Southern ports, seized rail and telegraph lines leading to the capital, and suspended the writ of habeas corpus (the power of a court to release individuals held by the police). Lincoln later defended his actions by claiming: "I felt that measures otherwise unconstitutional might become lawful by becoming indispensable to the preservation of the Constitution through the preservation of the nation. Right or wrong, I assumed this ground and I now avow it." In most instances the courts either avoided the constitutional issues or upheld Lincoln's actions. Lincoln had combined his constitutional prerogatives to justify his unprecedented actions.

> *Presidents have combined specific constitutional prerogatives so that the whole of their powers is greater than the sum of the individual powers.*

Many other presidents have managed to increase presidential power through the constant expansion and evolution of their constitutional prerogatives as commander in chief, foreign policy maker, and executor of the laws. Ironically, it is often acts of Congress that permit the president to expand his power at the expense of Congress. For example, during World War I, Congress granted President Woodrow Wilson the extraordinary combination of powers to conscript an army, license international trade, censor all communications with foreign countries, control enemy aliens within the country, and seize and operate the nation's water and rail transportation facilities as well as its telephone and telegraph systems.

During World War II, Franklin D. Roosevelt controlled the national economy by a systematic process of price and rent controls, federal rationing, plant and shipyard seizures, and material allocations. (Only some of these powers ever received congressional approval.) The most extreme application of his wartime powers came in Executive Order No. 9066 of February 19, 1942, under which approximately 112,000 Japanese Americans were removed from their homes in the "military areas" of the West Coast (Washington, California, Oregon, and parts of Arizona) and interned in special camps for the duration of the war. A month after the executive order was issued, Congress passed legislation approving Roosevelt's internment decision.

Such approvals for presidential actions are not always forthcoming. During the Korean conflict, for example, Truman overstepped the limits of "constitutional" authority by seizing most of the nation's steel mills—which were then on the verge of a strike. In *Youngstown Sheet and Tube Company v. Sawyer* (343 U.S. 579 [1952]) the Supreme Court declared the action unconstitutional.

In summary, successive presidents have combined their military, foreign, and executive powers to gain a wider range within which to operate. As the scope of these powers increased, their combined use resulted in new presidential prerogatives far beyond those specifically listed in the Constitution.

The President as Administrator of Domestic Affairs

The Constitution has given the president a unique role as an administrator of domestic affairs. In this capacity, the president has received three specific grants of power from Article II, Section 3, which deals specifically with the president's relations with Congress. These provide that (1) "he shall from time to time give to the Congress Information on the State of the Union"; (2) he shall "recommend to their Consideration such Measures as he shall judge necessary and expedient"; and (3) "he may, on extraordinary Occasions, convene both Houses, or either of them, and in Case of Disagreement between them, with Respect to the Time of Adjournment, he may adjourn them to such Time as he shall think proper."

Power to convene and adjourn Congress. The third of these cases can be covered rather quickly, because the evolution of this power has been away from presidential authority rather than toward it. By adoption of the Twentieth Amendment, Congress convenes each year in January and usually remains in session for nine months or longer, thereby providing few opportunities for calling it into session.

Because Congress is in session almost year-round, the power to convene Congress has meant little.

As with the presidential powers considered earlier, the first two powers enumerated under domestic affairs administrator also carry special import as a result of their evolution. Although neither the first provision that Congress shall be supplied with information nor the second, necessitating that it listen to the president's judgments, mandates either legislative direction or content, the exercise of these presidential powers has come to have that effect.

Power to address Congress on the state of the Union. The president's annual address to a joint session of Congress, by which he advises it on the state of the Union, began with Washington but fell into a prolonged period of disuse with Jefferson, who preferred to send written messages to Capitol Hill. The practice of a personal address was revived temporarily by Wilson and then more permanently by FDR and has been continued by each successive president, with the exception of Nixon during his second term. Delivering the State of the Union address has become a major television opportunity for the president. It allows him not only to influence the legislative agenda for the upcoming session but to appeal directly to the public to support his program.

Presidents use the annual State of the Union address to prepare Congress and the public for the president's legislative agenda.

Power to recommend legislation. Presidents now supplement the State of the Union address with actual drafts of bills. As part of this practice, which began with Theodore Roosevelt, the State of the Union address remains a philosophical statement but is followed by specific proposals to Congress. For example, in 1982 President Reagan used the State of the Union address to present the broad outlines of his "new federalism," which would reduce or eliminate many federal domestic programs. Later he presented Congress with

Most bills now originate in the executive branch.

draft legislation containing the specifics of which programs for states, municipalities, and individuals he wanted Congress to kill.

The evolution of the president's position as chief legislator has even been abetted by Congress. In 1921 Congress passed the Budget and Accounting Act, by which it required the president to supplement his State of the Union address with a detailed account of his proposals for the funding of both new and ongoing federal programs. The Budget and Impoundment Control Act of 1974 further legitimated the primary role of the president in the budgetary process. The Employment Act of 1946 required the president to analyze the nation's economy, with particular reference to maintaining full employment and production, and to make proposals for achieving those objectives. These acts have assisted in the evolutionary process by which the president has secured expanded prerogatives under Article II of the Constitution as the initiator of legislation. The constitutional provision that he shall "recommend measures" to Congress is now interpreted to include the planning and presentation of an entire program of legislation.

> *The president proposes the annual federal budget.*

Power to veto legislation. The Constitution clearly grants only one "official" authorization to the president regarding his role in the legislative process. Section 7 of Article I (which deals with Congress) limits presidential authority to the power to veto legislation. Significantly, this is one of the few constitutional prerogatives of the president that have not been substantially changed. He must still sign every congressional bill, or permit it to lie on his desk for ten days while Congress remains in session, for the act to have the status of a law.

> *The veto power gives the president the right to pass on every piece of legislation.*

In the event that the president decides that a bill as written should not become a law, even if his disagreement is with a single provision of the bill, he must return the entire bill to Congress in order to veto it. Neither the Constitution nor, quite understandably, Congress has given him the power of vetoing only selected parts of an act (an "item veto"). Reagan has repeatedly attempted to persuade Congress to grant him "item-veto" authority, arguing that he was challenging Congress to permit him to balance the budget by giving him the authority to veto individual items that would increase the federal deficit. Congress, viewing this as an unprecedented power grab on the part of the president, has refused to accept the "challenge."

Once vetoed, a measure must secure a two-thirds majority in each house of Congress in order to become law. If Congress has adjourned for the end of its session, however, the president may exercise his "pocket veto" by simply refusing to sign the bill in the requisite ten-day period.

Power to nominate judges. The same section of Article II that provides for presidential selection of ambassadors deals with the appointment of "Judges of the Supreme Court, and all other Officers of the United States, whose Appointments are not herein otherwise provided for, and which shall be established by Law. . . . " As we explain at greater length in the third chapter, the power to staff the judiciary is shared with the Senate because the president's nominees must be confirmed by the Senate. Normally, the president consults with the senators from the state where the vacant federal judgeship exists before a nomination is made. Although no one doubts the president's right to nominate whomever he pleases, no one doubts either the Senate's right to refuse to confirm a presidential nominee. Despite the evolutionary increase in presidential power, the president remains far from omnipotent.

> *The president nominates all federal judges, although his choices must be confirmed by the Senate.*

Power to command the executive branch. Besides presidential relations with Congress and the judiciary, Article II gives attention to the president's relations with members of the executive branch. In addition to the provision that "executive Power shall be vested" in the president, the article provides that "he may require the Opinion, in writing, of the principal Officer in each of the executive Departments." Except for these two provisions the Constitution is conspicuously silent on the president's relation to the bureaucracy. It assumes the presence of executive departments but makes no effort to define their composition, duties, powers, or responsibilities, and thereby leaves it to statute and the evolutionary process to provide for the bureaucracy's development. The result is that the president has wide latitude in deciding how he wishes to administer the executive branch of government. What Congress has done is strengthen the president's role as chief administrator simply by increasing the number of executive departments and the tasks they are expected to perform.

> *The president decides how laws are to be administered.*

Power to appoint bureaucrats. This increase in executive departments has been accomplished in accord with the provision that the president shall appoint "such inferior officers as [the Congress] may think proper." There was certainly no expectation by the Founding Fathers that the central government would experience the growth that has accompanied this nations's move into the twentieth century. Until acceptance of a merit-oriented civil service in 1883, presidents distributed literally thousands of patronage positions to loyal party followers. "To the victor belong the spoils" was a practice that was only partly curbed in 1883 when Congress passed the Civil Service Act (the Pendleton Act) following President James A. Garfield's assassination by a frustrated office seeker.

> *The president nominates the highest-level bureaucrats, although his choices must be confirmed by the Senate.*

The percentage of government positions open to presidential appointment has decreased with the extension of the civil service system, to the point that the number of political appointments is now relatively stable. When James Monroe was inaugurated in 1817, the *total* number of federal employees was only 6,500—which is approximately the number of new appointments that an incoming president can make today in a civilian federal bureaucracy that has grown to almost three million. The ground rules have changed with the continued expansion of the civil service, but the practice of presidential appointments to positions of importance in government has remained.

The question of who is to be hired for these 6,500 jobs involves negotiations between the White House staff, which wants to reward long-term loyal supporters of the president, and cabinet members, who often insist on taking primary responsibility for some major appointments in their own departments. In 1981, for example, Secretary of State Alexander Haig rejected White House suggestions that certain long-term Reagan supporters be given high-level State Department positions.

The Senate has traditionally supported the president's choices for executive positions, even if confirmation hearings sometimes become quite heated. This is not to say a president can be unmindful of the Senate's wishes. When President Reagan nominated Edwin Meese to become attorney general in January 1984, the Senate Judiciary Committee's investigation raised sufficient questions regarding his fitness for the office that a special prosecutor was appointed to investigate allegations that Meese had acted improperly as a presidential special assistant. Only after Reagan's reelection and the final report from the special prosecutor that cleared Meese did the Senate finally confirm him as attorney general in February 1985. The process took more than a year.

Although no cabinet-level nominee has been rejected by the Senate since 1959, when Lewis L. Strauss was turned down as secretary of commerce, presidential nominees have been withdrawn in the face of popular and congressional opposition. In addition, as the Meese case demonstrated, neither the Senate nor the president can take the confirmation process for granted.

The President as Head of State

Power to grant reprieves and pardons and to commission officers

The president's power to grant pardons has been used only in exceptional cases.

There are two remaining presidential powers enumerated in Article II, which correspond to the fifth constitutional role of the president: (1) the "Power to grant Reprieves and Pardons for Offences against the United States, except in Cases of Impeachment"; and (2) he "shall Commission all the Officers of the United States." These powers were obviously intended to be, and have largely remained, the ceremonial duties of any officer of government in whom are vested the powers of head of state. Occasionally there has been controversy over a "political" pardoning, such as President Gerald Ford's decision to grant a "full, free, and absolute pardon" to Nixon for all offenses he "committed or may have committed" while serving as president—a most exceptional case. Much less exceptional (indeed, more in accord with the tradition of presidential pardons) was Carter's first executive order, which he issued less than twenty-four hours after he assumed office. By "proclamation and executive order," Carter granted a "full, complete, and unconditional pardon" to those Americans who, without violence, had violated the Selective Service Act between August 4, 1964, and March 28, 1973. By this action, which applied to most Vietnam-era draft resisters (but not military deserters), Carter may have sought to start his presidency with an effort at putting Vietnam-era controversies to rest. Perhaps acting on similar impulses, early in his administration Reagan pardoned two former FBI officials who had been found guilty of authorizing illegal searches of the residences of antiwar activists. Presidents may use pardons to send political messages to the American people.

From our analysis of the president's constitutional powers and their evolution we have been able to identify at least the seeds that produced the current presidential roles of head of state, chief executive, commander in chief, chief administrator, and chief diplomat. However, the contemporary president's powers are even more extensive. Even careful reference to the Constitution cannot explain the development of the president's position of leadership in the American political scene or the constant blending, overlapping, and even conflicting nature of the roles he is required to fill—and it is to these that we now turn.

Presidential Leadership

The presidency provides an opportunity for leadership, but no guarantee of success.

No combination of constitutional, implied, or evolved presidential powers operates in a vacuum, without direction and force, or separate from the occupant of the Oval Office. The power of the president has increased over the years, in short, because of the men who have held the office. The judgment of history, by which presidents are labeled *strong* or *weak*, *capable* or *inept*, even *good* or *bad*, can often be reduced to a judgment of their leadership. Because of the unique nature of the office of president, the incumbent has the opportunity to lead the government, his own political party, and the American people. The ability with which various incumbents have handled this leadership role not only has determined their own places in history (subject, of course, to the vagaries of history itself) but has profoundly affected the possibilities open to their successors.

Leadership as Persuasion

We have already noted that the Congress is not in a position to compel presidential activity in many areas. Likewise, we should add that the president is unable to *compel* many people to do very much of anything. This statement may seem somewhat ironic, following as it does a section dealing with the evolution of presidential power, but it is accurate. As Richard Neustadt points out, the president rarely can compel people to act, but his position offers him advantages that, if he is skillful, he can use to *persuade* people to do what he wants them to do.

The president does not often rely on his formal authority in situations that call for presidential leadership. Many individuals he hopes to influence are not under his authority. Members of Congress, for example, are under no obligation to follow the president's suggestions. He cannot compel Congress to act; he must persuade it to do so. He can keep Congress from acting by using his veto power, but, ironically, the use of this power indicates that the president has failed to persuade Congress to pass a bill more to his liking. If the president's leadership had been more successful, he would not have needed to use the veto.

> *Successful presidential leadership is persuading others to do what the president wants.*

The president is unable to compel action on the part of individuals not under his authority; he even finds it difficult to compel action on the part of executive-branch officials who are. The president is at the top of a bureaucracy with millions of people, each responsible to his or her immediate supervisor. Presidential commands may be misunderstood or simply disobeyed, and the president may not have knowledge of the noncompliance. Senior members of his staff may initiate programs without his knowledge or consent. If the president decides to exercise his authority to fire cabinet officers, as Jimmy Carter did in 1979 with Transportation Secretary Brock Adams, Treasury Secretary W. Michael Blumenthal, and Health, Education and Welfare Secretary Joseph Califano, the incident may engender unfavorable publicity. If these persons were not the best possible candidates for their positions, why were they appointed in the first place? The use of the authority to remove a cabinet officer is not indicative of strong leadership but of a failure of leadership. It may suggest that the president has been unable to persuade a cabinet officer to do what the president thinks should be done.

> *The president cannot depend on his authority to accomplish a great deal.*

President's bargaining advantages in his relations with Congress. The president, in attempting persuasion, does have advantages, such as the constitutional prerogatives we have already outlined. In addition, there are many bargaining advantages that help him to persuade. There are, after all, presidential appointments to be made, invitations to be issued to important White House functions, presidential appearances during congressional campaigns for reelection, federal projects scheduled for construction or operation in congressional districts, "pet projects" on which presidential assistance would be helpful, budgets to be approved for both new and existing programs—the list goes on.

The president can provide or withhold that which a member of Congress needs or wants. In this area, presidents whose abilities to lead have been most pronounced are those whose decisions to provide or withhold have been most adroitly communicated. A presidential intervention that provides a member

> *The president's discretion in some budgetary matters is one of his persuasive advantages.*

[1]Richard E. Neustadt, *Presidential Power* (New York: Wiley, 1960).

of Congress with a federal project in his or her district does not need to be accompanied by the representative's promise of support—but that support had better be forthcoming. Kennedy, for example, was known to have excluded members of Congress of his own party from the speaking platform when he was touring constituencies because of their failure to support his program in the White House.

At times this congressional-presidential practice of *quid pro quo* (something for something) has become so blatant as to verge on outright trading. During the summer 1981 debates over Reagan's budget proposals that sharply modified Carter's fiscal year 1982 plan, several members of Congress from sugar-growing districts visited the White House. Reagan earlier had announced his desire to reduce sugar price supports because he believed such supports were inflationary. After these meetings, the president changed his mind on the supports, and the representatives came out in support of the Reagan budget. When asked whether his vote could be bought, Congressman John Breaux (D.-La.) replied, "No, it can be rented."[2]

Presidential popularity as a bargaining advantage. The president's national constituency provides him with another element of power that may be directly brought to bear on his relations with other elected officials because their constituencies must necessarily be included in his own. At least since Andrew Jackson, every president has understood and acted on this overlapping constituency in order to convince congressional recalcitrants that the administration's policies are the ones preferred by "the folks back home." Reagan often has repeated his contention that the 1980 and 1984 elections should be interpreted as "mandates" for the policies he favored and that members of Congress who opposed his policies were out of step with their constituents.

A popular president is likely to be persuasive; an unpopular president will have difficulty getting Congress to follow his leadership.

Appealing for national popular support is one of the most important elements in the president's arsenal of leadership tactics. In his war against renewing the charter of the Second Bank of the United States, Jackson used the veto as a means of gaining popular support. He sent Congress the most strongly worded presidential veto message it had ever received, but it was actually aimed at congressional constituents so they would pressure their representatives to vote against the measure the second time around. Wilson's "swing around the circle," a city-to-city tour to inspire popular support for the League of Nations, was a familiar tool in the hands of every president in the late nineteenth and early twentieth centuries.

By effectively using the mass media, a president can enhance his popularity and thereby increase his ability to realize his objectives in Washington.

As technological advances permitted more (and eventually more direct) contact with progressively larger audiences, the power of the presidential office kept pace. First newspapers, with their fiery editorials and selective perception of the news, assured the president of an audience wherever the

---

[2]Congressional *Quarterly Weekly Report,* July 4, 1981, p. 1169.

telegraph could reach a printing press. At least with Wilson, and possibly even Theodore Roosevelt, the presidential press conference became an established means of informing, pleading with, and "educating" the national constituency. The advent of radio provided first Calvin Coolidge and then, in full measure, Franklin D. Roosevelt with one of the most effective means of communication possible—a direct link between the citizen at home and the man in the White House. Roosevelt's "fireside chats" eliminated the journalistic middleman and brought the president into the living rooms of millions of Americans at once. Since the 1950s, through television, presidents are seen as well as heard at times of their own choosing, on topics they consider important, and under circumstances they deem most appropriate.

Most recent presidents have made extensive use of press conferences to get their messages across to the people. In his first term, Reagan was an exception; he averaged only seven press conferences per year, and, after 1981, the federal government actually stopped reporting presidential news conferences in its weekly compilations. To be sure, Reagan still uses the media more effectively that any other president in modern history, but at times of his own choosing, and in forums of his own selection. The traditional press conference, in which reporters are free to ask far-ranging questions on national and international policy, was not the forum of Reagan's choice in his first term.

These successive technological advances have not eliminated, but rather supplemented, the "swing around the circle." The president still travels to many parts of the country, aided by a host of helicopters, jets, and limousines, to present his views to his constituents in the hope that they will be convinced that his program is in their best interests and so inform their senators and representatives in Washington.

Yet, persuading Congress and the American people to follow his lead is far from the president's only concern. No president in his first term can dare to neglect the prospects of his reelection. If his electoral victory was relatively close in the last campaign, he will be eager to increase his popular support and enhance his image as the "representative" of all the people. This concern has become even more important as the electoral majority becomes less and less a reflection of the nation's numerical majority. If we were to combine all the votes cast for Richard Nixon and Hubert Humphrey in 1968, that number would still be less than the majority of American citizens, who either cast no vote at all or voted for a third-party candidate. In 1984, Ronald Reagan enjoyed a comfortable victory over Walter Mondale. However, although 59 percent of all who voted preferred Reagan, only 31 percent of all American adults voted for the former California governor. Almost as many Americans chose not to vote for anyone as chose to vote for Mondale and Reagan combined. These statistics are hardly likely to lull a president into complacency about his relations with the American people.

Such complacency is most easily avoided by the president's attention to *all* the overlapping roles that presidential leadership includes. As the only

The president's chances of reelection affect his ability to lead effectively.

> *Through his access to the mass media, the president can place issues on the national agenda.*
>
> *The effectiveness of the president's programs and actions has a large impact on his popularity.*

federal official with both the responsibility and the facilities to develop a comprehensive legislative program, he has the opportunity to place significant national problems on the political agenda and to frame them in a manner such that legislative majorities may be attainable. As the chief administrator, he can issue executive orders—such as Reagan's early decontrol of domestic oil prices—that may have the effect of increasing his popularity. The right to issue such orders either is inherent in his administrative responsibilities or stems from legislation in which Congress provides for presidential discretion over the timing and specificity of policy implementation. The decisions he makes regarding implementation can affect how the American people view their president.

The Presidential Political Context

Prestige: A function of the presidency, not the president. Presidential popularity, itself a source of extraconstitutional power, should be viewed more as a function of prestige of the office than merely a popular judgment of the incumbent. The adroit use of presidential invitations, the friendly phone call to an otherwise obscure public official, the appearance before a citizens' group, even the presidential press conference or televison appearance are all persuasive tactics available to any president. The incumbent benefits from the judicious use of such tactics—tactics that are his to use *only* because he occupies the Oval Office. It is the *president,* not a *specific* president, whose intervention often ensures the success of an otherwise doubtful program or policy. His personal prestige and status are automatically assured because he is "the president."

> *The prestige of the office of president gives its occupant opportunities to lead.*

One result of this prestige transferral can be seen in the president's role as a leader of public opinion. In May 1966, just before Lyndon Johnson ordered the bombing of Hanoi and Haiphong harbor, 50 percent of the American people favored such an action; one month later, after the presidential directive had been issued, the percentage rose to 85. Two years later, in March 1968, 51 percent of the electorate favored a limitation on the bombing; after this policy was initiated in April, only 26 percent of those polled were opposed to the new policy.[3] Many Americans support or oppose a particular policy simply because they desire to be in agreement with the president's position.

> *Some citizens support any program that the president believes is in the national interest.*

> *Many expect the president to be not just a political leader and a good administrator but a moral leader who will provide a model of good behavior.*

Elected from a nationwide constituency, the president is the only nationally elected official entitled to speak for all the people. In speaking for them, he is expected to lead, not only in terms of politics but in areas of ethics and morality as well. He is therefore understood to be a moral leader, to exemplify those qualities that serve as ideals for most Americans. Thus, FDR characterized the presidency as "preeminently a place of moral leadership."

---

[3]Figures taken from John E. Mueller, "Trends in Popular Support for the Wars in Korea and Vietnam," *American Political Science Review* 65 (1971): 369-370.

Many look to the president to solve all national problems; this is a source of power for the occupant of the office.

In addition, the American people look to the president for protection from economic ills, for social justice, for preservation of national security—in short, as the panacea of the political system. In this context, the very existence of the office of the president becomes a source of the incumbent's power with both Congress and the population at large.

To say that the prestige of the presidency is a source of power for the occupant of the office is not to say that unlimited power is in the hands of whoever occupies the office. The ability of a president to rely on the prestige of the office for support has its limitations. Richard Nixon, when under fire for a series of illegal actions during the Watergate crisis, argued that his critics were weakening the presidency, rather than merely attacking the current occupant of the position. Although this argument did garner Nixon some public support, the House Judiciary Committee voted to impeach him, and he resigned in disgrace. The prestige of the office is a great resource in the hands of a politically astute president, but his ability to use the resource wisely determines whether he is a powerful or a weak president.

American political parties are decentralized, and so power in the parties is at the state and local levels.

The president's position as head of one of the national parties is not a significant source of power.

The president as a party leader. Finally, we should mention the president's role as leader of his party. Actually, "party unity" in the United States is largely mythical because the parties are best characterized by decentralization (each "national" party is little more than a confederation of fifty state parties). Given the mythical nature of party unity, the president's position as party leader is, generally, quite insignificant. He no longer even controls the thousands of patronage positions once doled out to loyal party followers, the rise of the civil service system having drastically curtailed the "spoils system." The potential consequences of this lack of meaningful party unity and the president's inability to dispense favors as widely as he once could became evident in the summer of 1976: Gerald Ford, a nonelected but nonetheless sitting president, was nearly denied his party's nomination in the face of an extremely strong challenge to his position as party leader by Ronald Reagan.

The political milieu of presidential power. The president's role as party leader today is meaningful only in conjunction with the president's role as national leader in the field of public policy. By espousing a given public policy in the name of the party, the president can alter the public's *image* of the party and the party's composition. This was the tactic employed by FDR in the rejuvenation of the Democratic party in the early 1930s. By appealing directly to an urban-oriented clientele (including labor, blacks, ethnics, and intellectuals), he changed the composition of the Democratic party and set the tone of government policy as well.

Those who have wielded presidential power most skillfully over the years have done so within the context of decidedly political limitations. Working with a keen awareness of what is politically possible has usually allowed presidents to expand their range of alternatives; ignoring political possibilities

Strong presidents understand that politics is the art of the possible, that their actions must be grounded in realistic assessments of the perceptions of the American people.

Presidents are held accountable for the economic condition of the country; over time a stagnant economy weakens the president's popularity and therefore his ability to lead effectively.

Policy changes generally are incremental, slight movements from the status quo.

The Reagan budget victories of 1981 demonstrate that a strong president can bring about nonincremental changes.

has usually resulted in the loss of presidential power and prestige. Franklin Roosevelt's attempt to "pack" the Supreme Court by adding justices who would be more favorable to New Deal legislation is a case in point. The attempt, while perfectly legal constitutionally, was inappropriate in light of the political climate in which Roosevelt had to operate. Because he misjudged that climate, he not only failed to pack the Court but lost presidential prestige as well—even though he had just been reelected by the most substantial electoral majority in United States history.

The task of maintaining presidential power is made especially difficult by the existence of issues that the president cannot avoid. After a year or so in office the president is held accountable for the state of the economy. If the economic situation is perceived as poor, members of Congress increasingly distance themselves from the president because they are concerned with their own reelection. A president who is perceived as ineffective in dealing with national problems is not a powerful leader.

Aside from the current political scene, a president is also affected by agreements made by his predecessors—most notably in the area of foreign affairs. To disregard such inherited agreements can jeopardize the continuity of U.S. foreign policy and thereby cast doubt on the president's ability to execute his duties as chief diplomat. Such disregard may in fact damage the entire range of presidential powers, and yet the political climate demands that the incumbent not be frozen into the policies of his predecessors. A president may fail to recognize the necessity of altering his inherited foreign policy to accommodate domestic dissatisfaction—and this, too, would weaken presidential leadership.

The president is a *political* actor, and, as such, he must participate in the political process. This process often demands that conflicts be resolved by striking bargains between those who wish a certain policy continued without change and those who wish new policies implemented. The result of such bargains is *incrementalism*—the process of gradual policy alteration. As a result of the president's unique position in the American political scene, he is often able to institute dramatic policy changes and, in these instances, to overrride the effects of incrementalism. For a president to truly "lead," he must know when to use the powers of office to force rapid changes and when to settle for incremental changes.

An example of the effective use of presidential power to bring about nonincremental change is the victory of the Reagan administration in the budget battle of 1981. Reagan sought nonincremental shifts in federal spending priorities with unprecedented peacetime increases in defense spending and drastic reductions in spending for many social progams. He was able to persuade Congress to follow his bidding by shrewdly using his resources in four ways.

First, he reminded Congress of his great popularity at that time, so opposing his wishes might lead to defeats at the polls. Reagan acted quickly, early in his administration, while the traditional "honeymoon" period for new presidents still existed. Even the assassination attempt on Reagan in March 1981 effected an increase in his ratings in the polls, just after his popularity had begun to decline sharply. It is difficult for anyone to oppose a president who has recently been shot.

Second, the Reagan administration worked closely with Republican leaders in Congress to develop a strategy by which the massive spending changes would be accomplished through one vote, rather than many votes on individual programs. This enabled senators and representatives to avoid having to take an identifiable stand for or against cuts to popular programs.

Third, employing a tactic mentioned earlier in this chapter, Reagan invited small groups of legislators to the White House for personal chats. He used his personal charm as well as promises to support their pet projects to garner their votes: It is difficult to sit informally in the White House and say no to a popular, charming, wounded president.

Fourth, Reagan twice addressed the nation on television, urging citizens to contact their representatives and demand they support the president's program. Using his exceptional speaking skills, developed in his career as a professional actor, Reagan effectively persuaded the public to support his budget proposals. The president had used his power to command a national audience most adroitly.

In summary, we have argued that every president has resources that, if used effectively, permit him to persuade others to follow his lead. If the resources are not used effectively, the president will be able to carry out few of his plans. There are no guarantees, only opportunities.

Electoral Procedures
Presidential Eligibility

Constitutional provisions of presidential eligibility. As with presidential power, presidential selection cannot be fully understood by mere reference to the Constitution. The constitutional requirements of presidential eligibility are outlined in Article II, Section 1 and stipulate quite simply that the president be a natural-born citizen, at least thirty-five years of age, and a fourteen-year resident of the United States. The meaning of the first provision was questioned in 1968 when George Romney, born in Mexico of American parents, was being considered for the Republican nomination. Constitutional lawyers agreed, however, that any citizen born of American parents probably would be considered "natural born." Similarly, Herbert Hoover had not resided in the United States for the fourteen years immediately prior to his election, but the tenure provision is interpreted as requiring a total of fourteen years in any time sequence.

The Constitution places few limits on presidential eligibility.

Extraconstitutional considerations of presidential eligibility. Political and personal considerations have taken precedence over the bare constitu-

> *In practice only white males are eligible for the presidency.*

tional requirements. Of the thirty-nine presidents of the United States, twenty-five were lawyers, twenty-three served in Congress (four in the Continental Congress), thirty-three were able to trace their ancestry to prerevolutionary British stock, and of the remaining six, five were able to claim prerevolutionary Dutch or German heritage. Only John Kennedy, the lone Roman Catholic, could go back no further than a third-generation Irish immigrant. The log-cabin folklore has actually been true of Millard Fillmore, James Buchanan, Abraham Lincoln, and James Garfield and possibly also of Andrew Jackson and James Polk. William Harrison, Andrew Johnson, and Ulysses Grant dishonestly claimed during their campaigns that they too were of log-cabin birth. Marriage has not been seen as a requirement of the office; both Buchanan and Grover Cleveland were bachelors. Cleveland subsequently married (and Tyler and Wilson remarried) while occupying the office. Americans have also shown a marked preference for nominating generals after a "successful" war. Most predictably, yet often not mentioned, every major-party nominee for president or vice-president has been a white male, until 1984. Only with the nomination of Geraldine Ferraro as Mondale's running mate was this exclusive trend disrupted.

Presidential Selection

> *The electoral college as a deliberative body ceased to function after the Washington administration.*

According to the original prescriptions of the Constitution (Article II, Section 1), each state legislature was directed to choose a number of electors equal to its total number of representatives and senators. Each elector would vote for two persons (at least one of whom was not to be a citizen of that elector's state) for the office of president. It was to be understood that the electors were free agents who would choose, in the words of Alexander Hamilton, "characters preeminent for ability and virtue." A complete list of all persons voted for and the number of votes each had received was then to be sent to the president of the Senate. In the presence of Congress, the ballots of all the states were to be counted, and the person who had the majority of electoral votes was to be president; the runner-up, vice-president. In the event of a tie or the absence of a candidate with a majority of the electoral votes, the House of Representatives was to choose the president, and the runner-up was to be named vice-president.

The advent of political parties. This provision lasted only twelve years, until the crystallization of political parties around Jefferson and John Adams started the practice by which the electors in the several states pledged their support to one party or the other before their selection by the legislature. The overwhelming majority of electors in 1800 chose the "Democratic-Republican" (or "Anti-Federalist") ticket of Thomas Jefferson and Aaron Burr. The electoral lists received by the president of the Senate showed that the electors who supported this ticket had all cast one vote for Jefferson and one vote for Burr, so that the presidential candidate had the same number of votes as his running mate. The House was forced to select the president even though everyone knew that the electors wanted Jefferson as president and Burr as vice-president. The House quickly chose Jefferson, but the event precipitated passage of the Twelfth Amendment (ratified in 1804), designed to avert similar situations in future years. The new provisions mandated separate ballots for president and vice-president.

In the event of the lack of an electoral vote majority, as almost happened in 1968, the House will choose the president from among the top three contenders, and the Senate will select the vice-president from among the top two. The second and only time after 1800 in which the selection of the president fell to the House of Representatives occurred in 1824, when John Quincy Adams defeated Andrew Jackson in Old Hickory's first bid for the office.

> *A criticism of the electoral college is that it might again permit the loser in the overall popular vote count to win a majority of electoral votes and assume the presidency.*

Since the reforms of 1804, forty-five presidential elections have been conducted, and fifteen presidents, including Nixon in 1968, have been chosen without obtaining a majority of the popular vote. Of these fifteen, John Quincy Adams (1824), Benjamin Harrison (1888), and Rutherford B. Hayes (1876) actually received fewer popular votes than their major opponent. FDR's 1936 victory holds the record for landslides, with 61 percent of the popular vote and 98 percent of the electoral college total.

Current presidential nomination by political parties. The extension of the franchise and the development of the two major political parties have given rise to presidential candidate nomination by national party conventions. Nomination in conventions is by simple majority because neither party would willingly repeat the chaos of the 1924 Democratic convention. At that time, nomination required a two-thirds vote, and it took 103 ballots for the delegates to choose John W. Davis as their nominee.

> *Each party has its own system for choosing delegates to attend its national convention at which its presidential candidate is chosen.*

Convention delegate selection procedures. Each party has its own rules for selecting delegates to its national convention. With the general rules set by the national party organizations, the individual states have great latitude in deciding how delegates will be chosen to go to the national conventions. These rules are modified somewhat every four years as each party strives for a nominating system that will be fair to potential candidates, accurate in its representation of party supporters, and successful in giving the party's presidential nomination to the strongest candidate. Both parties have witnessed a rise in the number of delegates selected through primary election systems instead of caucus systems. In primary election systems, voters generally choose among delegate candidates pledged to support particular presidential hopefuls at the national conventions. In caucus systems, party members generally hold local precinct meetings to elect representatives to district party meetings, who in turn select representatives to state conventions.

Whereas caucus systems give crucial roles to party officials and others quite active in party affairs, primary election systems permit potential candidates to appeal directly to mass publics. Primary election systems permit potential candidates to use the media to attract votes to garner delegates without consulting party leaders. The rise of primary election systems has contributed both to the weakness of American parties and to the successful campaigns of the party "outsider," such as Carter, who had little support among party leaders.

> *The trend toward primary elections and away from caucuses has contributed to the decline of parties and the ability of "outsiders" to win presidential nominations.*

The two parties differ in the delegate selection procedures, primarily in the Democratic party's greater concern with the openness and representativeness of its system. Democratic conventions have more blacks, young people, women, Hispanics, and Native Americans than do Republican conventions. In the 1984 Democratic national convention, women accounted for almost half the number of delegates—quite a change from the older convention image of rooms filled with smoke and obese men.

Electoral college operations. Unlike the constantly evolving mechanisms for choosing convention delegates, the means of choosing electors have been virtually unchanged for over 100 years. This does not imply that the electoral college has not had its critics. Fears have been voiced that unpledged electors might begin to run in some states, thereby throwing the entire process into chaos. In addition, in most states there is no legal provision by which the pledged electors can be held to their announced candidate. This, combined with the possibility of throwing the election into the House of Representatives, has often served as an attraction to regionally based third-party candidates. Any hope of success held by the Dixiecrat party in 1948 and George Wallace's American Independence party twenty years later was based almost entirely on these strategies.

> *The candidate who wins a plurality of the vote in a state wins all of that state's electoral votes.*

The importance of any given state in the electoral college system rests on the number of electoral college votes to which the state is entitled. Electoral vote totals range from California's forty-seven (two for its senators and forty-five for its forty-five representatives) to three (two for its senators and one for its single representative) each in Alaska, Delaware, North Dakota, South Dakota, Vermont, and Wyoming. The unit rule electoral vote—which is observed in every state except Maine—dictates that the candidate who receives the most of a state's popular votes (a plurality[4] suffices) in a given presidential election receives *all* of the state's electoral votes. Winning California by the slightest of margins gives a candidate forty-seven electoral votes; winning Alaska by a 90 percent margin gives a candidate only three electoral votes.

According to the 1980 census, the ten most populous states (California, New York, Texas, Pennsylvania, Illinois, Ohio, Florida, Michigan, New

---

[4] A plurality winner is one who receives the greatest proportion of the votes cast, regardless of whether this proportion is a majority.

The Presidency   27

A successful presidential candidate must be able to win at least some of the large, urbanized states.

Jersey, and Massachusetts) account for 254 electoral votes—only 16 short of the 270 needed for election. It is crucial, then, that any presidential candidate carry these states—the nation's heterogeneous, urbanized, industrialized centers. Accordingly, electoral strategies are influenced by the electoral college system. No candidate can afford to ignore the issues of importance to the larger states, even if that candidate has a regional base of support such as Carter enjoyed in 1976. Carter managed to carry six of the ten largest states, which, combined with his support from the South and a few scattered states, permitted him to achieve a narrow electoral-vote victory over Ford. With 270 electoral votes needed for victory, Carter gained the White House by accumulating 297—a margin of only twenty-seven electoral votes, which could be offset by a single large state. The closeness of the race reinforced the necessity that each candidate for the presidency know how to appeal to the voters in the large states.

Electoral college reform?. Proposals for direct reform of the electoral college have been of three general types. The first would abolish the electoral college completely and establish a system of direct election. By this method, the candidate with the largest popular vote would be named president, but there is considerable disagreement over whether this should be a majority or whether a plurality would suffice. A second proposal would retain apportionment of the electoral college based on the state's congressional and senatorial seats, but the votes would be cast on a proportional basis, each candidate receiving the fraction of the electoral vote that would correspond to his popular vote within the state. The third proposed reform, a district plan, would give the electoral college vote to the plurality vote winner in each congressional district, the two corresponding Senate votes going to the plurality winner in the state as a whole. Under this proposal, a candidate would have to receive a plurality in *each* of California's forty-five congressional districts to capture all of that state's forty-seven electoral votes. This third proposal actually has been adopted by Maine: Reagan won all four of Maine's electoral votes in 1984 because he won victories in each of its two congressional districts and, therefore, in the state as a whole.

The electoral college is unlikely to be reformed because no one is sure of the practical consequences of the reform proposals.

These kinds of reform ideas have been in the political air for years and are particularly prominent after a close presidential election like that in 1976. Ford would have won that election if as few as 9,245 voters in Hawaii and Ohio had switched their votes to him from Carter, even though the latter had a 1.7 million-vote plurality nationwide. Despite bipartisan support for some kind of change in the system, we do not think it likely that the necessary constitutional amendment (which would affect Article II, Section 1) will be enacted in the near future. Political scientists disagree on the consequences of the proposals, and politicians, being no more certain, are not about to exchange a system with which they have grown comfortable for one whose political implications are obscure.

Term of Office and Succession
Term of Office of the Presidency

The Constitution provides that the president and vice-president shall serve concurrent four-year terms, and until ratification of the Twenty-second Amendment in 1951, there was no limitation on the number of terms an individual could serve in either position. By refusing to serve as president for more than eight years, Washington established a "voluntary" tradition that was to last until Franklin Roosevelt accepted the Democratic nomination in 1940 for an unprecedented third term (a record that would stand only until he extended it to four terms four years later—FDR was not one to be mesmerized by precedent). Since passage of the Twenty-second Amendment in 1951, no person may be elected to the presidency more than twice (reduced to once if he has served more than half of a term to which another person was elected).

A president can serve no more than two terms.

Succession to the Presidency

Article II of the Constitution stipulates that the vice-president shall assume the presidency in the event of death, resignation, or removal from office of the incumbent, and empowers the Congress to provide for the subsequent line of succession. The problem of succession has produced many proposed solutions, culminating in ratification of the Twenty-fifth Amendment in 1967. Because of the language of the Constitution, it was not clear whether the vice-president, on assuming the presidential office in the event of its vacancy, would be invested as president or only as acting president. Tyler settled this question when he insisted on being empowered with the fullness of the office after the death of Harrison in 1841. Harrison, the first president to die in office, died of natural causes, as did Zachary Taylor, Warren G. Harding, and Franklin Roosevelt; Lincoln, Garfield, McKinley, and Kennedy were assassinated; and Nixon resigned. On average, these presidents served less than one year of their four-year terms.

The presidency is not a healthful office: eight of thirty-nine occupants have died in office, and one resigned before completing his term.

Congressional attempts to stabilize the line of succession.
Prior to ratification of the Twenty-fifth Amendment, Congress attempted three times to settle the question of presidential succession. The Succession Act of 1792 placed the president pro tempore of the Senate and then the Speaker of the House of Representatives immediately after the vice-president in line of succession. This provision stood, unused, until congressional action in 1886 recognized the growth and importance of the executive branch and decided that the line of succession should run through the cabinet. The act provided for the secretary of state (followed by the rest of the cabinet in the order of the origin of their department's establishment) to assume office.

With Truman's assumption of the presidency in 1945 upon the death of Franklin Roosevelt, Congress again prepared to change the line of succession. Truman was reluctant to accept the provisions of the 1886 act on the grounds

> *The line of succession now runs from the vice-president, to the Speaker of the House, to the president pro tempore of the Senate, to the secretary of state, followed by other cabinet members rank ordered by the date their departments gained cabinet status.*

that they were "nondemocratic": he had the power to choose the secretary of state, therefore his own potential successor. The Succession Act of 1947 therefore retained all the provisions of its immediate predecessor but reinserted the Speaker of the House and the president pro tempore of the Senate (reversing the order of 1792) between the vice-president and the secretary of state. This provision was acceptable to Truman because it provided for officials who had at least undergone election to office, rather than appointment, to succeed to the presidency.

The provisions of 1947 stood until the assassination of Kennedy in 1963 highlighted the drawbacks of such an arrangement. As Johnson assumed the presidency, John McCormack, the Speaker of the House, was seventy-one years old, and his counterpart in the Senate, Carl Hayden, was almost eighty-seven. The obvious problem of their ages aside, could their selection for the office really be "democratic"? They held their positions of congressional authority at the behest of their colleagues; congressional leaders are elected to Congress, but not to their leadership positions, by the voters.

The Twenty-fifth Amendment.

Inspired by the long-standing custom by which each candidate for president selects his own running mate (originally by agreement and now through his party's nominating convention) and attempting to retain some degree of "democratic procedure," the states ratified the Twenty-fifth Amendment in 1967. According to its provisions, in the event of a vacancy in the vice-presidential office, the president is empowered to nominate a vice-president, who must then be confirmed by a majority of both houses of Congress. This ensures that the Speaker of the House will not succeed to the presidency unless both the president and vice-president die or resign simultaneously—on the presumption that there will always be time to appoint a vice-president. This amendment therefore addressed itself to presidential as well as vice-presidential vacancies, the latter having been more numerous than the former, numbering eighteen instances for a cumulative total of forty-five years.

> *A vacancy in the vice-presidency is filled by a presidential nominee confirmed by majority votes in the House and Senate.*

Upon the resignation of Spiro Agnew in October 1973, this newest succession procedure received its first trial. The speed with which the president acted—House Minority Leader Gerald Ford was chosen as vice-president designate within two days and confirmed by Congress within two months—demonstrated the viability of the amendment.

Less than two months later, the provisions of this same amendment were put into operation again. With Ford's accession to the presidency, the vice-presidential post again fell vacant. In August 1974, Congress received for confirmation the name of Nelson Rockefeller, and the United States, for the first time in its history, had a president and a vice-president chosen by Congress, not elected by the voters.

The office of the vice-president.

Having established the line of presidential succession, we should give some consideration at this point to the office of the

> *The vice-president has little authority or power.*

> *Each presidential candidate chooses his vice-presidential running mate, generally with the foremost purpose of balancing the ticket so as to win the election.*

vice-president, which its first occupant, John Adams, characterized as "the most insignificant . . . that ever invention of man contrived, or his imagination conceived." (Vice-President John Nance Garner, on a somewhat more graphic note, suggested that it was not worth a "bucket of warm spit.") The only constitutional provision other than succession delegated to the vice-president is the authority to preside over the Senate, where he votes only in event of a tie—hardly a provision of much importance.

Each party's presidential candidate generally chooses his vice-presidential running mate at the party's national convention, which then ratifies the choice. The candidate's choice of the number-two person is not often determined by the latter's qualities of judgment or expertise with which he or she might be expected to advise and be the confidant of the future president. Rather, the vice-presidential nominee is chosen for the political expedient of helping to get the ticket elected. All along, dating from the first presidential election, conventional political wisdom has dictated that there be some attempt to "balance" the national ticket in terms of age, temperament, ideology, and geographic origin.

The importance of political considerations in selecting vice-presidential candidates has not diminished with the advent of modern media campaigning techniques. In 1984, running against a president who was far ahead of him in the opinion polls, Walter Mondale selected Geraldine Ferraro, the first woman vice-presidential candidate put forward by a major political party. Her selection was clearly intended by Mondale to add a shot of adrenaline to his campaign. Ferraro did generate considerable enthusiasm and media attention (so much so that her husband's business dealings and their previous tax returns were called into question), but she did not generate sufficient votes for Mondale to defeat Reagan.

In 1968, Nixon's private polls convinced him that he would run best without a vice-presidential candidate because every well-known possibility alienated large groups of voters. Nixon responded to this dilemma by choosing Spiro Agnew, then an unknown figure in national politics. It was as close as Nixon could get to not having a running mate. Five years later Agnew resigned from the vice-presidency after pleading *nolo contendere* (no contention) to a criminal charge of tax evasion. Nixon's dilemma in 1973 was not the voters but mounting disclosures relating to Watergate. Under these circumstances, Agnew's successor would have to be someone who could help Nixon stem the impeachment tide in Congress. Nixon's logical, albeit futile, choice was Ford, minority leader in the House and a veteran of twenty-three years in Congress.

Traditionally the presidential nominee announces his choice for the vice-presidential nomination during his party's convention. In 1976 Reagan, a conservative, attempted to use the vice-presidential selection process as a tactic in his campaign for the Republican presidential nomination. Prior to the convention, Reagan announced that Richard Schweiker, then a liberal senator, would be his choice for the vice-presidential nomination and challenged Ford to announce his proposed running mate. This effort at broadening a candidate's appeal through the vice-presidential running mate was unique only because of Reagan's timing: the "balancing" customarily occurs after the presidential nomination has been secured.

In 1980 Reagan's behavior was more conventional. After receiving the presidential nomination, at the convention he chose George Bush as his running mate. Viewed as a more moderate Republican than Reagan, Bush added ideological balance to the ticket.

The president determines the nature and amount of authority that is exercised by the vice-president. Until Franklin Roosevelt's presidency, the vice-president did not even attend cabinet meetings, and Truman, although he attended, knew very little about U.S. foreign policy. He was completely ignorant of the substance of most strategy decisions about the conduct of the war, and even about the development of the atomic bomb until after Roosevelt's death.

More recent presidents have tended to elevate the vice-president to a more central role in their administrations, but he continues to function at the discretion of the president and not by right. In 1977, for example, Carter ordered the vice-president's office moved from the Executive Office Building across the street into the White House itself, because he intended that Vice-President Mondale would assume a central role in the administration. In 1981, Reagan appointed Bush to chair his administration's crisis management team over the objections of Secretary of State Haig. Although Mondale and Bush both had responsibilities denied to most previous vice-presidents, their responsibilities were given to them (and could be taken away) by the president—they were not theirs by vice-presidential right. In addition, we should note that the expanded vice-presidential role evidenced in recent administrations is primarily in the area of public relations and symbolic responsibilities. The vice-president's influence over the actual development of policy is conspicuously absent, nor is it likely to materialize. His nomination on the grounds of political expediency, his lack of an independent power base, and the nature of his duties all conspire to prevent him from evolving into a powerful political figure in his own right.

The only constitutional authority that has been added to the vice-president's office came with the ratification of the Twenty-fifth Amendment in 1967. Its passage stemmed from concerns over presidential disability—concerns that have surfaced periodically. During Wilson's second term, for example, his wife assumed many of the duties of the presidency while her husband was gravely ill. Years later, during Eisenhower's term of office, the problem of presidential disability arose again. A coronary thrombosis in 1955 followed in quick succession by an ileitis attack and operation in 1956 and a mild stroke the following year rendered Eisenhower temporarily incapable of discharging the duties of his office. The military command mode of operation

> *The current trend is toward greater involvement of vice-presidents in important executive activities; still, vice-presidents spend most of their time representing presidents at state funerals and making speeches.*

he had established from his first years in the White House rose to the occasion, and his "special assistant," Sherman Adams, through whom all presidential business had previously been channeled, made all necessary presidential decisions.

In each of these cases the then vice-presidents, Thomas Marshall and Richard Nixon, respectively, were either unwilling or unable to act according to the provisions of the Constitution. Article II stipulates that in the event of the president's "Inability to discharge the Powers and Duties of the said Office, the Same shall devolve on the Vice President," but it provides no means by which that disability is to be determined or the power transfer is to occur.

Passed in 1967, the Twenty-fifth Amendment permits a vice-president to assume the duties of a disabled president; this provision has never had to be used.

The Twenty-fifth Amendment therefore provides for two situations. First, it permits either the president himself or the vice-president (in concert with a majority of the cabinet or of any body designated by Congress) to inform the Speaker of the House and the president pro tempore of the Senate of the inability of the president to perform the functions of his office—at which point the vice-president shall become acting president. Second, a formerly disabled president can resume office by transmitting to the same congressional officers a declaration that he is again fit to discharge the duties of his office. This procedure was first used by Ronald Reagan during his cancer surgery in 1985. If the vice-president and a majority of the executive officers disagree with the president's declaration and within four days so advise the Congress, a vote of two-thirds majority in both houses, taken within twenty-one days of the receipt of the vice-president's message, is necessary for him to continue as acting president. If this element of constitutional authority had been granted to the vice-president earlier, perhaps history would remember Wilson's vice-president, Thomas Marshall, for more than his hopeful comment "What this country needs is a good five-cent cigar."

Impeachment and removal from office. The Constitution also provides that "the President, Vice President, and all civil Officers of the United States, shall be removed from Office on Impeachment [by the House of Representatives] for, and Conviction [by the Senate] of Treason, Bribery, or other high Crimes and Misdemeanors" (Article II, Section 4). The only president to be successfully impeached by the House was Andrew Johnson in 1868. He had requested and then demanded the resignation of Secretary of War Edwin Stanton in defiance of the Tenure of Office Act of 1867. By this act, passed over Johnson's veto, Congress had negated the presidential authority to remove members of the executive branch without senatorial approval. Johnson (following precedents established as early as Washington's first term) refused to accept this legislation as constitutionally valid.

Andrew Johnson was the only president to be impeached by the House, although he was acquitted by the Senate and remained in office.

In the face of heated partisan debate and intense congressional dissatisfaction with Johnson's "too lenient" reconstruction policies, the Supreme Court declined to rule on the question of constitutionality and set the stage for the trial in the Senate. With the chief justice presiding, in accord with the requirements of the Constitution, the Senate failed by one vote to muster the necessary two-thirds to convict Johnson of the charges that had been brought by the House (one of which included that he used improper language and spoke in a loud voice).

In contrast to the obvious "political" wranglings of the Johnson impeachment, the events that led to the only presidential resignation in the nation's history were relatively free of partisan overtones. On June 17, 1972 (five months before the presidential election), five men were arrested while planting surveillance equipment in the Democratic National Committee offices located in the Watergate apartment complex in Washington, D.C. An FBI investigation quickly unearthed financial links between the arrested men and the Committee for the Reelection of the President (CREEP) and, through it, to the White House itself. Top Nixon aides, acting on the president's orders, impeded the investigation.

Early in 1973 the web of White House inteference with the investigation began to unravel. Federal District Court Judge John Sirica refused to believe that the investigation had uncovered all the relevant facts, and the Senate voted seventy-seven to zero to establish a special select committee to investigate the incident. During the committee's hearings (at which the White House interference was documented), former presidential aide Alexander Butterfield disclosed the existence of a secret taping system in the White House by which presidential conversations had been recorded. When a special federal prosecutor attempted to gain access to the tapes through court action, he was fired by Nixon—an act that prompted the House of Representatives to empower its Judiciary Committee to begin an investigation into impeaching the president.

After the House Judiciary Committee voted to recommend impeachment to the entire House, Richard Nixon resigned from office.

The Judiciary Committee launched an extensive ten-month investigation. Even as the committee was deliberating, federal prosecutors continued to press for new evidence to convict the constantly expanding list of White House personnel who had conspired to obstruct justice by impeding the original investigation. On July 24, 1974, the Supreme Court ruled eight to zero that Nixon would have to surrender more tapes as evidence. Three days later the Judiciary Committee voted twenty-seven to eleven to recommend that the president himself be impeached on the same charge—obstruction of justice.

On August 5, 1974, the tapes that the Supreme Court had ordered released revealed that Nixon had ordered his top White House aid, H. R. Haldeman, to have the CIA block the FBI's investigation into the source of the Watergate funding. In light of this disclosure, congressional leaders informed the president that his impeachment by the House and conviction by the Senate was virtually assured. But impeachment would not be necessary—its threatened use was sufficient. Richard M. Nixon resigned the presidency on August 9, 1974, and Gerald R. Ford became the thirty-seventh president of the United States.

The Institutionalized Presidency
The President as Chief Executive

Theodore Sorenson, an assistant to President Kennedy, has accurately characterized the problems calling for a presidential decision as conflictual—that is, involving "conflict between departments, between the views of various advisors, between the administration and the Congress, between the United States and another nation, or between groups within the country: labor versus management, race versus race, or state versus nation."[5] How these conflicts are handled, who decides what is to be done, and the means by which decisions are reached and implemented are called the *institutionalization* of a particular presidency.

As the nation's chief executive, the president is "in charge" of the administrative and executive elements of the federal government. Each president has coped with his administrative responsibilities by using his own combination of cabinet officials and personnel from the Executive Office of the President. The cabinet, the existence of which is "assumed" by the Constitution, dates from the time of Washington. The Executive Office of the President (EOP), established in 1937, reached its peak in 1974 during the second Nixon administration—by which time it had grown to include more than a dozen agencies and 2,568 people, and had an overall budget of $106,700,000. The well-publicized abuses of presidential power, which could not have occurred without this growth, have induced subsequent presidents to trim these figures somewhat (e.g., just under 1,600 people in 1982), but they have been constrained in their cutbacks by the complexity of the task of overseeing the executive branch.

Each president sets up mechanisms by which he decides how his office will process information and make decisions; this is the institutionalization of his presidency.

Presidential styles. How a president utilizes his personnel and how he structures his organization are determined primarily by personal style. Eisenhower's administration was marked by heavy reliance on formally established bodies for advice and even decision making. The creation of the hierarchical structure on the military model was Eisenhower's brainchild—he did not inherit it. Nixon and Reagan both developed their organizational styles along the lines of the Eisenhower model. Reagan in particular has sought to involve himself only in major policy matters of program direction, not the specifics of bills and policy implementation. In contrast, Kennedy and Carter injected themselves into the decision-making process any time they had doubts about what might be happening.

Every president adopts an institutionalized presidency congenial to his executive style.

There is little agreement among scholars of the presidency on whether the active Roosevelt style or the passive Eisenhower approach is the more effective. Although Carter was praised for his extensive knowledge of public policy, he also was criticized for spending too much time on details and not

---

[5]Theodore C. Sorenson, *Decision Making in the White House* (New York: Columbia University Press, 1963), pp. 14-15.

marshaling his time to be able to deal effectively with major questions. Reagan has been praised for a great ability to build political support by focusing his energies carefully, but he also has been criticized for not learning the actual impact of his policy recommendations.

The degrees to which any president isolates himself from conflicting opinion, relies on formal channels, and attempts to maintain personal authority instead of delegating it are all measures of the tone of his administration. It is this tone that gives life and shape to the institutionalized presidency.

The Cabinet

Franklin Roosevelt once commented: "When I woke up this morning the first thing I saw was a headline in the *New York Times* that our Navy was going to spend two billion dollars on a shipbuilding program. Here I am the Commander-in-Chief of the Navy having to read about that for the first time in the press." His reaction dramatizes the president's lack of communication with the cabinet, the oldest element of the institutionalized presidency.

The president's cabinet includes the secretaries of the federal departments and the UN ambassador.

The cabinet was first formed as a four-member staff under Washington, from which it has grown to its current high of fourteen. Its present composition of members, all but one of whom is the administrative head of a sprawling federal bureaucratic structure, includes the United States ambassador to the United Nations, the attorney general, and the secretaries of state, treasury, defense, interior, agriculture, commerce, labor, health and human services, housing and urban development, transportation, energy, and education.

George Reedy, press secretary to Lyndon Johnson, described the cabinet as "one of those institutions in which the whole is less than the sum of its parts."[6] The same factor delineates both the individual strengths and the collective weakness of cabinet members: their relationship to their individual departments. We will analyze this relationship as the source of their power and influence in chapter 4 when we deal with the bureaucratic structure itself, but we find it to be analytically helpful to clarify that strength in relation to the collective impotence of the cabinet as an element of the institutionalized presidency.

The cabinet member's dilemma. The nearly three million civilian employees who work in cabinet departments wield tremendous power as a result of their acquired expertise, possession of the government's material resources, and a virtual monopoly on the capacity to act. The secretary must cultivate their confidence and respect, which he quickly loses if he fails to advance the departmental interests to which many of these men and women have devoted entire lives. Cabinet members change even more frequently than presidents, but their departments remain. Thus a cabinet officer, considered

[6]George Reedy, *The Twilight of the Presidency* (New York: New American Library, 1970), p. 77.

At cabinet meetings members have two roles: to represent the interests of their departments and to provide general advice to the president as part of his "team." These roles are often in conflict.

by the president as a "trusted adviser," is viewed by the department as "our man at the White House." This places cabinet members in an extremely tenuous political situation. If they take a parochial, "departmental" stance in cabinet consultations, their worth as presidential advisers on matters of more universal concern may be called into question by White House staff. This has been particularly true for the secretaries of the domestic policy departments during the Reagan administration; they were appointed to weaken programs in their departments, not to support program-expansion ideas of the civil servants.

If, however, a cabinet secretary fails to support departmental positions, especially the views of senior professionals, departmental personnel will believe that their "boss" is costing them influence with the president. They are likely to stall in implementing the secretary's administrative initiatives, to leak damaging information to the press or to Congress, and to engage in other behavior subversive to the secretary's position. Regardless of how a secretary handles this role of departmental representative to the president, the cabinet as a collective body of presidential advisers does not function well.

Conflicts between cabinet members and the White House staff are frequent as both vie for influence with the president.

The cabinet is often faced with disputes between members, resignations over administration policy (dating from Jefferson's resignation from Washington's cabinet over the economic programs advocated by Alexander Hamilton), the preemptive stature of other presidential officers (particularly the White House staff), and even the sheer uncertainty of individual cabinet members' positions. These problems increase their sense of frustration and often result in a retreat into their respective departments, leaving the institutionalized presidency to evolve other means of coping with its difficulties.

Use of the cabinet as an advisory body. Eisenhower was probably the last president to attempt to use his cabinet as an advisory body, establishing a special post of cabinet secretary to prepare agenda. Kennedy once referred to meetings of the cabinet as a "waste of time," and his successor never even discussed the conduct of the Vietnam War with the cabinet. Nixon's original pledge to revitalize the cabinet was quickly forgotten, as demonstrated by Interior Secretary Walter Hickel's complaint in 1970 that the president was inaccessible to cabinet members. Ford, Carter, and Reagan all made similar promises to involve the cabinet in the discussion of the most crucial matters. In practice Ford and Carter relied—and Reagan still does rely—for consultations on other arrangements, generally informal groups with memberships tailored to the subject matter and including people from the Executive Office of the President and one or two other trusted cabinet secretaries.

Recent presidents have made limited use of the cabinet as an advisory body.

The Executive Office of the President

Established by President Franklin Roosevelt by executive order under prerogatives granted him by the Reorganization Act of 1939, the Executive Office of the President (EOP) comprises staff agencies that aid the president in carrying out his duties. Table 1-4 (p. 41) lists the major components of the EOP, which has over 1,600 employees and a budget well over $100 million.

The White House Office. Taking precedence in the EOP is the White House Office (or White House staff), a circle of advisers with the most immediate access to and influence with the president. Its formal duties include advising the president on matters of public concern, briefing him on current activities and problems within the executive branch, acting as liaison with Congress, and providing him with advice on the full range of domestic, foreign, and national security affairs.

The White House staff is composed of close, long-term confidants of the president; they are the first to see him in the morning and the last to see him at night.

By controlling access to the president, the White House staff has great influence.

The main characteristic of the White House staff is a strong personal loyalty to the president. Unlike cabinet officers, staff members have no independent base of power from which to operate or bureaucracy to represent. Their position (like that of the vice-president) is determined by presidential style, but (unlike that of the vice-president) their relationship with the president usually dates from his earlier political career, so he trusts their judgment and advice. This closeness to the president is a source of substantial power for the White House staff. More than anyone else in the government, they are able to get the president's ear. The staff members also set the president's agenda, determining who gets into the Oval Office and which phone calls will be returned. By this role of "gatekeeper," the White House staff can structure the information that the president receives.

Some presidents delegate more authority to the White House staff than others do. Eisenhower and Reagan gave the staff more leeway to make decisions than did Kennedy, Johnson, Ford, and Carter. The extreme of staff autonomy among recent presidents, however, was Nixon's system. He exhibited the strongest trust in his staff, which was almost his sole source of advice on matters of national concern. In return, his staff exhibited such loyalty that one member suggested he would go so far as to run over his own grandmother if that would help the president. In addition, the power wielded by the staff was so pervasive that ranking members of the president's own party in Congress, and even cabinet members, complained that they had little access to the Oval Office.

For their zeal to protect the president from excessive criticism or too many visitors, some White House staffs have been criticized for isolating the president.

This type of staff system leaves open to serious debate the question whether the president gets the necessary information on which to make optimal decisions. In their zeal to serve him, staff members decide what information should be transmitted and what should be repressed. Their intervention may be overly officious, their confidence exceeding their competence. In their desire to remain in his favor (there is no job security for members of the White House staff), they may seek to shield him from all criticism. Consequently, the staff may isolate the president from the information he needs to avoid serious errors in judgment.

No treatment of the White House staff would be complete without mention of the president's special assistant for national security affairs. Under recent administrations he has assumed many of the duties of the secretary of

> *Over the years, each national security adviser, a member of the White House staff, has had squabbles with the secretary of state; this institutional arrangement, wherein the limits of the authority of their positions are not clear, almost guarantees such conflicts.*

state by taking a central role in the formulation of U.S. foreign policy. Thus, McGeorge Bundy under Kennedy, Walter Rostow under Johnson, and Henry Kissinger under Nixon became the "man in the basement" whose rivalry with the respective secretaries of state evolved into the merging of the two positions in Kissinger. This proved to be a short-lived marriage. In November 1975, after considerable intracabinet rivalry, Ford removed Kissinger from his post as assistant to the president, although Kissinger retained his position as secretary of state. Carter maintained the separation of the two positions when he assumed the presidency by appointing Cyrus Vance as secretary of state and Zbigniew Brzezinski as his special assistant for national security affairs. Their public squabbles over policy as well as over who should be presenting the administration's positions embarrassed Carter on several occasions. This problem continued in the early months of the Reagan administration as National Security Adviser Richard Allen publicly bickered with Secretary of State Haig. The appointment in 1981 of William Clark, a novice in foreign policy matters, to replace Allen provided at least temporary relief to this long-standing institutional dispute with the secretary of state. However, nothing was solved permanently. Other White House staff members leaked material damaging to Haig to the press, and in June 1982 Haig resigned after feuding with Clark. The White House staff will continue to vie with the secretary of state and other cabinet members for power and influence with the president.

Office of Management and Budget. Another important element in the EOP is the Office of Management and Budget (OMB), which is more powerful than any other single agency in its impact on the development and implementation of federal programs. From its inception it has coordinated the budget requests of all federal agencies. Without OMB clearance, no executive agency can request funds from Congress. And, as of 1970, no appropriated funds can be spent without OMB approval.

Established originally as the Bureau of the Budget under the control of the Department of the Treasury, the agency was transferred to direct presidential control at FDR's request in accord with the general trend toward presidential leadership in the legislative field. Since its reorganization and renaming by Nixon in 1970, OMB has become even more powerful. Its major responsibility is the supervision and control of the administration of the budget, and this responsibility has been constantly expanding in recent years in a White House attempt to control the bureaucracy.

> *OMB is the locus for executive decisions on expenditures as well as the linchpin in the president's effort at managing the federal bureaucracy.*

In preparing the federal budget, OMB gathers requests for expenditures from all departments and agencies of the government eighteen months before the beginning of a given fiscal year. It then coordinates those budget requests in accord with the president's determination of priorities. The director of OMB, nominated by the president with senatorial confirmation, then returns the "trimmed" budgets to each department for further consideration—

thereby initiating the continual process of request, consideration, and return that persists unabated until the presentation of the president's budget to the Congress for approval. At the same time, OMB is also responsible for improving governmental organization, developing information and management systems, and creating programs for the recruitment and training of federal career executives.

The "administrator" or "overseer" role of the OMB is intended to give greater emphasis to the management aspect of the government's operations. It is also an attempt to ensure planning and implementation on a coordinated basis with EOP direction and control. Reagan further strengthened OMB by ordering all federal agencies to clear changes in regulations or administrative procedures with OMB and its director, David Stockman. Under an even more far-ranging 1984 executive order, all federal departments and agencies were required to notify OMB at the beginning of the fiscal year of changes that they would propose during the upcoming year, and to provide OMB with early drafts of policy changes that were being considered. OMB thus has emerged at the center of Reagan's effort to gain tight control over the federal bureaucracy.

Council of Economic Advisers. Separate from OMB, but also concerned with the federal budget, is the Council of Economic Advisers, established under the EOP by the Employment Act of 1946 and currently operating under that statute and the Reorganization Plan of 1953. Its director and two other members are appointed by the president with senatorial consent and are asssisted by a small staff of economists and statisticians. The council relies heavily on the various federal departments and agencies for economic data, as does OMB, but unlike the latter, it cannot dictate appropriations and expenditures. It therefore enjoys a much more cordial relationship with its sources.

Unlike OMB, which has a large staff to gather information, the Council of Economic Advisers works with a small staff to develop an overview of economic conditions to be able to advise the president.

In accord with its broad responsibility to analyze the state of the economy, the Council of Economic Advisers issues yearly recommendations to the president on matters of economic growth and stability. It also prepares analyses of economic programs and policies of the federal government and submits advice on economic developments that, although general in nature, form the basis of the president's annual economic report to the Congress.

National Security Council. The National Security Council (NSC), established in the EOP by the National Security Act of 1947 (amended in 1949), advises the president with respect to the integration of domestic, foreign, and military policies relating to "national security." This phrase has been interpreted as including anything that would affect the functioning of the United States government as determined by the National Security Council itself. The anomaly here is that the same agency that defines the limits of national security also determines policies delineated by that definition.

The members of the NSC, by statute, include the president, the vice-

> *The National Security Council includes the heads of the essential agencies dealing with foreign affairs and military matters.*

president, the secretaries of state and defense, and any additional persons by presidential invitation. The NSC considers policies on matters of common interest to the departments and agencies concerned with the national security, but its utilization, as with every other element of the EOP, is a function of the personal style of the incumbent president. Eisenhower, for example, used the council extensively, developing an intricate substructure of boards and committees beneath it. Kennedy abolished the substructure, but during the Cuban missile crisis established an Executive Committee of the Council numbering sixteen members (which, when the crisis subsided, was just as quickly abolished). Nixon used the council for advice but frequently sought out non-NSC people like assistants H. R. Haldeman and John Ehrlichman for this purpose. Nixon revitalized the council and gave a central role to Kissinger—a role Kissinger continued to play under Ford even after being removed as special assistant to the president. Carter and Reagan returned to an earlier tradition of extensive use of the NSC, although neither developed the subcommittee structure used by Eisenhower. Again, it is the personal style of the president that dictates how, and how much, he uses specific elements of the executive branch.

> *The CIA is part of the Executive Office of the President under the National Security Council.*

The same statute that established the National Security Council placed the Central Intelligence Agency under NSC control. The CIA, whose director and deputy director hold presidential appointments with senatorial consent, coordinates intelligence activities of the several departments and agencies whose operations are in the interest of national security. It also performs additional services at the request of the NSC. After the 1970s revelations of illegal and bizarre CIA interference with Americans, Carter issued Executive Order 12036 on January 24, 1978, prohibiting the CIA from spying on any Americans except suspected foreign agents, terrorists, drug traffickers, and current or former intelligence employees suspected of endangering the agency. On December 4, 1981, Reagan rescinded the Carter limits on the CIA by his Executive Order 12333, which permitted the CIA to spy on Americans and to infiltrate domestic organizations, but "only if it is essential to achieving lawful purposes as determined by the agency head or designee." Because neither chamber of Congress objected within sixty days to this executive order, it went into effect. By such executive orders the president can modify the authorities of any unit in the Executive Office of the President, as long as the orders do not violate statutorily granted agency mandates.

Other elements within EOP. As summarized in table 1-4, the White House Office, the Office of Management and Budget (formerly the Bureau of the Budget), the Council of Economic Advisers, and the National Security Council all are elements of the Executive Office of the President with long histories and significant tasks. Each has substantial staffs on the EOP payroll as well as assistants "on loan" from various executive departments and agencies. Other elements are newer and smaller and do not enjoy the relative permanence that

Table 1-4
Executive Office of the President, January 1985

Office or Council	Year of Establishment	Statutory Head	Senate Approval?	Principal Task
White House Office	1789		No	Assist the president
Office of the Vice-President	1789	Chief of Staff	No	Assist the vice-president
Office of Management and Budget	1970[c]	Director[a]	Yes	Prepare and administer federal budget
Council of Economic Advisers	1946	Chairperson	Yes	Advise on economy and preparation of annual economic message
National Security Council	1947	President[b]		Advise on foreign affairs
Office of U.S. Trade Representative	1963	U.S. Trade Representative	Yes	Coordinate trade agreement programs and administer overall trade policy
Council of Environmental Quality	1969	Chairperson	Yes	Coordinate national environmental programs
Office of Science and Technology Policy	1976	Director	Yes	Serve as a source of scientific analysis and advice
Office of Administration	1977	Director[a]	No	Provide common administrative support services for entire EOP
Office of Policy Development	1978	Director[a]	No	Advise on and coordinate domestic policies

[a] Who is also an assistant or special assistant to the president.
[b] Staff operates under an executive director.
[c] The budgetary part of OMB's work had been done by the Bureau of the Budget, which had been in the EOP since 1946.

The president can reorganize the EOP or modify the mandate of units within the EOP by executive order, providing neither house of Congress objects within sixty days.

the principal agencies experience. Agencies are sometimes established within the EOP to demonstrate special presidential concerns with a problem. The Office of Drug Abuse Policy, for example, established by Nixon and abolished by Carter, would fall into this category.

The EOP is subject to administrative reorganization at any time, provided only that the president submits to Congress any reorganization proposals, which automatically become effective if neither house rejects them within sixty days. This provides each president with the flexibility necessary to manage his responsibilities according to his own best judgment. This flexibility can produce drastic changes in the composition of the EOP. Nine of the nineteen organizations in the EOP when Carter took office in 1977 were eliminated within six months. Functions performed by these now-defunct offices were transferred either to cabinet departments or to other offices within the EOP. Reagan generally felt comfortable with Carter's organization of the EOP, although he moved quickly to abolish the Council on Wage and Price Stability (COWPS), an agency he found ideologically distasteful. COWPS employees who monitored wage and price fluctuations lost their jobs, while COWPS employees who were working on measuring the impact of governmental regulations were transferred either to OMB or to a new task force on regulatory reform.

Commissions. The task force on regulatory reform, chaired by Vice-President Bush, is an example of a special ad hoc entity that the president may establish at any time. Usually called commissions, they are composed of citizens appointed by the president and supported by paid professional staffs. These presidential commissions operate within the EOP until their reports are completed and presented to the president for his consideration. They carry no real authority and are rarely significant in the determination of presidential policy. They are frequently established not so much to provide a source of information for presidential action as to convey the impression of presidential concern. They therefore tend to reflect more heavily the attention to public relations than to public policy, as the fate of recent commission reports demonstrates.

When faced with public pressure to "do something" about a problem, presidents sometimes establish commissions charged with preparing reports to the president.

The Kerner Commission blamed white racism for the widespread urban riots of 1966-1967 and called for massive federal programs to combat the emergence of what it saw as "two Americas": one white and the other black and poor. The report's failure to heap lavish praise on Lyndon Johnson's civil rights accomplishments resulted in a lukewarm presidential endorsement of the report itself and no subsequent attempt to initiate its proposals. The Commission on Obscenity and Pornography, appointed by Johnson, reported in 1970 that pornography was not causing crime, a conclusion that was termed "morally bankrupt" by Nixon. Similarly, Nixon announced even before the Commission on Drug Abuse presented its report that he would not abide by its recommendations if they included the legalization of marijuana.

Removal of personnel. Before leaving the institutionalized presidency, it is in order to mention the fate of the Tenure of Office Act of 1867, in defiance of which Andrew Johnson removed a subordinate and precipitated his own impeachment the following year. The act was declared unconstitutional by the Supreme Court in *Myers v. United States* (272 U.S. 52 [1926]), in which Chief Justice Taft reaffirmed the position taken by George Washington in his battle with the first Congress on this point: the president must have the power to dismiss members of the executive branch on his own authority because he is responsible for the work of the departments involved.

The president can fire high-level administrators he previously appointed.

Conclusion

The office of the presidency provides an opportunity for leadership.

In summary, the president's use of political power takes precedence over the exercise of his constitutional authority. Through a series of power evolutions (which reflect the overall development of the American political system) and in response to initiatives not of his choosing, each successive president has been faced with the problem of molding an institution capable of responding to the vagaries of the American political climate. How the incumbent reacts to this challenge is a function of the individual rather than of the office. The means of presidential leadership are available, but their use is dependent on the individual's ability and political expertise.

To rise to the presidency, the exercise of good political judgment is essential, but the political judgment needed to get elected is not the same as that needed to govern effectively; to lack the latter results in deteriorations in popularity and ineffectiveness in persuasion.

One cannot attain the presidency without a good deal of political expertise, yet one of the persisting ironies is that many who have reached the presidency have demonstrated a decided *inability* to exercise the kind of leadership one would expect from those with such political experience. The history of Lyndon Johnson's presidency stands as the clearest possible example that shrewd politicians do not necessarily become strong presidents. Lyndon Johnson's knowledge and mastery of the wily maneuverings on Capitol Hill served him well in his first years in office. His personal knowledge of legislators, the reputation and prestige he had commanded on the Hill, and his long experience in the art of bargaining coupled with his new, though tragically attained, office produced expectations of an extended honeymoon with Congress. He continued many of the tactics that had earned him a place among the Senate's most illustrious floor leaders in history, but he fared poorly in the end.

Johnson's inability to recognize the differences between senatorial and presidential leadership and to read and react to the signs of popular dissatisfaction with an increasingly futile war in Southeast Asia made it impossible for him to achieve presidential leadership in domestic affairs at a critical period of American history. This failure resulted in a nation racked by conflict at home and abroad and a man broken in body and spirit. The powers of the office are available to those who know how to use them, but only a sensitive understanding of social and political realities will combine with these powers to produce an outstanding leader.

We need not applaud strong presidents if we judge their objectives harmful to our nation.

In contrast to the nation's dissatisfaction with Johnson's foreign policy, Richard Nixon enjoyed overwhelming support for his direction of foreign affairs. During the Nixon presidency, the United States finally extricated itself from the longest war in its history, established better relations with nations that had once been overtly hostile (including the People's Republic of China), and generally assisted in reducing international tensions. But Nixon's foreign policy "successes" will not, for all their contributions, determine his place in history. By virtually ignoring domestic problems, isolating himself from political realities, failing to provide the moral leadership demanded of the occupant of the Oval Office, and taping his own conversations in which he apparently directed a conspiracy to obstruct justice, Nixon missed his opportunity to lead the American people.

If the powers of the presidential office can be used insensitively, as Johnson demonstrated, Nixon showed that they can, likewise, be misused. This misuse of the powers of his office combined with a total disregard of social and political realities to produce the only presidential resignation in American history.

Carter brought to the presidency great intelligence and enormous energy, yet his administration produced few examples of successful presidential leadership (such as Carter's cajoling the Senate into ratifying the Panama Canal Treaty). His inability to present to the people a clear vision of where he sought to lead them brought about public perceptions of Carter as indecisive, weak, and even inept. The more these perceptions took hold, the harder it was for Carter to persuade Congress and his own executive appointees to follow his lead, thereby reinforcing the perceptions.

Reagan faces a situation that most modern presidents have not faced: a second ("lame-duck") term of office. He can ignore many of the more "political" aspects of the presidency because he will never again be eligible for election to the office. Yet, as his second term advances, his power may be limited by the certainty that someone else will take over the presidency on January 20, 1989. How he handles the advantages and disadvantages of his "lame-duck" second term will determine the level of effectiveness of his leadership. The United States has had thirty-nine presidents; the number who have exerted effective leadership is considerably less. Whether Reagan uses the advantages of his lame-duck presidency to exert effective leadership must be left to the judgment of history.

Selected Additional Readings

The authors found the following works to be most helpful in the preparation of this chapter and recommend them to students who want additional information on the presidency:

Barser, Harold M. *The Impossible Presidency*. Glenview, Ill.: Scott, Foresman, 1984.

DiClerico, Robert E. *The American President*. 2d ed. Englewood Cliffs, N.J.: Prentice-Hall, 1983.

Edwards, George C. *The Public Presidency*. New York: St. Martin's Press, 1983.

Koenig, Louis. *The Chief Executive*. 4th ed. New York: Harcourt Brace Jovanovich, 1981.

Neustadt, Richard E. *Presidential Power*. New York: Wiley, 1960.

Page, Benjamin I. and Petracca, Mark P. *The American Presidency*. New York: McGraw Hill, 1983.

Case History: "Superfund" 1980, 1985

On December 11, 1980, President Carter signed into law the Comprehensive Environmental Response, Compensation and Liability Act of 1980 (CERCLA—popularly known as the "Superfund" law), which had been passed by an overwhelming majority of Congress the week before. This is the first of four end-of-chapter segments that document the national government's involvement in that historic legislation, and with its reauthorization in 1985. Each segment deals with the role of the institution that is the principal theme of the chapter to which it is appended. Notations in the margins refer the student to those points in the text that develop and explain the powers or activities documented in the case history. Our treatment of the one case history in four segments is intended to encourage the student to realize the interrelated nature of the institutions under consideration in this text.

Part I: The President

In 1976 the U.S. Environmental Protection Agency (EPA) and the New York State Department of Environmental Conservation (DEC) initiated an investigation of purported chemical contamination at a site known as Love Canal in Niagara Falls, New York. Within two years, New York's Commissioner of Health had declared a health emergency at the site, 237 families had been evacuated, and the nation learned that past practices in the disposal of toxic and hazardous waste promised to haunt the country in the future. In fact, the Surgeon General of the United States said in June 1980 that toxic chemicals would pose a major threat to health in the United States during this decade. By mid-1985 the EPA had announced that it expected that the total number of sites around the country that could eventually "leak" toxic chemicals into the environment could exceed 22,000.

16, 17 Throughout this chapter we have emphasized that no president exercises power in a vacuum, that the president responds to and assists in the initiation of the political climate in which his actions take shape and have their meaning. Carter's assessment of the extent of the hazardous materials disposal problem in the United States was based on the reports of the EPA and on the growing popular concern that abandoned waste sites may exist in many communities. His own involvement in the problem at Love Canal began with his declaration of a national disaster there in August 1978. Tons of toxic chemicals had been dumped at Love Canal in the 1940s, primarily by the Hooker Chemical Company, which later gave the land to Niagara Falls. The county subsequently built an elementary school directly over the location in which many of the toxic substances lay buried. A community of more than 200 homes grew up around the school. By the mid-1970s the residents were experiencing health problems and abnormal births. New York State spent $23 million to help relocate the families and control the spread of the chemicals.

12 By early 1979 Carter had asked Douglas M. Costle, the EPA administrator, to prepare a bill for submission to Congress that would address cleaning up abandoned hazardous waste sites. A special task force was set up within EPA to draft the legislation. By early June the proposed legislation was on Carter's desk.

12 On June 13, Carter sent his proposal to Congress. The bill was designed to help prevent future disasters like the one at Love Canal, but it went far beyond the dangers inherent in chemical contamination. Proposed as the Oil, Hazardous Substances and Hazardous Waste Response, Liability and Compensation Act, the bill was designed to provide the first comprehensive program to address releases of oil and hazardous substances from spills and from inactive and abandoned sites into navigable waters, ground waters, land, and air. The intention was to fill the gaps in the federal government's authority to respond in cases of both oil and hazardous substance releases into the environment. The bill would have established a $1.6 billion fund (dubbed "Superfund" because of its size), of which 80 percent would be provided by fees levied on oil refiners and chemical manufacturers. The remainder of the fund would come from tax revenues. Under the Carter plan, fishermen could be compensated for the loss of income resulting from an oil spill on surface waters but no provisions were made for compensating the public from the fund for damage to health as a result of the release of hazardous materials into the environment.

12, 13 On August 2, 1979, Carter sent a special "Environmental Message" to Congress. He called for passage of the bill, which would permit identification of hazardous sites across the country, establish a uniform system of reporting spills and releases, provide for federal emergency response authority to clean up or contain and mitigate the effects of such releases when those responsible were either unwilling or unable to do so, provide stronger authority to compel the responsible party to take action, provide for monetary compensation in limited cases, and establish fees for industry and state cost-sharing provisions to complement the federal government's tax contributions.

Through the remainder of 1979 and virtually all of 1980, Carter's bill was completely stalled in Congress. In the case study at the end of the next chapter, we will detail the development and substitution of different bills for the Carter proposals. Here we point to some of the problems Carter's bill faced and indicate why his original proposal failed.

16, 19   We have noted that the president's power is not absolute but, rather, that he depends on his ability to persuade others to act as he wants them to act. He ignores signs that others are not disposed to do so at his own peril, as the case of the Carter Superfund proposal indicates. Carter's bill was aimed at cleaning up both abandoned hazardous waste sites and oil spills, but linking these two problems in the same piece of legislation had been unpopular in Congress; an oil spill liability bill had died in the final days of the 95th Congress in 1978 when the House refused to accept a Senate proposal that would have included chemical spills and sites in the same bill.

In the end, Congress exerted its own leadership potential, proposed several versions of the Superfund bill, and passed one of these—which it sent to Carter on December 3, 1980. The president signed the

13   legislation eight days later, and the Comprehensive Environmental Response, Compensation and Liability Act of 1980 (CERCLA) became law.

With the signing of any bill into law, the president's responsibilities regarding its implementation begin. Under ordinary circumstances, legislation passed by Congress empowers "the president" to take certain action. There are places where federal officials other than the president are mentioned in CERCLA, but these are clearly exceptions. Thus, for example, Section 106 (c) of CERCLA specifies that "the Administrator of the Environmental Protection Agency shall, after consultation with the Attorney General, establish and publish guidelines... to effectuate the responsibilities and powers created by this Act." But most of the powers granted in this and other legislation are not so specific. Rather than authorizing the "Administrator of EPA" or the "Attorney General" to act, most of the provisions of CERCLA and of other laws authorize "the president" to take specific actions. It falls to the president to delegate to subordinate federal officials in various agencies the powers originally delegated to him by Congress. This redelegation of

14   authority, accomplished by means of executive order, can be a powerful political tool in the hands of an administration.

When Carter signed the Superfund legislation into law, he was already a "lame duck" president—he had lost the election to Ronald Reagan, who would assume the presidency on January 20, 1981. Unless an executive order redelegating the president's authorities as outlined in CERCLA was issued by the White House before January 20, none of the federal agencies that might be involved in implementation of the new law would be certain of the extent of their authority. They would be unable to take any new actions in the area of hazardous waste cleanup other than to implement those sections of the law that, like Section 106 (c), specified a particular federal official other than the president.

Senior management and staff from several affected federal agencies worked closely with the White House staff during the waning days of Carter's administration to try to iron out the details of an executive order in regard to CERCLA. Finally, on January 19, 1981—the day before he left office—Carter signed Executive Order 12286, which delegated authority to various federal agencies to implement CERCLA.

We have noted that an executive order is a political tool in the hands of an administration. If a president "favors" a particular federal agency, he is able to make considerable delegations to it, thereby increasing the agency's role in implementing federal legislation and concomitantly increasing the agency's size, power, and prestige. Conversely, if an agency is "out of favor" with the White House, the president may delegate authority to others and leave the errant department with little to do. If it has no functions, no "authority" to act, a federal agency will shrivel and die: its personnel lose their jobs or are absorbed by other agencies.

Under Executive Order 12286, Carter assigned a central role in implementing CERCLA to the Council on Environmental Quality (CEQ). CEQ was given the responsibility of amending and publishing the National Contingency Plan (NCP). Section 105 of CERCLA says that "the President shall...revise and republish the national contingency plan for the removal of oil and hazardous substances, originally prepared and published pursuant to Section 311 of the Federal Water Pollution Control Act, to reflect and effectuate the responsibilities and powers created by this Act." For years, the federal government had been responding to environmental emergencies under the authority of the national contingency plan, and the important responsibility of revising it to cover the new power to respond to hazardous materials releases into the environment passed to CEQ.

When the new administration took over on January 20, 1981, it was soon apparent that some of Reagan's advisers and White House staffers were unhappy with Carter's "lame-duck" executive order. On August 14, 1981, Reagan signed Executive Order 12316, which rescinded the Carter order.

Two features of EO 12316 demonstrate the political nature of executive orders: the role of the Office of Management and Budget and the absence of CEQ. Under the Reagan order all regulations and guidelines regarding the implementation of CERCLA must be approved by OMB. This is consistent with the general shift of power to that office that we noted earlier in this chapter. In addition, some of the new president's close advisers were mistrustful of CEQ; they considered it to be duplicative of functions performed in other federal agencies, and to have "liberal leanings." By the time the new executive order was signed, the writing was already on the wall: CEQ was being reorganized and weakened considerably. The authority to revise and republish the National Contingency Plan was delegated to the Environmental Protection Agency (EPA)—after review and approval by OMB. Executive orders, originating from the president, do not require congressional approval.

During the next five years, Reagan's involvement with Superfund would be substantial, and it would be the basis of one of the longest-running scandals of his first administration, with charges of mismanagement and an antienvironment bias. One key element of the scandal was the claim, made by EPA Administrator Anne M. Gorsuch in 1982, that certain Superfund records held by the agency would not be provided to Congress because they dealt with "sensitive enforcement matters" and were, therefore, covered by the doctrine of "executive privilege." On December 16, 1982, the House of Representatives voted to hold Gorsuch in contempt of Congress for her refusal to deliver the requested documents. Although the contempt charge was dropped in August 1983, it was instrumental in causing her resignation, the firing or resignation of at least twenty-four other senior-level policy-making and political appointees at the agency, the conviction of one former assistant administrator of perjury, and the concentration of public attention on the agency's activities (especially Superfund) for several years.

Partially as a result of the scandal involving EPA's handling of the popular Superfund program, Reagan announced in his State of the Union address in January 1984 that his administration would seek reauthorization and expansion of CERCLA when it expired in September 1985. This announcement was important for several reasons. First, with many policy items competing for inclusion in this annual message to Congress, an item must be perceived by the administration as having important policy implications in order for the president to mention it; this put CERCLA in that category. Second, the announcement permitted the EPA to devote considerable resources to determining its preferred position on the size of the reauthorized fund, to deciding upon the changes in the law that it wanted to see, and to lobbying congressional staff regarding reauthorization proposals. We shall deal in some detail with these activities in the case study at the end of Chapter 4, but mention them here because of the "legitimacy" accorded them by Reagan's announcement of support for reauthorization in his State of the Union address.

"Support" does not necessarily mean that the president is ready to propose legislation. CERCLA Section 301(a)(1) required the president to send to Congress in December 1984 a complete evaluation of the Superfund program, along with recommendations for reauthorization. Of course, 1984 was an election year; there were considerable political pressures being exerted by industry, environmental groups, members of Congress, and by the media to act on reauthorization prior to submission of the Section 301 evaluation. Some Democrats were eager to embarrass Reagan during the campaign—hoping that a Superfund debate prior to the election would rekindle memories of the 1983 EPA scandal. Others wanted the Superfund debate to take place in 1984 because they believed that Reagan could not afford to veto a strong Superfund bill before the election, given all the trouble Superfund had caused him earlier. As Representative Dennis E. Eckart (D.-OH) expressed "I can't think of a better bill to lay on Ronald Reagan's desk as he speaks so piously of his new, reborn concern with the environment."

The president was successful in delaying renewal of Superfund until 1985. Congress was unable to agree on a bill reauthorizing it during 1984 (we will deal with the reasons for this in the case study section at the end of the next chapter). The Section 301 evaluation was submitted in December as required by law, and it formed the basis of the administration's reauthorization proposal in 1985. Although many members of Congress wanted to force the president to act in 1984, he was able to use the requirement that Congress itself had placed in the law (that the Section 301 studies be submitted to them in December of that year) in order to force Congress to conform to his timetable. Superfund, greatly expanded and considerably stronger, was reauthorized in 1985.

Chapter 2

The Congress

Congress retains a key role in government.

The twentieth century has seen the weakening and demise of legislatures in much of the world as power has gravitated to presidents, premiers, and prime ministers. One legislature that remains an essential force in governmental policy making is the Congress of the United States. Congress may not be as powerful in relation to the presidency as it was in the age of Daniel Webster, but it has retained a central role in the government. As Richard Neustadt writes, "A President will often be unable to obtain congressional action on his terms or even to halt action he opposes. The reverse is equally accepted: Congress is often frustrated by the President. Their formal powers are so intertwined that neither will accomplish very much, for very long, without the acquiescence of the other."[1]

Congress and the president are dependent on each other.

Congress changes more slowly than the presidency.

The presidency changes, sometimes abruptly, as each incumbent stamps it with his own personality. Congress, however, has demonstrated continuity in its procedures, rules, and general nature regardless of who is elected and which party controls the congressional leadership. Of course, Congress has changed since its beginnings as a tiny body of twenty-six senators and sixty-five representatives, but the changes have been much more evolutionary than revolutionary. We feel secure in predicting that the Congress of 1995 will fundamentally resemble the Congress we describe in this chapter.

Constitutional Prerogatives

The Constitution gives Congress prerogatives and powers.

The Constitution grants Congress the authority to legislate, to police itself, and to impeach and try errant national officials. Table 2-1 summarizes Congress's constitutional duties.

The Authority to Legislate

Power to enact legislation. Article I of the Constitution states that "all legislative Powers herein granted shall be vested in a Congress of the United States, which shall consist of a Senate and a House of Representatives." This

---
[1] Richard Neustadt, *Presidential Power* (New York: Wiley, 1960), p. 37.

Table 2-1
The Congress: Constitutional Prerogatives and Powers

Authority to Legislate	Authority to Impeach and Try
Power to enact legislation (Art. I, Sec. 1)	Power to impeach and try (Art. I, Secs. 2 & 3)
...expanded by commerce clause (Art. I, Sec. 8)	Authority to Police Itself
...expanded by "elastic clause" (Art. I, Sec. 8)	Power over its own operations (Art. I, Sec. 5)
Power to override presidential vetoes (Art. I, Sec. 7)	Power over electoral procedures (Art. I, Sec. 4)

Congress can pass laws only in policy areas listed by Article I, Section 8 of the Constitution.

Most government tasks initially were left to state and local governments.

Modernization increased demands on the national government; the Constitution did not prevent Congress from changing to meet these demands.

Under its power to regulate commerce, Congress has passed much legislation affecting the economy.

Minimum wage legislation is an example of how the commerce clause permits broad congressional activity.

clause does not grant Congress the right to pass any law it deems wise, but only those pertaining to the specific powers "herein granted." Section 8 of this same article spells out the areas in which Congress may act. The Constitution provides for a national government acting to perform only specifically designated functions (coining money, establishing post offices, maintaining the armed forces, and so forth), thereby leaving most governmental functions to the states (for example, building schools, maintaining police forces).

What this country has experienced in the two centuries since the writing of the Constitution is the development of an intricate, highly industrialized society requiring many services at all levels of government. The Constitution has provided sufficient flexibility for Congress to adapt itself to respond to modern national needs. Two clauses in particular, in Section 8 of Article I, have permitted Congress to broaden greatly the scope of its legislation: the commerce clause and the "elastic" or "necessary proper" clause.

The commerce clause. The commerce clause simply states that Congress shall have power "to regulate Commerce with foreign Nations, and among the several States, and with the Indian Tribes." This clause has been the constitutional justification of much legislation in the economic realm, including minimum wage, labor, and antimonopoly legislation. Thus, although not given the explicit authority to prescribe working conditions or set a minimum wage, Congress enacted the Fair Labor Standards Act of 1938. Passage of this act eliminated child labor in factories and mines, mandated overtime pay after forty-four hours at the regular wage, and set a minimum wage of twenty-five cents per hour. Fred W. Darby, an employer in the lumber industry, claimed that Congress lacked the authority to pass such legislation. However, the Supreme Court ruled (in *United States v. Darby,* 312 U.S. 100 [1941]) that so long as Darby's lumber products were shipped in interstate commerce, Congress did have the authority to set working standards by making it a crime to send products made in violation of those standards into another state.

Because so much activity in America directly or indirectly involves interstate commerce, the commerce clause allows Congress to legislate in almost any economic realm it chooses.

The "elastic clause." The "elastic clause" merely states that Congress may "make all Laws which shall be necessary and proper for carrying into Execution the foregoing Powers." If Congress were limited to the specific, delegated powers of Section 8 (establishing post offices, coining money, and so on), the power of the national government would be extremely constrained. Instead, Justice John Marshall ruled in *McCulloch v. Maryland* (4 Wheaton 316 [1819]) that the "necessary and proper" clause should be interpreted to allow Congress "implied powers" (powers not specifically delegated, but reasonably implied in the execution of those delegated powers). Thus, Justice Marshall ruled that Congress had the authority to incorporate a national bank (even though the Constitution mentions neither banks nor incorporation) as an implied constitutional power derived from the enumerated powers to tax, to borrow money, and to regulate commerce. His decision established the legal grounds for congressional legislation in a wide range of areas not mentioned in the Constitution. Such legislation is viewed as a "necessary and proper" extension of Congress's constitutional prerogatives.

Congress can pass laws "necessary and proper" to carry out its specific powers effectively.

McCulloch v. Maryland determined that Congress has the right to act in areas reasonably related to its specific powers.

In the twenty decades since the writing of the Constitution, the United States has become a nation characterized both by substantial cultural diversity and by a highly integrated economy. These interrelated factors have meant that almost no problems or situations are matters of purely local or state concern, that almost everything has national implications—from a strike of migrant workers in California to a cutback in production of a logging company in Maine. The Constitution has provided Congress with the specific right to pass legislation relating to commerce, war, and finances, and this right has been broadly interpreted by Congress in the extension of its legislative prerogatives. This interpretation, as upheld by the courts, places only one limitation on the legislative power of Congress: it may not infringe on the rights of states and individuals explicitly granted elsewhere in the Constitution.

Congress now has the right to legislate in all areas, but its laws cannot take away rights explicitly granted in the Constitution to states and individuals.

Power to override presidential vetoes. Although all bills must be passed by Congress to become law, we have seen that the Constitution does not place the entire legislative process in the hands of the Congress. Thus, we must explore the relationship between congressional actions and presidential vetoes. After a bill passes both the House and the Senate, it is sent to the president, who has three alternatives: he can sign it, he can veto it, or he can do nothing. If he signs it, the bill becomes a public law. If he vetoes it, the bill is returned to Congress, which may modify the bill in light of the president's wishes or may attempt to override his veto—a difficult course of action. The difficulty arises from the constitutional provision (Article I, Section 7) that

Overriding a presidential veto requires a two-thirds majority in each house of Congress.

requires a two-thirds majority in each house to override a presidential veto.

Relying on his battery of persuasive tactics, a president can usually persuade either one-third of the senators or one-third of the representatives to support his veto; hence, overridden vetoes are rare. From the administration of George Washington through Ronald Reagan's first term, only ninety-six presidential vetoes were overridden by Congress. Not surprisingly, the president who most often found his vetoes overridden was the impeached and almost convicted Andrew Johnson. Congress overrode fifteen of his twenty-nine vetoes. Gerald Ford, another president who fought bitterly with Congress, found that twelve of his sixty-six vetoes were overridden. In his first term, Ronald Reagan had four of his thirty-nine vetoes overridden.

> *Congress rarely overrides a presidential veto.*

When the party controlling the presidency also controls both houses of Congress, successful overrides by Congress are even rarer than they are during periods of split party control. Of the more than 600 vetoes by Franklin D. Roosevelt, the Democrat-controlled Congress managed to override only nine. Congress overrode none of John Kennedy's twenty-one or Lyndon Johnson's thirty vetoes and only two of Jimmy Carter's thirty-one.

> *When the same party controls both the presidency and Congress, overrides almost never occur.*

The president's third course of action upon receipt of a bill from Congress is to sit back and do nothing with the bill for ten days. Ironically, it is not the action of the president but the condition of the Congress that determines the fate of the bill in this instance. If Congress remains in session, the bill automatically becomes law at the end of the ten-day period. (Presidents often use this tactic of "permitting" the bill to become law without actively supporting its passage. It is thus a demonstration to Congress that the president is not really pleased with the legislation but that his opposition to it is either too mild to warrant a veto or futile in face of a larger than two-thirds majority in both houses.)

> *If a president does not sign or veto a bill within ten working days after receiving it from Congress, the bill automatically becomes law.*

Pocket vetoes. If Congress adjourns within ten days of sending a bill to the president, the bill does not become law unless the president signs it. Presidential inaction while Congress is in session results in a "pocket veto"—that is, Congress by its adjournment has prevented the president from returning the bill (which he presumably "stuffs in his pocket" and quietly ignores). It is therefore only at the end of a congressional session that a president can veto a bill by his inaction. In the flurry of legislative activity that usually marks the end of the term, many bills have been passed that subsequently faced pocket vetoes. Forty-two percent of presidential vetoes have fallen into this category and have contributed significantly to the low success ratio of congressional overrides mentioned above. Of Franklin Roosevelt's 631 vetoes, 261 were of the pocket variety—by far the largest number of any president. Grover Cleveland, however, holds the record for most pocket vetoes per year, with 136 vetoes of end-of-term bills during his eight years in the White House.

> *If Congress adjourns within ten days after sending a bill to the president and he does not sign it, the bill is "pocket vetoed"; Congress, having adjourned, has no opportunity to override a pocket veto.*
>
> *Pocket vetoes account for 42 percent of all vetoes.*

These records will probably stand, because recent presidents have made less use of the pocket veto: Richard Nixon used it only nineteen times, Ford

To avoid a veto, Congress often changes a bill to reflect the president's wishes.

twenty-two, Carter eighteen. This reduced use is indicative of the persuasive capability of the modern presidency. By threatening to veto a bill while it is still under congressional consideration, the president is often able to persuade Congress to change those features of the bill to which he objects. No one is more aware of the difficulties inherent in overriding a presidential veto than the members of Congress, who seek to avoid the prospect whenever possible. A president is not at all reluctant to brandish an impending veto if the bill in question is not modified to reflect his views. Thus, in the face of a threatened veto in 1981 by Reagan, Congress changed the bill funding the Legal Services Corporation to remove those elements that most displeased him.

The president cannot veto part of a bill; he either signs the entire bill or vetoes it.

A rider is a provision of a bill not necessarily germane to the purpose of the bill.

The president works with his supporters in Congress to stop the attachment of riders he does not favor to bills he does favor.

Item vetoes. Although the Constitution does provide the president with veto power, it does not provide him with an *item* veto. The president must either sign an entire bill or veto an entire bill; he cannot sign certain sections of the bill while vetoing others. This lack of an item veto encourages Congress to propose riders (legislation not necessarily germane to the bill to which it is affixed) that may be displeasing to the president. Thus Congress will attach legislation that, in isolation, would be vetoed by the president to bills particularly favored by him. He is unable to separate the rider from the bill to which it is attached and must therefore sign or veto it in its entirety. A powerful president will, as we noted in the last chapter, have enough support in Congress to avert the attachments of riders to his proposed legislation.

The Authority to Impeach and Try

Although Congress has the right to impeach and remove derelict officials of the executive and judicial branches, it has rarely done so.

Besides granting to Congress the right to legislate, the Constitution also grants the right to remove national officials judged guilty of "high crimes and misdemeanors." The House of Representatives *impeaches*, a confusing word that means to bring to trial for consideration for removal. Following a successful impeachment by the House, the Senate acts as jury in the trial proceedings, by which a two-thirds vote is required to remove the offending public official from office. Impeachment proceedings have very rarely taken place, for the threat of impeachment is usually sufficient to cause the tainted official to submit his resignation, as we have already seen in the case of Richard Nixon.

The Authority to Police Itself

Congress has the right to deny a seat to a member chosen in a fraudulent election but generally accepts the judgment of state authorities.

Power over its own operations. Constitutional prerogatives also include Congress's right to determine its own internal procedures and the legitimacy of its members. Although this latter prerogative permits it to deny a seat to a member whose election involved irregularities, Congress generally has accepted without investigation the winner declared by state authorities.

This authority to police itself includes the right to set salaries ($75,100 in

Congress sets the salaries of its members.

Legislators must disclose personal finances; they cannot keep "slush funds," accept expensive gifts from lobbyists, or engage in "lame-duck" travel.

In spite of ethics codes, scandals continue to occur, although only a small number of legislators have been involved.

Congress requires lobbyists to register.

The most successful congressional lobbyists are often former members of Congress.

Congress grants access to the floor to all former members.

For federal elections, Congress mandates secret ballots, single-member districts, and a common date (the Tuesday after the first Monday in November).

1985) and benefits, including a generous pension plan. In 1981 Congress greatly expanded its members' remuneration by legislating a tax deduction for all expenses incurred while in Washington and by providing for automatic raises pegged to the inflation level. In 1982, in response to public outcries, it rescinded the special tax deduction.

Congress has set limits on the conduct permitted members. Members must make full financial disclosures of assets and liabilities. They cannot keep unofficial office accounts ("slush funds" whose sources and distributions are unreported) and cannot receive gifts valued over $100 from lobbyists. In addition, members are prohibited from "lame-duck" travel (trips taken at government expense by legislators about to retire). Because Congress has in the past been reluctant to investigate the ethics of its members, the rigor of enforcement of these rules is in doubt.

Despite the existence of codes of ethics, scandals have continued to generate negative publicity for Congress. In 1980 the House went so far as to expel Rep. Michael Myers (D.-Pa.) after his conviction in the "Abscam" affair. Myers, the first member of Congress ever to be expelled for official corruption, was among six representatives and one senator filmed accepting bribes offered by undercover FBI agents posing as wealthy Arab sheiks. All seven legislators are out of political life.

Congress has also exercised its power over its own operations by requiring lobbyists in Washington to register. Because the First Amendment to the Constitution prohibits Congress from restricting lobbying ("Congress shall make no law . . . abridging . . . the right of the people . . . to petition the Government for redress of grievances"), reformers have instead sought to control the excesses of pressure groups by restricting gift giving (as with the $100 restriction) and by requiring public disclosure of lobbying activities. The Lobbying Disclosure Act of 1946 requires all Washington lobbyists to specify their employers and their legislative interests. This at least provides the public with information on who is lobbying for what. Not surprisingly, often the highest-paid and most influential lobbyists are former members of Congress; their contacts and access to the floor (open to all former members) make them highly sought after as lobbyists.

Power over electoral procedures. Finally, the Constitution provides that Congress can determine "the Times, Places, and Manner of holding Elections." In the absence of congressional action, each state legislature makes these determinations for the election of its U.S. senators and representatives. Congress has exercised its option to standardize electoral procedures by mandating single-member districts (only one winner in each district) for representatives (1842), the secret ballot (also called the Australian ballot) (1872), and the time of the election (the Tuesday after the first Monday in November). In 1940 Congress passed the Hatch Act, which prohibits federal government employees from participating in political campaigns. The law is so strict that a postal employee cannot even put up a lawn sign supporting a candidate. There have been efforts to reform this act so that federal employees might enjoy the same political rights as other Americans. However, concerns that poorly written reforms might subject federal employees to the kinds of political pressures that characterized the spoils system have hampered these efforts.

Article I, Section 4 has permitted Congress to pass legislation prohibiting corporations and unions from making campaign contributions and limiting the size of individual contributions. The law has a loophole that permits the creation of political action committees (PACs) through which corporations and unions funnel large sums into politcal campaigns. Although critics have argued that the great influence of PACs perverts democratic norms of elected officials responsible only to their constituents, Congress recently has shown little interest in reforming the campaign finance laws. In part, Congress's tolerance of PAC spending may be a consequence of the tendency of most PACs to give most of their money to incumbents rather than to challengers.

> *The Hatch Act prohibits federal government employees from involvement in campaigns.*
>
> *Congress can regulate campaign contributions.*
>
> *PACs buy influence through campaign contributions.*

Congressional Leadership

Noting that the Constitution grants Congress prerogatives enabling broad legislation, impeachment, and control over its own elections and membership tells us that Congress has the potential for real leadership, but it tells us little about whether Congress has chosen to exert this leadership. As in the case of the presidency, we must look beyond the Constitution to view Congress as leader.

> *The formal powers granted Congress by the Constitution give Congress an opportunity for leadership.*

The Roles of Congress

Can Congress really lead the American people in the sense that the president can fulfill a leadership role? Congress differs from the presidency in that it does not speak with one voice, but with a chorus composed of 435 representatives and 100 senators. Congress cannot unanimously urge the adoption of a single, coherent, integrated program of government. But Congress can execute adeptly five functions that, taken together, give it an immense capacity for leadership. These functions are (1) representation, (2) creation and clarification of issues, (3) oversight of government, (4) legitimation of governmental policies, and (5) lawmaking. In performing these functions, Congress not only can provide and act on alternatives to specific executive proposals but can guide the general direction of national policy as well. When it does so with clarity and vigor, the result is congressional leadership.

> *Congress can do more than just react to executive branch initiatives.*

Representation. One basic function performed by Congress is that of representation. The president and vice-president are the only elected officials

> *Local interests have their views aired by their representatives.*

with a nationwide constituency and therefore can claim to represent the interest of all Americans. But, in representing all Americans, they cannot grant a special voice to the farmers of Kansas or to the lobster fishermen of Maine. Senators and representatives are expected to provide such a voice and to be supportive of the needs of their respective constituents. Thus, the senators and representatives from Maine are expected to be knowledgeable about problems in the lobster industry and to press for national efforts to alleviate these problems, while the members from South Carolina are expected to present the position of the textile interests. Congress is a place where the diverse interests of our large nation are given open representation. This does not mean necessarily that Congress will pass legislation favorable to lobstering or to the textile people, nor does it mean that all local interests are represented (local interests in the same district often oppose each other, with the representative supporting one interest and ignoring the other). Instead, we can safely conclude that most interests (at least those supportive of a particular representative in the district) are likely to receive a public presentation of their views in Congress.

> *A member of Congress, to garner support for bills of particular concern to his or her constituents, may agree to support the particular concerns of other members in return for their votes; vote trading, also called "logrolling," occurs most often in "pork-barrel" votes.*
>
> *On most issues, constituents either lack firm opinions or are divided.*

This situation in which some issues carry regional significance for some representatives and are not salient at all for other representatives allows for bargaining among members of Congress. Because textiles are not salient to the representatives from Maine, they might be willing to trade their vote on a textile bill in return for support of the South Carolina representatives on a lobster bill. This form of vote trading is most common in "pork-barrel" legislation (bills involving public works projects).

Congress performs this representative function without many of its members seeing themselves as instructed delegates who mirror the will of the majority of their constituents. In fact, there is rarely a dilemma between voting one's own judgment and voting constituents' opinion. On most issues, voters exhibit neither knowledge nor concern. Even when a majority of voters have an opinion on an issue, a given constituency may be equally divided on two sides of the issue. We are also faced with the question of whether senators and representatives accurately know the views of their constituents. Members of Congress do not take periodic, professionally prepared surveys of their districts. Rather, they depend on mail questionnaires, which are notoriously biased, partly because conservatives[2] are more likely than liberals to respond

---

[2]*Conservatism*, as the term is used in this chapter and in contemporary parlance, refers to a series of positions on issues generally, including opposition to government regulation of the economy, heavy government spending on social programs, and civil rights legislation and enforcement. In contrast, liberalism is the political view that looks to government as a positive force that can ameliorate wrongs and provide opportunities for individuals otherwise disadvantaged in society. Liberals generally favor social programs and civil rights legislation. On the issue of military spending, conservatives tend to support most proposed new programs, and liberals generally oppose large increases in military spending. Conservatives generally support government programs to promote prayer in public schools and to outlaw abortion; liberals tend to oppose government involvement in these areas.

to such questionnaires. So, not knowing how their constituents really stand on issues, most members of Congress assume (often correctly) that they themselves reflect the actual views of their constituency. They see no conflict between voting their own opinions and voting according to constituency opinion back home.

The electoral process enhances the extent to which individual members represent the majority sentiment in their districts. Conservative districts elect conservative representatives who, by voting conservatively, have no conflict between their constituents' views and their own. Similarly, liberal districts elect liberal representatives, who only rarely find themselves at odds with their constituents.

Issue creation and clarification. A second congressional function is the creation and clarification of issues. Congress provides a forum for the public expression of diverse views. It acts as a sounding board for new ideas, many of which later are enacted into law.

In the public nature of almost all its debate, Congress differs considerably from the executive branch, where private debate beforehand usually enables it to present a united front to Congress. Although Congress used to conduct many of its important debates in closed committee meetings, new rules passed in the mid-1970s opened to the public all but the small number of meetings concerned with national security matters. Even markup sessions (when bills are actually drafted) are now open to the public. And, of course, debate on the floor remains open.

Hearings are ostensibly investigations to gather information for the writing of approved legislation, but they also serve to focus public attention on problems or new issues. In recent years, congressional hearings have publicized such issues as sexual harassment on the job, abuses involving pension funds, and the impact of the Voting Rights Act. Early in the 1970s, hearings focused national attention on the campaign abuses of the Nixon administration. In the 1960s Congress instigated a national debate through its hearings on the war in Vietnam. The hearings of the Senate Foreign Relations Committee largely began the nationwide questioning of the wisdom and morality of the involvement of the United States in that tragic war.

Oversight of the executive branch. A third valuable function performed by Congress is that of "watchdog" or "overseer" of the executive branch. Each substantive committee is expected to oversee the activities of the executive branch that fall within its subject area. Thus, for example, the Armed Services Committees in both houses are expected to maintain vigilance over military activities. Reports that Congress was weak in its oversight function led the House in 1974 to require substantive committees to develop plans specifying how they will fulfill their oversight function for each two-year period. As a

---

Because members of Congress do not take frequent, professional polls, they often do not know where their constituents stand on issues.

Because most districts elect representatives who agree with the predominant constituency sentiment on issues, most representatives rarely face the dilemma of voting their conscience versus constituency opinion.

Congress provides a public forum for the discussion of issues and ideas.

Congress opens almost all committee meetings, even markup sessions, at which committee members work out the actual wording of bill modifications.

Hearings often publicize problems and issues.

Every substantive committee is responsible for oversight activities in its area of specialization.

safeguard, the House Committee on Government Operations (in addition to its own broad oversight activities) supervises and coordinates the oversight activities of the substantive committees.

Committee hearings often investigate executive branch behavior.

Committees use their powers of investigation to review executive actions. Administrative officials and other interested parties are required to attend hearings where they must answer questions put to them by legislators. Subjects of investigation in the early 1980s have included U.S. involvement in El Salvador (both by the Inter-American Affairs Subcommittee of the House Foreign Affairs Committee and by the Foreign Operations Subcommittee of the House Appropriations Committee) and the food stamp program (by the House Agriculture Committee's Subcommittee on Department Operations). These and similar investigations have helped Congress learn about many executive branch activities.

Casework provides oversight information to members.

Oversight also is performed as an unintentional outgrowth of the casework that members perform for constituents. Annually each member's office handles thousands of requests from constituents who seek information or assistance in dealing with the federal bureaucracy. Through these communications members discover problem areas in the implementation of federal programs.

The GAO audits the executive branch and performs inquiries requested by Congress.

Another means by which Congress fulfills its oversight function is the General Accounting Office (GAO), which audits the executive branch, conducts inquiries, and gathers information at the request of Congress or even of individual members. Headed by Comptroller General Charles A. Bowsher whom the president appointed for a fifteen-year term with Senate approval, the GAO is designed primarily to provide nonpartisan information on the spending behavior of the executive branch. The GAO works closely with the Congressional Budget Office to supply the Budget Committees with up-to-date information on how money is being spent.

Congress's control of appropriations is the key power that makes oversight important.

Congress's control of appropriations is its real strength in carrying out its oversight responsibilities. Congress takes its oversight responsibilities seriously because members know that they have the power to reduce or even to stop the funding of programs they find to be inefficient. The executive branch, knowing that Congress has this power, tries to convince the legislators that programs are being effectively administered in line with congressional intentions. The oversight function is thus a never-ending review of executive branch performance where the stakes are the expansion, reduction, and elimination of federal agencies and programs.

Legitimation of government policy. A fourth function of Congress is legitimation of government policies. If people believe that governmental policies are passed by a legislature fairly elected in open, free elections, they are very likely to believe that the policy decisions of the government are legitimate, that the government has a right to do what it is doing. Because people believe that most of the policy decisions of the government are arrived

People feel a responsibility to obey federal laws because Congress is a representative institution whose members are freely elected.

at "justly" through a representative institution, they also usually feel obligated to obey those decisions—even decisions they would otherwise consider absurd. Thus Congress aids in the peaceful resolution of conflicting interests. A citizen who disagrees with governmental policies knows that a peaceful remedy—electing members of Congress who agree with him or her—is available. The existence of this electoral remedy, which is not available in nations like Chile, Poland, and Libya, legitimates the regime.

Lawmaking. A fifth function of Congress, and its most obvious, is that of lawmaking. Congress considers thousands of bills each year, only a small number of which are enacted into law. Congress's lawmaking function involves not only passing bills but modifying and rejecting them as well. Although major legislation increasingly originates in the executive branch, Congress rarely accepts the executive's versions without making important substantive revisions. Sometimes, as in the case study at the end of this chapter, Congress substitutes its own version of a bill for the one offered by the president, and often it rejects executive proposals entirely. In fact, some of Congress's finest hours have come in its rejection of politically popular but ill-conceived bills. Annually, for example, Congress rejects bills that would infringe on the constitutional rights of unpopular minorities, such as the American Communist party, the Ku Klux Klan, and the Gay Activist Alliance.

In the previous chapter we stressed that one cannot profitably think of the president as "switching" from one role to another in the process of leadership. His roles often overlap and merge with each other, and congressional functions should be viewed in a similar light. Thus, we might refer to the national budget, involving as it does the expenditure of almost $1 trillion, as an important "law" that the Congress must pass every year; yet the process by which the Appropriations Committee of the House reviews the budget requests of the various agencies, bureaus, and departments of the executive branch forms an integral part of the "budgetary process" as well. This close scrutiny represents at least two congressional functions: overseeing the executive branch and enacting legislation.

These five roles may still not equal the leadership potential of the president, but the potential for leadership that Congress does possess is obviously immense. When Congress is maximizing its leadership capabilities, it is giving a clear voice to the demands of all Americans, clarifying important issues, keeping a keen oversight of the executive branch, legitimating possibly unpopular yet wise government policies, and passing progressive laws. When Congress is failing to exercise its leadership responsibilities, it is failing to represent many Americans, confusing and badly articulating issues, giving unbridled rein to the executive branch, failing to justify government policies adequately, and passing foolish laws. That Congress fulfills its leadership roles vigorously is clearly of the greatest importance.

Congress rejects most bills that are offered.

Congressional actions often involve more than one function.

Congress has the potential for leadership.

Electoral Procedures

Apportionment

Senators and representatives are elected for different periods of time to bodies of different sizes. These differences of tenure and size give rise to operational differences between the two houses, some of which can be seen in table 2-2.

Each state, regardless of size, has two senators.

Senate apportionment. There are 100 senators, two from each state. This method of apportionment of the Senate gives each state equal representation, regardless of a state's population. Thus, the composition of the Senate is undemocratic in that the one-person, one-vote premise of democracy is ignored. The senators from California, for example, represent over 24 million Americans, whereas the senators from Alaska represent fewer than a half-million. The Founding Fathers, however, believed that this "undemocratic" apportionment of the Senate was so important that it is the one provision of the Constitution that cannot be amended. Article V, which describes the amending process, includes the provision that "no State, without its Consent, shall be deprived of its equal Suffrage in the Senate."

House apportionment. The House of Representatives comprises 435 members elected under the one-person, one-vote rule, but with the added

Table 2-2
House-Senate Differences

House	Senate
Larger (435 Members)	Smaller (100 members)
Two-year term of office	Six-year term of office
More centralized power	Less centralized power
Acts more quickly	Acts more slowly
More rigid rules	More flexible rules
More impersonal	More personal
Policy specialists	Policy generalists
Smaller constituencies	Larger constituencies
Less prestige	More prestige
Younger	Older
Wider minority representation	Narrower minority representation
Less reliance on staff	More reliance on staff
More committees	Fewer committees

stipulation that each state must have at least one representative. Congress itself determines the size of the House, which started with 65 members in 1790 but has remained at 435 since 1912. Every ten years each state legislature redraws congressional district boundaries so that each district contains close to the same number of people, around 600,000 in the 1980s. Of course, the six states with only one representative (Alaska, Delaware, North Dakota, South Dakota, Vermont, and Wyoming) face no redistricting tasks. In those states (and in Washington D.C., which has one nonvoting representative), House candidates must run statewide.

Each state has the number of representatives proportionate to its population.

Every ten years census results are used to reapportion the House.

House and Senate compared. The smaller size of the Senate gives each senator more prestige than each representative. Being 1/100th of a legislative body is more important than being 1/435th. The Senate's smaller size also permits it to be less formal, more personal than the House—which needs its more rigid rules just to avoid chaos. Senators are usually generalists who try to learn a little about many policy areas; representatives often focus on a smaller number of issues of particular interest to them or their constituents. The larger size of the senatorial constituency—an entire state—makes it less likely that a senator will represent the parochial interests of a subregion or have a narrow, localized viewpoint.

Senators have more prestige than representatives.

The Senate runs itself more informally than does the House.

Single-Member Districts and Plurality

Both senators and representatives are elected from single-member districts. (Although each state's two senators share the same "district," they are not elected simultaneously.) These districts operate on a "winner-take-all" plurality basis. This means that each district elects only one representative: the candidate who receives the greatest proportion of the votes, regardless of whether this proportion is a majority. In an election with four candidates receiving, respectively, 35 percent, 30 percent, 25 percent, and 10 percent of the votes cast, the candidate with 35 percent of the votes would be elected; there would be no runoff election between the first two finishers. Because of this system of elections, a minor party can win 25 percent of the vote in every congressional district and still fail to send even one of its candidates to Congress.

Each district elects only one person to Congress. A plurality wins, for there are no runoff elections.

Alternatives. If, instead of the present system, members of Congress were elected under a system of proportional representation, a party winning 25 percent of the vote nationwide would hold 25 percent of the seats in Congress. The current system greatly increases the proportion of seats in the legislature that the most popular party wins and discourages the efforts of third or fourth parties by making it highly unlikely that a minor party could win any seats at all.

The single-member, plurality-wins system rewards the most popular party with extra representation in Congress and severely penalizes third parties.

If the electoral system were changed to require an absolute majority for election, a system of runoffs (or successive ballots) would have to be initiated.

Voters would know that on the first balloting they could vote for a minor-party candidate without "wasting their votes," for the likelihood would be great that neither major-party candidate would win 51 percent of the vote on the first ballot. Voters would then still have a chance to vote in the second balloting between the two "real" candidates. If an absolute majority were required for election, the proportion of votes going to minor parties would thus be higher than the proportion minor parties receive under the current electoral system. This would encourage minor parties and at the same time weaken the dominance of the two major parties.

Tenure

Senate tenure. Senators are elected for six-year terms staggered in such a way that every two years one-third of the senators are up for reelection. A senator elected in 1986 does not have to face reelection until 1992, an appealing prospect to politicians accustomed to running for office every other year.

Senators have six-year terms.

House tenure. Representatives are elected for two-year terms, so most of them are thinking seriously about the next campaign by the day they are sworn into office. Incumbent representatives rarely lose their bids for reelection. While in office most legislators make skillful use of franking privileges (free mailing), casework opportunities (information and assistance to individual constituents), and media communications to their districts. In the past decade over 90 percent of House incumbents who have sought reelection were successful, and most of the contests were not close; in 1984 only 12 percent were won by less than 55 percent of the vote. In contrast, in the 1980s incumbent senators—whose stands on controversial issues are more visible—have been victorious in only two-thirds of their races; over one-third of the winners have squeaked by with under 55 percent of the vote.

Representatives have two-year terms.

House members usually are reelected; only two-thirds of Senate incumbents win their races.

Senators and Representatives
Characteristics

In terms of age, race, sex, and wealth, the members of Congress are not representative of the American people. Instead, they resemble mid- to upper-level managers found in American corporations.

Age. Not surprisingly, members of Congress are older than most Americans: the average age of senators in the 99th Congress (1985-86) was fifty-five; of representatives, fifty-one (data as of January 1, 1986). Congress in the 1980s is younger than it was in the 1960s and 1970s. This change reflects the increasingly competitive nature of elections in the South (which regularly used to send many septuagenarians and octogenarians to Congress), and the

Members of Congress are typically older than other Americans.

decision of many older incumbents to take advantage of the generous pension benefits that Congress has made available to long-term members who retire.

The leadership of Congress is older than the rank-and-file membership. In 1986 Speaker of the House Thomas P. ("Tip") O'Neill (D.-Mass.) was seventy-three; Senate Majority Leader Robert Dole (R.-Kan.) was sixty-two. The average age of committee chairpersons, powerful leaders in Congress, was sixty-one in the Senate and sixty-two in the House. In general, the top leadership of Congress resembles that of the executive branch and large corporations in that white men in their late fifties and early sixties predominate.

Congressional leaders are typically in their late fifties or sixties.

Sex and race. By saying men, not people, predominate, we do indeed mean men. In 1986 there were only twenty-two women in the House (5 percent of the membership) and two in the Senate. None held a leadership position either in her party or in committee. Thus, Congress is a group led by late-middle-age men, and is a group that for the most part is white. In 1986, for example, there were only twenty blacks (two of them women) in Congress, including Walter E. Fauntroy, the nonvoting delegate from Washington D.C. All twenty were representatives, composing 4 percent of the House membership.

Few women are in Congress.

Few blacks are in Congress.

Wealth. Members of Congress are not only older and more likely to be white and male than the general population but also much wealthier. In 1986, 44 percent of representatives and 61 percent of senators were lawyers. Thirty-three percent of representatives and 30 percent of senators listed their occupation as banker or businessman. Congress had only five engineers, two labor leaders, three clergymen, and thirty-one farmers.

Half the legislators in Congress are lawyers.

The Ethics in Government Act of 1978 requires members to disclose within broad categories their investments and sources of unearned income, such as stock dividends. So, although it is impossible to know exactly how wealthy our legislators are, we do know that approximately 10 percent are millionaires. Most members invest in stocks or bonds, and 63 percent of representatives and 76 senators have real estate investments besides their personal residences or vacation homes. Although a few members have not amassed great savings, most have well surpassed the wealth of working-class and middle-class Americans.

Most legislators have accumulated substantial wealth.

The "typical" member. The "typical" member of Congress is fifty-two years of age, Protestant, white, male, a lawyer, and an investor in real estate and stocks. Less affluent people are rarely found in Congress, and women and blacks have only token representation. That these groups often feel unrepresented and left out of congressional decision making is not surprising. After all, the vast preponderance of the verbiage in Congress is by affluent white males.

The "typical" member is a middle-aged, white, male, affluent lawyer.

Activities

How does the "typical" member of Congress spend his time? The image of long hours spent in debate on the floor of Congress is inaccurate. Instead, senators and representatives have harried schedules involving committee work and constituent service in addition to floor action. Our typical member reaches the office quite early in the morning to review the mail and do legislative homework before committee meetings begin, usually around 10 A.M. Although members do have staffs who open the mail and respond to many constituent requests, each legislator must prepare the daily schedule—and it involves some difficult decisions. Should he speak before the Rotary Club back in the district at its annual "Hurrah for Capitalism!" luncheon in two months, or will Congress still be in session (possibly holding an important vote), or should that time be spent with his often-neglected family?

> *Most members spend little time debating issues on the floor.*

Legislative homework. The member may also spend this morning time gathering information on bills, especially those under consideration in the committees to which he is assigned. In addition, he is likely to find lobbyists waiting to talk with him on these same bills. And although the lobbyists are not likely to change his vote on pending legislation, they gladly provide him with information that they believe he needs to do his job.

> *Considerable work on writing and evaluating bills is done prior to formal committee meetings.*

Committee meetings. Then at 10 A.M. the member is likely to have a committee meeting in which several proposals to amend a bill originating in the executive branch may be discussed and voted on. Most committee meetings adjourn just before noon, at which time the House usually convenes. While the House is in session, the few members actually in attendance will not be paying much attention to the debate because the real work of Congress is done in committees. Instead, the typical member is probably conversing with lobbyists in the lobby next to the floor (whence the word *lobbyist* was derived), speaking with constituents visiting the Capitol, meeting with his office staff, or listening to a party leader attempting to persuade him to side with the leadership on an upcoming vote.

> *Most serious work in Congress occurs in committee.*

Floor appearances. Only when the bells in the House office buildings ring, signifying a floor vote, does the typical member join his fellow legislators, who temporarily leave their other duties and appear in the chamber. Having been previously briefed by staff on the nature of the proposed legislation, he will not cast his vote capriciously. Thus, he has made optimum use of his time by not "wasting" it on the floor.

Constituent service. After the House adjourns for the day, the member is likely to return to the office to catch up with work. He may have to contact one of his supporters in his district to find out whether rumors that he is going to face a tough primary election challenge are true. He may return a call from a

Members of Congess and their staffs devote major efforts to helping individual constituents deal with the federal bureaucracy.

financial backer in his district who is upset over the member's recent voting record and must be assuaged. Then there are the ever-present groups of tourists visiting Washington who want to be assured that "their" representative in Washington is working for them. Before leaving his office, the representative may attempt to intercede with officials on behalf of a constituent. This might mean several calls to the Veterans Administration, for example, to remedy the inexplicable termination of disability payments due a constituent who lost his foot in Vietnam.

Campaigning, in the form of speaking before interested groups, never stops.

Public appearances. But quite often the typical member's day is still not finished. He may find to his regret that he committed himself to speak briefly at a banquet—perhaps at the annual convention of the National Association of Beet Growers, because there are important beet farmers in his district. He is subjected to a meal of questionable chicken (served, of course, with beets), after which he delivers an impassioned plea for legislation proclaiming the beet our national vegetable. When he returns home after the speech, he probably reads memos prepared by his staff on the merits of amendments to legislation coming up for a vote the following day.

The job of the representative, to be done competently, requires enormous amounts of energy and work. The representative is further pressed when the demands of the job in Washington are supplemented by almost-weekly travel back to the district to attend town meetings or for similar occasions. Because so many of our legislators are independently wealthy and have professional abilities that are attractive to private employers, perhaps it is surprising that more of them do not quit their often-frustrating jobs. Instead, most members leave Congress either by involuntary retirement by the voters or after reaching their sixties, seventies, or eighties.

The Leaders of Congress

Each house has its own leaders and its own system of leadership. The power of the leadership in the House in relation to rank-and-file members is greater than the power of the leadership in the Senate in relation to rank-and-file senators. In both houses the leadership may be conveniently defined as elected party leaders and committee chairpersons. Table 2-3 lists elected party leaders in both houses.

Leaders of the House

Speaker of the House. The Speaker of the House is elected by House members in a straight party vote, the only vote that determines the party identification of members for organizational purposes. Each party caucus (the assembly of all members of the party in the respective houses of Congress)

Table 2-3
Leaders of Congress, 99th Congress (1985-1986)

	Democrats	Republicans
Senate		
President*		George Bush
President Pro Tempore*		Strom Thurmond, S.C.
Minority Leader	Robert C. Byrd, W. Va.	
Majority Leader		Robert Dole, Kan.
Minority Whip	Alan Cranston, Calif.	
Majority Whip		Alan K. Simpson, Wyo.
House		
Speaker	Thomas P. O'Neill, Mass.	
Majority Leader	Jim Wright, Texas	
Minority Leader		Robert H. Michel, Ill.
Majority Whip	Thomas S. Foley, Wash.	
Minority Whip		Trent Lott, Miss.

*Largely symbolic, very little power in these offices.

> At the turn of the century, the Speaker ruled the House.
>
> In the 1910 revolt against Speaker Cannon, power shifted to committee chairpersons.

nominates one of its members for the speakership, with the majority party of course able to elect its nominee. Between 1890 and 1910, the Speaker was immensely powerful, controlling appointments to committees as well as chairing the powerful Rules Committee. Democrats and dissident Republicans revolted against this concentration of power in the hands of Thomas B. Reed and Joseph G. ("Uncle Joe") Cannon and succeeded in removing many formal powers from the Speaker. Control of the House shifted from the Speaker to committee chairpersons, who reached their positions through operation of the seniority rule. According to the seniority rule, the member of the majority party with the longest service on each committee became its head and was given broad powers of control over the actions of the committee. From 1910 until the 1970s, power in the House of Representatives was decentralized to committee chairpersons.

> The Speaker did retain some powers: presiding over sessions and assigning bills to committee.

During this period of a weakened speakership, the Speaker, whose office is provided for in the Constitution ("The House of Representatives shall choose their Speaker and other Officers," Article I, Section 2), nonetheless remained an important officer. He presided over the House, allowing him to recognize or ignore members who wish to speak, appointed members of special or select committees, and assigned bills to committees. This last power sometimes enables a Speaker who favors a bill to send it to a committee also likely to favor it rather than to one that is likely to kill the bill. The content of some bills is sufficiently broad to enable the Speaker to choose between at least two committees.

By the mid-1970s, House Democrats came to believe that a strong, more centralized leadership would enable Congress to deal more effectively with the president. They created the Democratic Steering and Policy Committee, chaired by the Speaker, and assigned it the responsibility of making committee assignments for Democrats. (These appointments had formerly been made by the Democratic members of the Ways and Means Committee.) The Speaker not only chairs the Steering and Policy Committee but directly appoints eight of its thirty-one members.

The Speaker also was given the right to nominate all of his party's members, including the chair, of the powerful Rules Committee, which, as discussed on page 78, has great influence over the flow of legislation in the House. In addition, the Speaker's power has been enhanced by the expansion of the Democratic whip system, which is a useful tool in the Speaker's efforts to effect legislation. Finally, the new budget process discussed on pages 90–93 gives the Speaker an opportunity to coordinate and oversee the behavior of House committees. By granting the Speaker these new powers with the Steering and Policy Committee, the Rules Committee, the whip system, and the budget process, the Democrats strengthened his leadership role.

The Speaker is elected to office by a secret ballot of the majority caucus, which has been Democratic since 1955. Tip O'Neill assumed the speakership in 1977 upon the retirement of Carl Albert (D.-Okla.). This was a continuation of a tradition in which the majority leader succeeds to the speakership. In 1985, Speaker O'Neill announced his intention to retire at the end of the 99th Congress in 1986.

House majority leader. The majority party also selects, in caucus, a House majority leader who functions as a key party strategist. Together with the Speaker and the members of the Rules Committee, he schedules debate and negotiates with the opposition party and with committee chairpersons on procedures. A post-World War II tradition has initiated the ascent of the majority leader to the speakership upon the retirement of the Speaker. Jim Wright (D.-Tex.) became majority leader in 1977 and will probably be chosen Speaker in 1987.

House majority whip. The third leader of the majority party in the House of Representatives is the majority whip, a word derived from the British "whipper-in" (the chap in the fox hunt who attempts to restrain the hounds from straying). In the House the whip rounds up members for votes. He also conducts "straw ballots" (polls to determine voting intentions) for the leadership. These straw ballots affect both bargaining efforts and the timing of legislation on the floor, so that only bills favored by the leadership will be

---

The Speaker has great influence on the Democratic Steering and Policy Committee.

The Speaker nominates the members of his party who are to serve on the powerful Rules Committee.

Changes in the whip system and the budget process have enhanced the Speaker's ability to coordinate policy.

The majority caucus elects the Speaker by secret ballot.

Normally the majority leader succeeds the retiring Speaker.

The majority leader coordinates party strategy and tactics with the Speaker.

The majority whip leads the whip organization of the majority party.

The whips gather information for the leadership on how party members intend to vote.

enacted. As we have already noted, the Speaker in conjunction with the majority leader nominates the whip, a chief deputy whip, and three other deputy whips, who must then be approved by the entire caucus. The leadership also appoints regional whips, each of whom has responsibility for a state or group of states. Thomas S. Foley (D.-Wash.) became majority whip in 1981 after the incumbent whip, John Brademas (D.-Ind.), lost his seat in Congress in the fall of 1980 general election.

The minority party's organization resembles that of the majority party.

House minority leader. The organization of the leadership in the minority party closely parallels that of the majority party, except that the minority party lacks a Speaker. For instance, today the Republicans have a minority leader who would become Speaker should the Republicans gain control of the House, an event not experienced since 1954. When the president and the minority leader in the House are members of the same party, the latter is expected to support the president's program and attempt to work toward its enactment. In 1981 the Republicans elevated their whip, Robert H. Michel (R.-Ill.), to replace retiring minority leader John Rhodes (R.-Ariz.).

The minority leader heads the minority party in the House; only the majority party chooses a Speaker who presides over the entire House.

The minority whip heads the whip organization of the minority party.

House minority whip. The duties of the minority whip are the same as those of the majority whip. In today's Democratic-controlled House, he is responsible for finding out how Republicans in the House plan to vote, information he relays to the minority leader. The minority whip is aided by regional and assistant whips. The assistant whips report to the regional whips, who, in turn, advise the leadership of the expected voting patterns of minority-party members.

Leaders of the Senate

President of the Senate. The Senate's structure of leadership parallels that of the House, but there are important differences. The vice-president holds the constitutionally delegated office of president of the Senate, with authority to preside over debate—a rather impotent prerogative. The Senate's rules have developed in such a way that the presiding officer is denied even the power to structure debate. The position is so meaningless that the gavel is usually wielded by freshman senators, who are expected to devote a certain amount of their time to presiding. The only important function fulfilled by the president of the Senate is to vote in the event of a tie, a rare occurrence, to which the vice-president is quickly alerted by the leadership.

The presidency of the Senate offers little power.

The president of the Senate has little involvement in Senate activities, except to cast tie-breaking votes.

President pro tempore of the Senate is an honorary position.

President pro tempore. The president pro tempore of the Senate, a position provided for by the Constitution, has little real power because the office is largely ceremonial in nature. Its weakness stands in stark contrast to the very powerful position of Speaker of the House. Elected by the majority party, the president pro tempore is traditionally the majority party member with the greatest amount of seniority. When the Republicans gained control of the Senate in 1981, Strom Thurmond (R.-S.C.), at age seventy-eight, became president pro tempore. Thurmond at that time had served continuously in the Senate for twenty-five years.

Senate majority leader. The real power of the leadership in the Senate is found in the offices of the majority and minority leaders. In the 1980 elections Republicans captured both the presidency and control of the Senate, and so the role of majority leader Howard Baker (R.-Tenn.) was to work with the president to help win passage of the administration's program of legislation. Toward this end the majority leader uses his ability to schedule floor action so that issues come up at the most propitious time for the administration. Other sources of power are his memberships on both the Republican Policy Committee (which coordinates Republican positions on issues) and the Republican Committee on Committees (which makes the party's committee assignments). How a majority leader chooses to use these positions is a matter of personal choice and style. After Baker retired in 1984, new Majority Leader Robert Dole (R.-Kan.) worked to fashion bills that Senate Republicans could support. Through his low-key manner of conciliation and compromise, on several important bills he was able to unite his party in the Senate, at times even over President Reagan's opposition. His ability to soothe and cajole was a major factor in building coalitions that turned proposals into legislation. Just as with the presidency, although the office provides significant resources to an individual who wants to use them to exert strong leadership, only the occupant of the office can determine how best to use its opportunities for persuasion.

When his party controls the presidency, the majority leader coordinates strategy with the White House.

The majority leader schedules bills for consideration on the floor.

The office legitimates efforts by the majority leader to persuade other senators in his party to vote as he suggests.

Senate minority leader. Baker had been minority leader during the Carter years when the Republicans were in a minority in the Senate. During those years he had the same bases of power within his party, but did not control scheduling, a power of the majority leader, and faced a different task: the presentation of policy proposals representing Republican alternatives. After the 1980 Republican victories at the polls, Baker switched positions with Robert C. Byrd (D.-W.Va.), who had been majority leader. Byrd assumed the role of minority leader, attempting to influence legislation (especially regarding issues on which Republican senators were divided) and presenting criticisms and Democratic alternatives to Reagan proposals. This role, similar to that of the "Loyal Opposition" in Great Britain, is required of the "out" party when the other party controls the executive branch.

The minority leader presents his party's alternatives to the majority's positions.

Senate whips. The whip organizations of both parties in the Senate parallel those in the House, although the job is easier in the Senate because there are fewer members to survey. In 1986 the Senate majority whip had to know the voting positions of only fifty-three Republican senators, in contrast to the 253

Whips gather information on Senators' voting intentions.

Democratic votes that his counterpart in the House had to ascertain. The Senate minority whip had to report on only forty-seven Democratic votes, while the House minority whip had to find out the views of 182 Republicans.

The Senate whip positions do seem to offer entry to higher positions of Senate leadership. Byrd had been whip at the time he was elected Democratic leader in 1977. Ted Stevens (D.-Alaska), who had been the Republican whip in the previous Congress, lost the race to become Republican leader in 1985 to Dole by only three votes. In 1986 the whips were Alan K. Simpson (R.-Wyo.) and Alan Cranston (D.-Calif.). Part of the rationale for their elections was to provide geographical balance with their respective majority and minority leaders. Especially in the case of the liberal Cranston, the whip selection also created ideological balance with the more conservative Byrd. Considerations of ideological and geographical balance are common in choosing whips.

Whips often provide geographical and ideological balance with other party leaders.

Senate/House Comparison

The Senate, as we noted earlier, is smaller and less formal than the House. Thus, leadership in the Senate is less a matter of holding a position (the Speaker of the House is almost certain to be very powerful) and more a matter of strength of personality and individual will. Senators tend to be prima donnas who can be led only by accomplished students of human nature who tailor their approaches to the whims, needs, and pathologies of individual senators. The majority and minority leaders are viewed by their colleagues as senators who have special coordinating and spokesperson roles. In contrast, the Speaker is viewed by his colleagues as much more than just another representative with some special responsibilities. Symbolic of the high position of the Speaker is the custom of not voting except to break a tie. Party leaders in the Senate, in contrast, vote along with all other senators.

As stated in the discussion of the speakership, House reforms of the 1970s both increased the power of the Speaker and decreased the power of committee chairpersons. The net effect was to centralize power in the elected leadership and to expand the roles of individual members. Reforms in the Senate followed one of these trends but not the other: the roles of individual members were expanded at the expense of committee chairpersons, but the centralized leadership was not significantly strengthened. The Senate used to be dominated by a small group of committee chairpersons; it is now a much more egalitarian institution.

Leadership in the Senate differs by party in that the Democrats have a highly centralized formal leadership, with the minority leader also serving as chairperson of both the Policy Committee and Steering Committee. For the Republicans these chairs are occupied by separate individuals, neither of whom is the majority leader.

The party caucus is the assembly of all members of the party in the

Leadership in the Senate depends on the abilities of leaders to use interpersonal skills effectively.

Leadership in the House comes more with positions, although interpersonal skills in persuasion are also important.

Trends in the House have been toward increasing power in the speakership and assuring the rights and expanding the roles of individual members.

Trends in the Senate have been toward increasing the roles of individual members but without increasing the power of the leadership.

In the Senate, Democratic party leadership is centralized in the minority leader; in contrast, the Senate Republican party leadership is less concentrated in the majority leader.

Caucuses debate party positions and strategies; in voting on the floor, members are not required to support party positions.

Caucuses have important roles in electing party leaders and committee chairpersons.

Most of the work of Congress is done in committees. Except for controversial issues, committee decisions are generally respected by the entire House or Senate.

Chairpersons preside over meetings and have much influence in deciding how committees deal with bills.

respective houses of Congress. Membership is determined by party self-identification, with members very rarely excluded even when their activities have been supportive of the other party.

In meetings of the caucus (or conference, as the Republicans label their caucus), party policy is debated and positions taken, even though members cannot be bound to vote the party's positions. This lack of ability to bind caucus members to the party line led to former Speaker Sam Rayburn's characterization of caucus meetings as "a waste of time."

This unflattering characterization may still hold for the majority of caucus meetings. The exceptions are the organization meetings conducted at the start of each two-year Congress. These meetings are clearly important in both the Senate and the House. The majority party, meeting in caucus, determines committee chairpersons and committee structures by which each chamber organizes its work. In approaching the legislature's task, both chambers make the committee the chief workplace.

Committee Chairpersons as Leaders

Neither Congress nor congressional leadership can be understood without reference to the chairpersons of the twenty-two standing committees of the House and the fifteen standing committees of the Senate. The only way for Congress to deal rationally with the more than 10,000 bills introduced each two-year period is through a stong committee system. The decisions made in committee to report out some bills (a vote by the committee to permit the bill to be passed on to the entire House or Senate for consideration) and to kill others are generally respected by the chamber as a whole.

Powers of chairpersons. The committee chairpersons usually have great influence in their respective committees. In addition to presiding over meetings, they (more than any other committee members) influence the scheduling of meetings, determine which bills will be considered and when, and appoint and direct the committee's staff. Most chairpersons have a broad knowledge of the subject area within the jurisdiction of their committees, an expertise usually quite respected by committee members.

Congressional reformers in the 1960s felt that some committee chairpersons were misusing their powers by failing to be responsive to the wills of their committees. For instance, some chairpersons refused to hold hearings on bills they viewed negatively, or stacked the hearings so that only one side's position was presented. Committees passed committee "bills of rights" in the 1960s guaranteeing that at least minimal standards of procedural fairness would be maintained. Chairpersons must now regularly schedule meetings, hold hearings on bills when requested by a majority of the committee, and share with committee members the hiring and utilization of committee staff.

Committee "bills of rights" help to ensure that committee chairpersons are responsive to the wills of their committees.

Characteristics of chairpersons. Tables 2-4 and 2-5 illustrate that, in the 99th Congress, all chairpersons in the House were Democrats and all in the Senate were Republicans. Although no written rule requires this, long tradition dictates that the majority party in each chamber controls all the committee chairs. Thus, the Republican capture of the Senate in 1980 cost all Democratic chairpersons their positions. Except for the exclusion of Republicans from chairs in the House and Democrats from chairs in the Senate, the committee chairpersons listed in the two tables do not obviously stand out as greatly distinct from the general membership of Congress. This is quite a change from similar data for the 1960s and 1970s, when chairpersons were substantially older than their colleagues and much more likely to be Southerners. Chairpersons are still older (an average of sixty-one years of age for Senate chairpersons in comparison with fifty-one for the House), although the

> *The majority party in each chamber elects the chairpersons of all committees.*

Table 2-4
House Committees, 99th Congress (1985-1986)

			Chairperson	State	First Elected
Exclusive	Appropriations Rules Ways and Means	A member of any one of these is not permitted to serve on any other committee.	Jamie L. Whitten Claude Pepper Dan Rostenkowski	Miss. Fla. Ill.	1941 1962 1958
Major	Agriculture Armed Services Banking, Finance, and Urban Affairs Education and Labor Foreign Affairs Energy and Commerce Judiciary Public Works and Transportation	A member of any one of these is permitted one other membership which must be on a nonmajor committee.	E. ("Kika") de la Garza Les Aspin Fernand J. St. Germain Augustus F. Hawkins Dante B. Fascell John D. Dingell Peter W. Rodino James J. Howard	Tex. Wis. R.I. Calif. Fla. Mich. N.J. N.J.	1964 1970 1960 1962 1954 1955 1948 1964
Nonmajor	Budget* District of Columbia Government Operations House Administration Interior and Insular Affairs Merchant Marine and Fisheries Post Office and Civil Service Science and Technology Small Business Standards of Official Conduct Veterans' Affairs	Members may serve on two (or, occasionally, three) of these committees.	William H. Gray III Ronald V. Dellums Jack Brooks Frank Annunzio Morris K. Udall Walter B. Jones William D. Ford Don Fuqua Parren J. Mitchell Julian C. Dixon G.V. ("Sonny") Montgomery	Pa. Calif. Tex. Ill. Ariz. N.C. Mich. Fla. Md. Calif. Miss.	1978 1970 1952 1964 1961 1966 1964 1962 1970 1978 1966

*Unique committee composed of five members of Appropriations and Ways and Means, respectively, one member from each party's leadership, and twenty-one other members of Congress. Service for any member of Congress on the Budget Committee is limited to six years in any ten-year period.

> *Chairpersons are somewhat older than rank-and-file members.*
>
> *In the 1960s and 1970s chairpersons were quite often Southerners and in general were much older than other members.*
>
> *All chairpersons are experienced members of Congress because of the seniority rule.*
>
> *The member of the majority party who has been on a particular committee the longest normally becomes its chairperson.*

differences, especially in the Senate, are not large. These changes reflect the Republican takeover of the Senate, the increasingly competitive nature of statewide elections in the South, and the increasing degree to which older members choose retirement. Tables 2-4 and 2-5 also illustrate the experience of chairpersons by listing the year each was first elected to the House or Senate. Seniority dictates that chairpersons be experienced members of Congress.

Selection of chairpersons by seniority. Predictions about the nature of future committee chairpersons can be made with accuracy because of the means by which they usually are selected. One becomes a chairperson through *seniority,* an important concept for understanding Congress. The member of the majority party who has served continuously on a given committee longer than any of his colleagues can expect to become the chairperson. This practice, which cannot be found in any written rule of Congress, is followed by both parties. Thus, any member knows that by remaining on the same committee year after year and living long enough, he or she will probably become the committee's chairperson when his or her party controls that house of Congress. By the same token, a competitive district, which sometimes elects Democrats and sometimes elects Republicans, will never have its representative become a committee chairperson.

Table 2-5
Senate Committees, 99th Congress (1985-1986)

			Chairperson	State	First Elected
Major	Agriculture, Nutrition and Forestry	Senators may serve on two of these committees.	Jesse A. Helms	N.C.	1972
	Appropriations		Mark O. Hatfield	Ore.	1966
	Armed Services		Barry Goldwater	Ariz.	1952
	Banking, Housing and Urban Affairs		Jake Garn	Utah	1974
	Budget		Pete V. Domenici	N.M.	1972
	Commerce, Science and Transportation		John C. Danforth	Mo.	1976
	Energy and Natural Resources		James A. McClure	Ida.	1972
	Environment and Public Works		Robert T. Stafford	Vt.	1972
	Finance		Bob Packwood	Ore.	1968
	Foreign Relations		Richard G. Lugar	Ind.	1976
	Governmental Affairs		William V. Roth	Del.	1970
	Judiciary		Strom Thurmond	S.C.	1954
	Labor and Human Resources		Orrin C. Hatch	Utah	1976
Minor	Rules and Administration	Senators may serve on one of these committees.	Charles McC. Mathias	Md.	1968
	Veterans' Affairs		Frank H. Murkowski	Alaska	1980

Critics have argued that the seniority system has promoted members not on the basis of their abilities and performances but solely on the basis of time on the committee.

In response to critics, Congress now submits each nominee for committee chairperson or ranking minority member to a secret ballot vote of the nominee's party caucus in the House or Senate.

In 1975 and 1985 four imcumbent House chairpersons lost their chairs through vote in the Democratic caucus.

Chairpersons now know that they must be responsive and fair to the members of their committees or face possible removal from their leadership positions.

Although chairpersons no longer can do whatever they want at little risk of losing their positions, the seniority rule is still used in almost every instance to select the chairperson.

Criticisms of seniority system. Critics have long argued that the seniority system results in the promotion to chairperson of some members who have been unresponsive to committee majorities and almost incompetent in the handling of committee business. The critics point to examples of chairpersons who have been alcoholic, senile, or just inept. Defenders of the seniority system point to the many talented chairpersons and argue that any other means of selecting chairpersons would involve a large expenditure of valuable time in rancorous deal making and other politicking that would upset the harmony of Congress. The rationale is that the enormity of the task facing Congress requires that conflict among members be minimized, even at the cost of sometimes having feeble or reactionary chairpersons.

Modification of seniority system. Partly as a response to the criticisms of reformers, the seniority system has been modified. Although the assumption is still that the most senior majority-party member on a committee will become its chairperson and the most senior minority-party member on a committee will become its ranking minority member, the seniority system no longer operates automatically. Every nominee now must undergo a vote of the full party caucus by secret ballot. In 1975 the House Democratic caucus actually selected new chairpersons of the Agriculture, Armed Services, and Banking committees over the opposition of incumbent chairpersons. In 1985 the House Democratic caucus ousted the frail, elderly Melvin Price (D.-Ill.) as chairperson of the Armed Services Committee, reaching down to Les Aspin (D.-Wis.), the seventh-ranking Democrat on the committee, in its search for a vigorous leader. Democratic leaders were quick to state that the action was an exception to the continued use of the seniority system.

Although all our examples and the denials of chairs to most senior members have come from the House Democratic caucus, House Republicans as well as Senate Democrats and Republicans all vote in caucus for their head committee positions.

Leadership by Tradition

Seniority. Seniority, an unwritten rule in both the House and Senate, is a key to understanding Congress. Seniority is part of the informal structure, a series of customs followed by all but a few members. Seniority is more than just a means by which committee leaders are chosen. It includes the notion that new members especially should respect the institution and its ways of doing things. In rhetorical exchanges they should seek to avoid insulting language, instead referring to each other in glowing terms, such as "The distinguished senior senator from New York who has often enlightened us. . . . " This broadened concept of seniority also includes notions of deference to more senior members and an appropriate term of apprenticeship before assuming a public leadership position on issues. These seniority norms have weakened a great

Seniority also means respecting congressional traditions, waiting to take leadership positions, and deferring to more experienced legislators.

Seniority norms are stronger in the House than in the Senate.

For low-level federal appointments, the president must get the approval of the senators or senator of the president's party from the state to which the appointment is made; if a senator from the relevant state disapproves the nomination, the entire Senate will vote to reject the nominee.

deal in the Senate in recent years as Senate membership has turned over rapidly and brash new senators have not been reluctant to speak out. The idea that new senators should be seen but not heard is no longer widely shared in the Senate. In the House, although the seniority tradition has weakened somewhat, a strong degree of deference to more experienced representatives is still the norm.

Senatorial courtesy. One unwritten rule that maintains its full force in the Senate is the practice of senatorial courtesy. The Senate will refuse to confirm a presidential nomination for lower offices such as district court judge or United States marshal unless the nomination has first been cleared with the senators of the president's own party from the state to which the appointment is to be made. Thus, when President Ford nominated William Poff of Virginia to a district judgeship in 1976, Ford sought the approval of the Republican senators from Virginia; and when Senator William Scott (R.-Va.) informed the Judiciary Committee that he disapproved of the nomination, the committee failed to recommend Poff to the entire Senate, thereby killing the nomination. This was done as a matter of courtesy to the objecting senator. This practice of senatorial courtesy began in 1789 with the rejection of the nomination of Benjamin Fishbourne of Georgia for the post of naval officer of the port of Savannah. The senators from Georgia were able to persuade the Senate to reject the nomination made by Washington. Since that time presidents, mindful of the power of senatorial courtesy, have sought the approval of the appropriate senators before making nominations. Senatorial courtesy, in effect, gives any senator of the president's own party a veto power over the appointment of federal job vacancies within his or her state. The practice does not extend, however, to appointments to the Supreme Court or to cabinet departments which serve more than one state.

Congressional Committees

Woodrow Wilson wrote in 1885 that "Congress in session is Congress on public exhibition, whilst Congress in Committee rooms is Congress at work." Although somewhat overstated, Wilson's characterization is still largely valid for the U.S. national legislature.

House Committees

Rules, Appropriations, and Ways and Means are the most powerful House committees; members serving on one of these committees are not permitted any other committee assignment.

In the previous section on congressional leaders we discussed chairpersons, for they are indeed leaders of Congress. Although all chairpersons are poweful within their committees (and in this sense leaders), not all committees are equally powerful or important. In the House of Representatives three committees—Rules, Appropriations, and Ways and Means—stand out.

These committees are considered so prestigious that membership on one of them precludes membership on any other standing House committee.

House Rules Committee. The House Rules Committee is one of four nonsubstantive standing committees (a committee that does not consider the actual substance of legislation) in the House. The Rules Committee decides which bills get to the floor for debate. When a substantive committee has reported out a bill, it goes to the Rules Committee, which may kill the bill (recently this has been infrequent) or give it a "rule"—that is, set the time allowed for floor debate, the terms of the debate, and the degree to which the bill may be amended on the floor. It is the Rules Committee that has consistently decided not to allow tax bills to be amended on the floor, a decision that prohibits recorded votes on tax loopholes.

The debate over the rule granted to the 1981 budget reconciliation bill illustrates the control the Speaker has gained over the Rules Committee and the critical importance of the rule assigned by the committee to the passage or defeat of bills. As part of the budget process in 1981, Congress had voted instructions to fifteen House committees to make budget reductions. The resulting bill was the most comprehensive budget provision ever passed by Congress. The members of the Rules Committee were divided on what sort of rule would garner the most support for substantive changes in the bill on the floor. Speaker O'Neill finally persuaded the committee to adopt a modified closed rule that would have permitted separate votes on several amendments. Realizing that they did not want to face individual votes on cutting popular programs such as Social Security and student loans, Reagan and House Republican strategists favored a rule that would have accepted or rejected the entire package of budget cuts in a single vote. Republicans challenged the rule adopted by the Rules Committee when the bill reached the floor of the House. By a 217 to 212 margin, with twenty-nine conservative Democrats voting with the Republicans, the committee-assigned rule was overturned and replaced with a "closed" rule that required an "up" or "down" vote on the entire package, with no amendments. If the Republicans had not won this procedural vote on the adoption of a rule relating to the amendability of the bill, the outcome of the 1981 budget battle could have been dramatically different, for some of the massive cuts in popular programs probably would have been scaled back. After winning the procedural vote, the Republicans had little difficulty winning acceptance of the president's entire package.

House Ways and Means Committee. A second powerful House committee is the Ways and Means Committee, which deals with all revenue bills. All measures to change our tax laws originate in this committee in accord with the constitutional mandate (Article I, Section 7) that "all bills for raising Revenue shall originate in the House of Representatives." Although the executive branch and the Senate Finance Committee also are heavily involved in tax

---

Bills go from substantive committees to the Rules Committee, which decides how and when bills will be debated on the floor.

The nature of the "rule" given to a bill by the Rules Committee influences how the bill may be amended as well as the bill's ultimate passage or defeat.

Rules given to bills by the Rules Committee can be challenged, although such occurrences are rare.

Congressional action on all tax bills originates in the Ways and Means Committee.

legislation, and tax bills require full House and Senate approval just like other legislation, the Ways and Means Committee has traditionally been the key battleground on taxes. Because seemingly innocuous changes in obscure sections of the complex tax code can mean billions of dollars to individual industries and companies, lobbyists exert great energies to influence committee members. The extent of these efforts can be seen in the case study at the end of this chapter.

House Appropriations Committee. The third of the big three House committees is Appropriations. Bills dealt with in substantive committees, passed by Congress, and signed by the president become laws; yet, these laws do not actually appropriate funds. Funding is accomplished only with the completion of the budgetary process (discussed fully late in this chapter), in which the Appropriations Committee plays a crucial role. Each item in the budget, which is several thousand pages in length, is reviewed by a subcommittee of Appropriations and then by the committee as a whole. The committee members believe strongly that they must preserve the watchdog function of Congress by guarding the treasury against waste by the bureaucracy. The committee calls many witnesses, especially executive branch officials, who are asked to justify items in the president's budget or the conspicuous absence of items. During the years of the conservative Reagan administration, executive officials were often asked to explain why the president's proposed budget did not include sums sufficient to administer adequately programs mandated by Congress. Scrutinizing the budget constitutes almost all of the activity of the Appropriations Committee. It is such an enormous task that committee members have the reputation of being among the hardest-working members of Congress.

The Appropriations Committee reviews the annual federal budget in detail.

Subcommittees of the Appropriations Committee hold hundreds of hearings at which administration officials are asked to justify the president's proposed budget.

Other House committees. Rules, Ways and Means, and Appropriations are exclusive committees; members of any one of these committees are, with rare exceptions, not permitted to serve on any other committee. The House also has eight major committees, membership on which limits additional committee assignment but does not exclude it (table 2-4). The eleven remaining committees are nonmajor, and members usually serve on two of these. All major and nonmajor committees are substantive with the exceptions of Budget and Standards of Official Conduct. This last committee proposes standards of ethics to be passed on by the entire House and occasionally conducts inquiries into alleged breaches of those standards.

Members may serve on only one of the eight "major" committees.

Competition to serve on the more popular committees is stiff.

Usually the competition for assignments to exclusive and major commitees is stiff. One exception recently has been assignment to the Judiciary Committee. Many members of Congress seek to avoid service on this committee, which traditionally has handled highly controversial matters, such as reform of the federal criminal code, gun control, and abortion.

Much of the work assigned to House committees is decentralized further

> *Subcommittees do much of the work of Congress.*
>
> *The proliferation of subcommittees in the 1970s further weakened the power of committee chairpersons.*

to the 140 subcommittees. During the 99th Congress every committee except Standards of Official Conduct had at least two subcommittees; Appropriations topped the list with thirteen. The subcommittees act as miniatures of the larger committees, complete with powers of investigation. However, subcommittees do not report their actions to the Speaker or the Rules Committee but back to the full committee for further action. The many subcommittees mean large numbers of subcommittee chairpersons who hold hearings and deal with bills. Because committee chairpersons usually have little control over what subcommittees are doing, subcommittee proliferation has further weakened the power of committee chairpersons.

Senate Committees

> *Sentors serve on two major committees and up to eight subcommittees.*
>
> *Limitations on the number of committee assignments and chairs each senator can hold ensure that even the most junior senators get some choice assignments.*
>
> *The Senate has no exclusive committees equivalent to Rules, Appropriations, and Ways and Means in the House.*
>
> *There are so many subcommittees that senators sometimes find themselves with two or three subcommittee meetings scheduled simultaneously.*
>
> *Staff does considerable work for senators at subcommittee meetings.*

The smaller size of the Senate results in fewer committees and subcommittees, but senators still serve on two major committees and up to eight subcommittees (table 2-5). These limits were established in 1977 when the Senate also set the maximum number of subcommittees that a senator could chair at three. The reforms did open up some choice committee seats and subcommittee chairs to junior senators—seats that had previously been held by senior senators serving on more than three committees or holding more than three subcommittee chairs. As in the House, power has been decentralized in the Senate.

There are no committees in the Senate that are exactly comparable to the Rules, Ways and Means, and Appropriations committees of the House. The Senate Rules and Administration Committee is a minor committee; in the Senate, bills are not given a "rule" by the Rules Committee because they come directly from the substantive committees to the floor, where debate and amendments are always in order. The Senate counterpart to the House Ways and Means Committee is the Finance Committee, an important committee but one that lacks the constitutional authority to originate tax bills. The Senate Appropriations Committee is ostensibly the counterpart of the House Appropriations Committee, but the Senate committee lacks the size needed to scrutinize carefully the entire budget. The Senate Appropriations Committee therefore limits its activities primarily to reviewing the actions of the House and to attempting to reinstate funds for a few pet projects or to remove funds from less favored ones.

Subcommittees proliferated in the Senate in the 1970s, as they had in the House. During the 99th Congress, the fifteen Senate standing committees had 102 subcommittees, a particularly large total when one recalls that there are only 100 senators. With senators serving on up to eight subcommittees, subcommittee meetings frequently have only one senator in attendance. The absent senators generally send staff members to report back on subcommittee activities.

The smaller Senate gives less deference to committee decisions than does the larger House. Accordingly, the committee system is somewhat less important in the Senate, although it is still an essential element of the legislative process. Most bills die in committee, where fundamental modifications of administration bills also take place. In the Senate, as in the House, Congress in committee is Congress at work.

> *Committees are more important in the House because the smaller Senate does more of its work on the floor.*

Appointments to Committees

Size of committees. The size of committees varies by chamber (House committees are larger) and by workload (in 1986 House Appropriations, with fifty-seven members, was the largest). The division of committee seats between Democrats and Republicans in the Senate is made on the basis of the party proportions. For example, the 99th Congress had nine Republicans and eight Democrats on the Foreign Relations Committee, proportions reflecting the Republicans' fifty-three to forty-seven advantage in the entire Senate. The same procedure is applied in the House, except that the majority party controls two-thirds of the seats on the Rules Committee. Thus, the Democrats in the 99th Congress had 58 percent of the seats in the House, and nine of the thirteen members of Rules were Democrats.

> *Committee seats are divided between the parties in proportion to their overall strengths in each chamber; the "exclusive" committees in the House are exceptions to this proportionality principle.*

House appointments. Committee assignments in the House are decided by each party's Committee on Committees. For the Democrats, the Steering and Policy Committee (composed of the Speaker; ten other Democrats with official positions, such as chairs of important committees; eight members appointed by the Speaker; and twelve members elected by regional caucuses) acts as the Committee on Committees at the start of each Congress. The composition of the committee ensures that appointments will be responsive to the desires of the Democratic leadership. For the Republicans, the minority leader appoints the members of the Committee on Committees (one from each state that has at least one Republican representative), which functions to ratify appointments made by its own executive committee. In the executive committee, members of large states dominate because each is allotted the number of votes equal to the number of Republican representatives from his or her state. For example, in 1985 the executive committee member from California had eighteen votes because eighteen of California's forty-five representatives at that time were Republicans.

> *Each party has a committee that determines which party members will serve on which committees.*

Seniority, of course, remains the key to assignment; freshman members are rarely appointed to Rules, Ways and Means, or Appropriations. But, once assigned to a committee, a junior representative will not be dropped if a more-senior representative seeks the seat. The only occasion on which members are bumped from committees is when their party loses seats in an election with the result that the party also loses proportional seats on each

> *More senior members get the more prestigious committee assignments.*
>
> *Members, building up expertise, often remain on the same committees for many years.*

committee. Then straight seniority operates, and the least-senior members are automatically removed. Even when a party loses many seats, members are rarely bumped from their committees because it is likely that one or two other committee members are not returning, either voluntarily or through election defeat, to each committee.

Seniority aside, other considerations come into play in making committee assignments, particularly when assigning freshman members. The Committee on Committees take into account party standing (party dissidents do not do well in committee assignments), geographical balance on committees with vacancies, and interests of the applicant's district. When Shirley Chisholm, a black Democrat from Brooklyn, was initially elected to Congress, she found herself appointed to the Agriculture Committee—an assignment that helped the geographical balance of the committee but did little to relate to the interests of her constituents. In a rare instance of willingness to reverse its decision, the Democratic Committee on Committees transferred Chisholm to the Veterans' Affairs Committee after she agreed to support the leadership's choice for majority leader.

Senate committee appointments follow the same general norms as House appointments.

Senate appointments. In making Senate committee appointments, the Republicans set up their Committee on Committees of around fifteen members who get on the committee either through their holding other high party office or by appointment by the Republican conference chairperson. In 1985 the Republican conference chose John H. Chafee (R.-R.I.) conference chairperson. Among his first important actions was appointment of Republican senators to their Committee on Committees. The Democrats used their twenty-five-member Steering Committee, chaired by Minority Leader Byrd during the 99th Congress, to decide which Democrats would serve on which committees. Both parties have adopted rules that ensure that each senator will be appointed to a prestigious committee before any senator receives a second-choice appointment. This is in accordance with a tradition begun in the 1950s under Democratic Majority Leader Lyndon Johnson. Although the Senate does not have committees as exclusive as House Rules, Ways and Means, and Appropriations, there is a recognized hierarchy from the prestigious Foreign Relations Committee to the minor committees such as Rules and Administration or Veterans' Affairs.

Every senator is assured at least one choice committee appointment.

The Foreign Relations Committee has been a cradle of presidential aspirants.

The Foreign Relations Committee is a particularly choice appointment, in part because of the Senate's special responsibilities in the ratification of treaties and in part because of the overwhelming importance of foreign affairs in the nuclear age. In the 1980s debates in the Foreign Relations Committee focused attention on the strife in Central America and on proposals to reach disarmament agreements with the Soviet Union. With the great importance of foreign affairs in mind, it is perhaps not surprising that several recent Democratic presidential aspirants had at one time been members of the Foreign Relations Committee.

Other Committee Features

Open committee meetings. Reformers in Congress have long sought to open committee meetings to the public. By the mid-1970s "sunshine" resolutions had passed in both chambers so that now only a few meetings, generally dealing with national security, are closed to the public. Even markup sessions, when bill modifications are discussed prior to voting in subcommittee or committee, are open. The reformers in the 1960s and early 1970s expected that open meetings would be attended by the press, public interest watchdog groups, and generally interested citizens. Instead, many meetings are attended primarily (if not entirely) by special interest lobbyists concerned with the bills under consideration. Nevertheless, Congress in committee has become more visible to anyone who wants to observe. On any day Congress is in session, a visitor to Washington can watch a committee or subcommittee at work—one of the Capitol's free and often entertaining shows.

Almost all committee and subcommittee meetings are open to the public.

Joint committees. In a discussion of committees, mention must be made of both joint committees and special or select committees. Joint committees, composed of members from both chambers, are organized to perform studies and routine oversight activities. The 99th Congress had four joint committees. The Joint Economic Committee supervises economic studies; the Joint Taxation Committee functions as the formal "home" for staff who work for both chambers' tax-writing committees; the Joint Library Committee supervises the Library of Congress; and the Joint Printing Committee directs the Government Printing Office. Although these joint committees have long histories, other joint committees usually are organized to investigate a particular problem and are in existence only long enough to hold investigatory hearings and report their findings.

Joint committees include as members both senators and representatives.

Joint committees have specialized objectives that range from studying a particular problem to administering the Library of Congress.

Special or select committees. Special or select committees usually are temporary bodies set up to investigate a particular problem. One well-known special committee was the Senate Select Committee on Presidential Campaign Activities, popularly known as the Watergate Committee, which examined the campaign abuses of the Nixon administration. Some select committees, such as the Senate Select Small Business Committee, Senate Select Committee on Intelligence, and the House Select Committee on Narcotics Abuse and Control, have lasted for several years. These committees differ from standing committees in that they lack the authority to deal with bills directly and may only investigate and make recommendations to the standing committees.

Select committees are found in both the House and Senate.

Select committees usually coordinate policy recommendations for groups (e.g., the aged or Native Americans) over which no single standing committee has jurisdiction.

Subpoena power. All congressional committees—standing, select, and joint—have the right to subpoena witnesses for purposes of investigation toward the preparation of legislation. Reluctant witnesses may be granted

Every committee has the power to subpoena witnesses to gather information for legislative purposes.

varying levels and types of immunity from prosecution in the courts, thereby forcing them to testify by removing the option of taking the Fifth Amendment—a respondent's refusal to answer questions on the grounds that such responses may tend to incriminate him or her. A witness who, granted immunity, still refuses to testify (as did Watergate burglar and conspirator G. Gordon Liddy in 1973 before the House Armed Services Committee) may be cited for contempt of Congress and immediately imprisoned.

Scores of staffers, both professional and clerical, are assigned to every committee.

Staff. Another source of strength for committees is extensive staffing, although the 6,000 committee staffers are a smaller crew than the 12,000 personal staffers hired by individual senators and representatives. Divided into Republican and Democratic staffs on each committee, congressional committee staffers include secretaries as well as professionals such as doctors, scientists, and lawyers. Their work involves research, arranging hearings, drafting bills, and keeping committee members informed. With the enormous demands on elected members, staffers play a crucial role in enabling committees to perform their legislative tasks. Professional committee staff often serve for many years and provide the "institutional memory" of the committee on the laws over which the committee has jurisdiction.

In a short book on the nuts and bolts of American politics, we have devoted an entire section to committees, and a large part of our section on congressional leaders deals with committee chairpersons. This is because the leaders of committees are leaders in Congress, for the key locus of power is the committee. This situation will become even more obvious in the forthcoming descriptions of how a bill becomes a law and of the budgetary process.

How a Bill Becomes a Law

Bills can be blocked at several points on the route toward passage.

Only a small percentage of bills introduced eventually become laws.

Of the 10,559 bills and joint resolutions introduced during the 98th Congress (1983-84), only 623 were enacted into law. To become a law, a bill must pass through the series of roadblocks shown in figure 2-1, any one of which may kill it. It is indeed a hazardous route from introduction to final passage. Not every congressional pronouncement is a bill: congressional action also takes the form of simple, joint, or concurrent resolutions (table 2-6). However, because the treatment of a resolution in each house is the same as that of a bill, we shall confine ourselves to following a bill's progress through Congress. The great majority of major legislation is introduced in the form of a bill.

Only a member can formally introduce a bill.

Most bills have similar versions introduced in both houses, and any member of either house can introduce a bill. Although most bills, as we have seen, have their origin in the executive branch, only members of Congress may introduce a bill. The administration usually seeks powerful leaders on committees relevant to the substance of a bill to handle its introduction. Members of the executive branch cannot themselves introduce a bill, nor can they seek recognition even to speak on the floor.

The Congress 85

Figure 2-1. How a bill becomes a law.

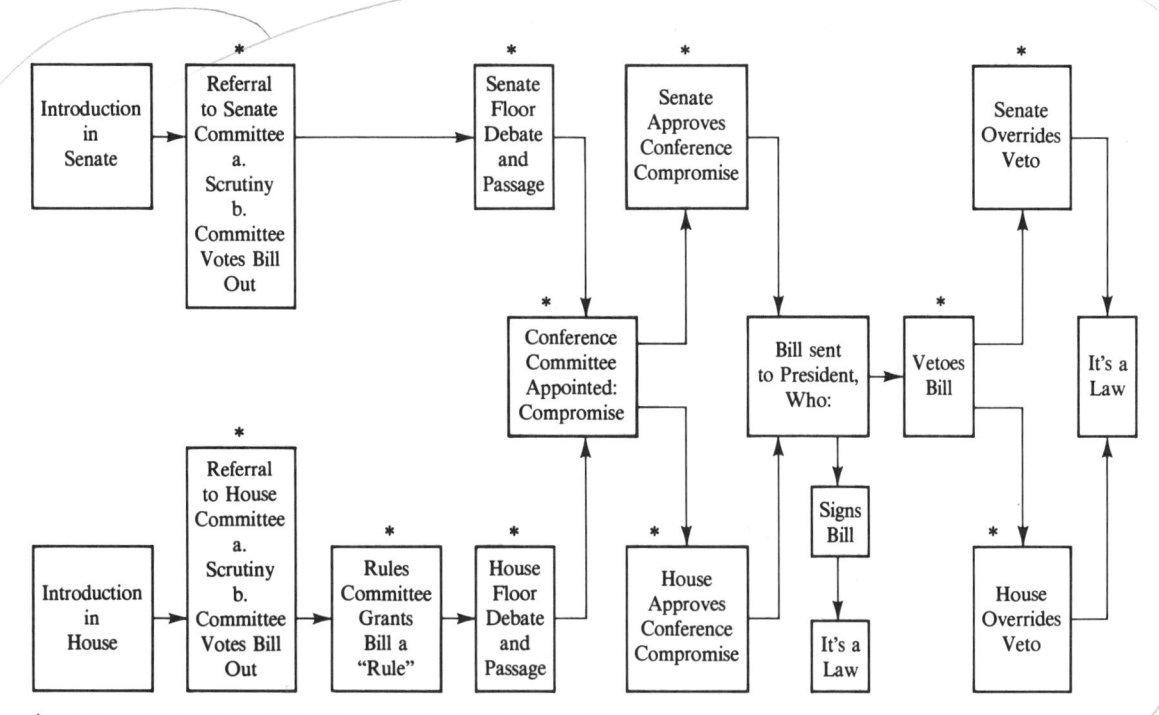

*Legislative roadblocks: points in the legislative process at which a bill may be killed.

Table 2-6
Congressional Bills and Resolutions

Measure	Nature	Necessary for Passage	Force of Law?
Bill	Broad, general legislation such as the Superfund Act of 1980	Majority vote in both houses and the president's signature	Yes
Simple resolution	Changes in the rules of one chamber or expressions of sentiment, such as the determination of the daily meeting time in the Senate	Majority vote in one house	No
Concurrent resolution	Changes in the rules of Congress or expressions of sentiment, such as a proclamation of congratulations to an astronaut	Majority vote in both houses	No
Joint resolution	Limited, specific legislation, such as a special appropriation for flood victims	Majority vote in both houses and the president's signature	Yes
Joint resolution to amend the Constitution	Changes in the Constitution, such as the Twenty-second Amendment (limiting any president to two terms)	2/3 vote in both houses and ratification by 3/4 of the states	Yes

Referral to Committee

Most bills die in committee.

In the stage of the legislative process that follows the introduction of a bill, a number is assigned to the bill, and it is referred to a committee, the place where most bills die. In the House the bill is referred to a substantive committee by the Speaker; in the Senate referral is by agreement between the majority and minority leaders. This right of referral is a source of some power, for the Speaker may kill a bill or greatly enhance its chances of passage by his choice of committee. As we see in the case study at the end of this chapter, committees can claim to have jurisdiction over a bill, but the Speaker reserves the authority to refer bills to committee. However, in most instances the subject matter of the bill gives the Speaker little leeway in referral.

Subcommittee scrutiny.   After a committee receives a bill, it usually refers it to a subcommittee, which studies the bill and often holds open hearings on its provisions. The subcommittee (or the committee as a whole if the bill has not been referred to a subcommittee) usually requests comment on the bill from agencies of the executive branch affected by the proposed legislation. The subcommittee then reports its recommendations back to the full committee, including proposed amendments to the bill. If the bill has been substantially amended, the committee often discards the original and replaces it with a "clean bill" (complete with a new number) incorporating all the proposed changes.

Subcommittees perform much of the detailed review of bills.

The committee must then decide whether it wishes to report out the bill. Although a bill may be reported out unfavorably, or with no committee or subcommittee recommendation, most bills that pass this stage have the support of a majority of the committee. The bill is reported out with amendments (without amendments if it is a "clean bill") and with a report detailing the committee's justifications for supporting the bill. A minority report stating the reasoning of committee members who oppose the bill usually accompanies the positive report. Of course, the chances are the committee will never report out the bill because 90 percent of all bills are killed in committee. Committees are the graveyard of proposed legislation.

If committees refuse to report out bills, those bills die.

Discharge petitions.   A member of Congress who is disgruntled that his pet bill is bottled up in committee has little recourse but to try informally to influence the committee to report out his bill. There is a way of discharging a committee from its jurisdiction over a bill, but the method is rarely successful. In the House a member may file a discharge petition if a committee has failed to report out a bill within thirty days. Such a petition requires that its sponsors obtain 218 signatures—a formidable task in a chamber whose members have a very strong respect for the judgments of committees. Since the House adopted the discharge procedure in 1910, fewer than thirty bills have been discharged, and only two of these have become law. The discharge procedure is used mainly as a threat to encourage reluctant committees to report out bills.

A total of 218 representatives can pry a bill out of committee if they sign a discharge petition, but this procedure is rarely used.

Members are reluctant to challenge committee decisions not to report out a bill.

In the Senate the motion to discharge a committee from its jurisdiction over a bill may be made by a single senator, but senators are even more likely than representatives to reject discharge. In the history of the Senate only fourteen bills have been pried from committees through discharge motions, and only six of these bills subsequently were passed by the Senate. Only one actually resulted in a law; it permitted the government to mint a special medal commemorating a state of Florida celebration in 1964, hardly a landmark piece of legislation.

Bills Reported Out of Committee

Calendars are lists of bills awaiting action on the floor.

Rules are determinations made by the Rules Committee that set the limits for floor debate.

In the House bills reported out of committees go to the Rules Committee, which decides when and how the bills will be debated on the floor.

The Rules Committee works closely with the House majority leadership to organize floor proceedings.

In the Senate bills go directly to the floor after being reported out by committees; the majority party leadership determines when bills will be scheduled for floor actions.

House bills reported out of committee are placed on one of five calendars (lists of bills pending floor action). As table 2-7 shows, the Union Calendar (money matters) and House Calendar (other major proposals) contain the major bills. Bills on the House Calendar pass through the Rules Committee, which gives the bill a "rule"—needed to set the limits of the bill's amendability and the length of its debate. Bills on the minor calendars (Private and Consent) do not need a rule, and bills on the Union Calendar are given special status by which both Appropriations and Ways and Means can bypass the Rules Committee and send their bills directly to the floor. This prerogative is rarely exercised because both of these committees prefer to go through the Rules Committee to obtain a rule limiting amendability and debate time.

The Rules Committee is an arm of the leadership. However, if the Rules Committee should refuse to grant a rule to a bill, the bill could be pried from the committee by means of a discharge petition (this has never been done) or by a mechanism known as "Calendar Wednesday." On Wednesday the list of substantive committees is read so that any of their bills on the House or Union Calendars may be brought up for immediate consideration, bypassing the Rules Committee. The availability of Calendar Wednesday procedures is a factor encouraging the Rules Committee to grant a rule to almost any bill.

Bills that are held up in the Rules Committee are those with lukewarm support and those on which the leadership and many representatives do not want to have to take a public stand through a vote on the floor. The private death of a bill in the Rules Committee allows House members to equivocate on their position on an issue without the embarrassment of a public vote.

The Senate has ony two calendars: the Regular Calendar, composed of all bills voted out by committees, and the Executive Calendar, containing all nonlegislative measures, such as treaties and presidential nominations (table 2-7). As previously mentioned, the Senate does not have a rules committee granting each bill a rule limiting amendability and debate. All bills go to the floor open to amendment and limitless debate. The only exception to this direct referral to the floor occurs when another committee also claims jurisdiction over a bill and wishes to hold hearings. Although he often confers with the minority leader, the majority leader decides the order in which bills are considered on the floor of the Senate.

Table 2-7
Congressional Calendars

	Name	Nature of Contents	Vote on Floor Necessary for Passage
House Calendars	Union	Monetary considerations (revenue and appropriations, such as tax bills)	Majority
	House	All major nonmoney matters (such as antidrug legislation)	Majority
	Private	Individual claims (such as bills to permit particular persons to immigrate)	Unanimous
	Consent	Noncontroversial matters (such as naming a government office building in honor of a distinguished citizen)	Unanimous
	Discharge	Successful discharge petitions (very rare)	Majority
Senate Calendars	Regular	All legislative matters	Majority
	Executive	Treaties and presidential nominations	Treaties: 2/3 Nominations: majority

Floor Action

House floor procedures. Debate on the floor of the House usually involves only a small number of representatives until there is a vote or quorum call, at which time members rapidly file into the chamber. A quorum is 218 members, an unwieldy number for the transaction of business when one considers the myriad demands on a representative's time.

To avoid the unreasonable quorum and at the same time permit interested or affected representatives a chance to debate the merits of a bill, the House "dissolves itself" into the Committee of the Whole House. There are no assignments to the Committee of the Whole; the quorum is reduced to 100 members, and any interested representative may request debate time. When debate is in the House sitting as the House of Representatives, the length of debate is determined by the "rule" or, if there is no rule, one hour is allocated to each member. When debate is in the Committee of the Whole, the length of the debate is agreed on and divided equally between supporters and opponents of the bill. After general debate is completed, the bill is read section by section for amendment. Each proposed amendment is debated for ten minutes, the time being divided equally between its supporters and opponents.

After the Committee of the Whole has debated and possibly amended the bill, it dissolves itself by "rising" (thereby reestablishing the larger quorum) and reporting its recommendations to the entire House. The House, sitting now as the House of Representatives, then begins its considerations of the bill by voting on each of its provisions, section by section (and therefore on any

Most floor debate is tightly structured by the "rule" granted each bill by the Rules Committee.

Noncontroversial votes are often by voice; other votes are almost always electronically recorded and then published so that citizens may know how members are voting.

amendments that were adopted by the Committee of the Whole). The House then votes on the bill as a whole, either sending it back to a substantive committee (thereby effectively killing it) or passing it. Votes on minor and procedural matters on which there are few disagreements are usually by voice vote in which members shout "yea" or "nay" in chorus. Votes on important procedural questions and major bills and their amendments are usually recorded by electronic voting devices. On demand of forty-four members (one-fifth of a quorum), any vote must be electronically recorded, thus exposing the members' voting decisions to the scrutiny of their constituents.

Senate floor procedures are less structured, with unlimited debate permitted.

Filibustering is a tactic used in the Senate by which opponents of a bill try to keep the Senate from voting on it by continuous speeches.

Filibusters are broken when 60 senators vote for "cloture."

Filibusters are used by senators only when they feel that the Senate is about to pass a particularly disastrous bill.

Senate voting resembles House voting, except that the smaller body conducts roll calls by reading through the list of senators rather than electronically tabulating votes.

Senate floor procedures. Floor procedures in the Senate reflect its relatively small size. Debate and amendability are unlimited, which gives minority opponents the opportunity to attempt to talk a bill to death by not permitting it to come to a vote. The use, or threatened use, of this tactic, (called *filibustering*) by Southern senators in the 1950s and 1960s led to the defeat of many civil rights bills. These senators knew that if the bills came to a vote, they would pass with solid majorities. Once recognized by the chair, a filibuster talks for a couple of hours, then yields the floor to a fellow filibuster, who yields only to another filibuster, and the process continues.

A filibuster can be broken only when sixteen senators petition for a vote of "cloture" to halt debate to bring the bill to a vote. Proponents of the bill must then win the support of at least sixty senators on the cloture vote. If they fail to invoke cloture after a couple of attempts, the proponents have to resign themselves to the success of the filibuster; the bill will not be put to a vote.

Before 1975 cloture required support from two-thirds of the senators present and voting. This difficult standard and the Senate's traditional respect for the rights of strong-willed legislative minorities meant that between 1917 and 1975 only 21 of 100 cloture attempts were successful. Successful cloture votes include the Civil Rights Acts of 1964 and 1968 and the Voting Rights Act of 1965, all dramatic victories by liberal reformers. Since 1975 almost half the cloture attempts have been successful, and liberals often find themselves on the side of the filibusters. For example, 1981 and 1982 Senate liberals filibustered to defeat bills designed to promote prayer in schools and to end federal involvement in school desegregation efforts.

The final vote in the Senate is by voice, by division (members supporting a bill stand and are counted; then the process is repeated for opponents) and by roll call. Only roll-call votes, which may be demanded by 20 percent of the senators present, record the vote of every senator for the public record.

Conference Committees

A bill passed by both the House and the Senate is still not ready to be sent to the president. Most bills are modified during the process of consideration, which means that the House and the Senate rarely pass the same version of a bill. If the House and Senate versions differ, the bill is sent to a conference

When the House and Senate have passed different versions of the same bill, a conference committee is formed to reconcile differences.

committee composed of members of both chambers selected by the presiding officer of each chamber. Usually senior members of the relevant substantive committees are appointed to the conference committee, which normally is able to arrive at a compromise bill. The committee writes an explanatory report noting changes from each house's version and justifying these changes. The Senate and the House then vote separately whether to accept or reject (they cannot amend) the report of the conference committee. If the report is accepted, the bill is sent to the president and the conference committee dissolves. If either chamber rejects the report, the conference committee tries again to prepare a compromise bill able to pass both bodies.

Final Action

To become laws, all bills must either have the president's signature or must pass by two-thirds margins in both chambers to override presidential vetoes.

Once both chambers have passed identical versions of the bill, it is sent, as we have seen, to the president. If he decides to veto the bill, he returns it to the chamber in which it originated along with a message outlining his objections and the reason for rejection. Party leaders may not schedule an override attempt if they know they lack the votes. If party leaders in either chamber believe they can muster the necessary two-thirds majority to override, they schedule an override attempt. If the attempt is successful, the bill is sent to the other chamber where another successful override vote would make it a law. Unless both houses vote to override the veto, the bill is dead and can be revived only as a new bill requiring the same lengthy process of analysis as any other new bill.

The Budgetary Process
Appropriations

General laws authorize expenditures but do not actually appropriate money; the annual budget is the law that actually provides the authority for the Treasury to release funds.

The budgetary process is an extremely important aspect of the government's work. A president who wants to help handicapped youngsters may have a bill introduced for this purpose into Congress. The bill may then pass into law. The legislation authorizes expenditure of up to a certain amount, but not a penny will be spent unless Congress subsequently *appropriates* money for the law's purpose in the annual budget. There are many laws authorizing the government to spend millions in programs for which little or no money is ever appropriated. Thus, an interest group arguing on behalf of handicapped youngsters must do more than persuade the president and Congress to pass legislation authorizing a new program; the interest group must make certain that the program, once authorized, is actually funded.

The authorization process involves the substantive committees (for example, Agriculture or Armed Services) that decide if a program is desirable. The appropriation process involves the Appropriations Committees and the Budget Committees that determine to what extent programs already authorized can be afforded within the budget.

The Timetable

The budget, by which Congress appropriates almost $1 trillion, is the one piece of legislation that Congress must pass every year. Before the passage of the Budget and Impoundment Control Act of 1974, Congress approached the budget in much the same way it does most bills: the process was handled by various committees among which there was little centralized coordination.

The Budget Act established a timetable (outlined in table 2-8) designed to ensure that Congress allow itself sufficient time to work on each stage of the budgetary process. The first stage, ending April 15, is information gathering, analysis, and discussion; the second stage, ending May 15, is adoption of budget ceilings for each of the sixteen functional areas of the budget. The third stage, ending in early September, is enactment of spending legislation. The final stage, which is intended to produce a reconciliation bill by September 25, involves reassessments of spending and revenue levels.

Congress first decides how much money it wants to spend overall and then breaks this down into target sums of money to be spent in each of

Table 2-8
Congressional Budget Timetable

Deadline	Action to Be Completed
November 10	President submits Current Services Budget, an estimate of the cost of continuing existing programs for the next fiscal year.
January 18[a]	President submits his budget proposal.
March 15	All committees submit budget estimates and advice to the budget committees.
April 1	Congressional Budget Office reports on fiscal policy to the budget committees.
April 15	Budget committees report First Budget Resolution.
May 15	Deadline for congressional committees to report new authorizing legislation.
May 15	Deadline for Congress to pass the First Budget Resolution.
Labor Day + 7[b]	Deadline for Congress to complete action on all spending bills.
September 15	Congress completes action on Second Budget Resolution.
September 25	Congress completes action on reconciliation bills for any changes made in spending by any committee.
October 1	Fiscal year begins.

[a]Or fifteen days after Congress convenes.
[b]Seven days after Labor Day.
Source: Adapted from U.S. Congress. Senate, Committee on the Budget, Congressional Budget Reform, 93rd Congress, 2nd sess., March 4, 1975. p. 70

In the spring Congress decides how much money overall it wants to spend in the fiscal year starting October 1.

In the summer Congress scrutinizes the budget and enacts spending legislation.

In the early fall Congress brings the spring spending figure into line with the spending legislation passed over the summer.

The budget process has not worked out as intended in the 1974 act.

Reconciliation forces committees to follow spending guidelines.

Continuing resolutions are sometimes used for spending decisions.

twenty-one functional areas. The Budget Act provided two new committees—the Senate and House Budget Committees—to report out recommended limits on spending to the floor of each chamber. The law requires that the committees report by April 15 and that Congress agree on targets by May 15.

After the budget resolution is passed by both chambers the Appropriations Committees know how much must be cut from or added to the president's budget proposals to equal the amounts in this first concurrent budget resolution. Subcommittees of the House Appropriations Committee are especially thorough in their scrutiny because they have traditionally viewed themselves as guardians of the federal treasury. The Appropriations Committees report out to the floor of each chamber expenditure bills that, by law, must be passed by seven days after Labor Day (the first Monday in September). All that remains is for Congress to pass a second concurrent resolution by September 15, again setting limits on spending and the amount of deficit. If any amounts in this second concurrent resolution differ from amounts in the expenditure legislation adopted during the summer, Congress must reconcile the differences before the start of the new fiscal year on October 1.

The budget process illustrates that structures created for one purpose may have quite unintended consequences. The Budget Act intended "reconciliation" to be a minor accounting procedure that would make sure that amounts in the Second Budget Resolution, passed in September, would be consistent with amounts in appropriations bills. Instead, since 1980 reconciliation has become the device by which, at the time of the First Budget Resolution in the spring, Congress forces appropriations bills to fall within specific spending limits.

The first major use of the reconciliation procedure occurred in 1981, when President Reagan achieved massive cuts in domestic spending. Reconciliation compelled committees to reduce the amounts budgeted for programs under their jurisdiction. Rather than forcing members of Congress to vote on proposed cuts in individual popular programs, reconciliation permitted the entire package of changes to pass with only one vote. Although Congress has not since used reconciliation to produce drastic changes, it continues to use it to enforce overall spending limits on committees.

The budget process also illustrates that Congress can choose to ignore its own rules. The deadlines listed in table 2-8 have often been missed. Congress has even failed to pass one or more of the thirteen regular appropriations bills by the October 1 start of the fiscal year. When this has happened, Congress has passed continuing resolutions, stopgaps that keep government agencies in operation for short periods until the regular appropriations bills are passed. In recent years, however, several continuing resolutions have been major laws that authorized and appropriated money and modified policy directions. During times of moderate economic growth and great pressure for large increases in military spending as well as for the maintenance of government benefits people have come to expect, congressional budget making is a struggle.

Congressional Budget Office. The Budget Act also created the Congressional Budget Office (CBO) to provide Congress, most specifically the Budget Committees, with technical information about the economy. Critics have argued that the president had the Council of Economic Advisers and the Office of Management and Budget (OMB) with its large staff of experts to advise him, but Congress lacked sufficient professional staff to make judgments independent of information provided by the executive. The OMB provides a point of coordination for executive branch preparation of the budget; the CBO, together with the Budget Committees, now performs similar functions of coordination and information generation for the legislative branch.

> *The Congressional Budget Office provides economic information to the budget committees and any other committee or member who requests information.*

Conclusion

Congress moves with great deliberation. Major new ideas receive very detailed scrutiny and require a strong consensus before they are enacted into legislation. In the early 1970s reformers who believed that the snail's pace of Congress kept it from dealing responsibly with national problems led a struggle to change Congress. Although the reformers were not entirely successful in getting everything they wanted, many reforms that have had a substantial impact were enacted. The net effect has been to increase both the power of the party leadership (especially in the House) and the ability of younger members (especially in the Senate) to participate fully in the legislative process. Conversely, the reforms have decreased the power of committee chairpersons in the House and the "inner club" of senior senators who used to run the Senate. The reforms of the budgetary process have added to the ability of Congress to deal systematically with the annual budget, and, by substantially increasing its professional staff, Congress has enhanced its ability to process information relevant to its legislative tasks.

> *Reforms in the 1970s strengthened the power of the leadership as well as the ability of individual members to participate fully in legislative tasks.*

The effects of these reforms can be overstated. The leadership has been strengthened, yet the process by which a bill becomes a law still involves many roadblocks, any one of which can prove fatal to a bill. Congress is a "rubber stamp" for no one, including its own leadership. If there is no consensus among our legislators on what is to be done with public problems (or, for that matter, no consensus on what constitutes public problems), it is difficult to see how any set of reforms will enable Congress to produce consistent and coherent public policies. Congress is a representative body, and so its policies may be expected to reflect a lack of harmony when its members are sharply divided along several dimensions. Conversely, Congress can act quickly and decisively when consensus exists. In 1981 strong presidential leadership combined with conservative majorities in both the House and Senate to enact significant changes in fiscal policy. The political strength of Reagan and his allies in Congress overcame structural obstacles to massive changes in spending and taxing. But, in Congress, the policy process never ends. The degree to

> *Bills still can be blocked at several points in the legislative process.*
>
> *The incoherent nature of much public policy reflects the absence of a consensus in Congress on what should be done; when such a consensus exists, however briefly (e.g., in 1981), Congress can act swiftly and boldly.*

which these new policies satisfy the expectations of the American people will largely determine the president's political popularity and thereby delimit his ability to get what he wants from Congress. Politics and structure will continue to interact to produce public policy.

Selected Additional Readings

The authors found the following works to be most helpful in the preparation of this chapter and recommend them to students who want additional information on Congress:

Congressional Quarterly. *C Q Guide to Current American Government, Fall 1985.* Washington, D.C.: Congressional Quarterly, 1985.

Dodd, Lawrence C., and Oppenheimer, Bruce I. *Congress Reconsidered,* 3rd ed. Washington, D.C.: Congressional Quarterly, 1985.

Oleszek, Walter J. *Congressional Procedures and the Policy Process.* 2d ed. Washington, D.C.: Congressional Quarterly, 1984.

Smith, Steven S., and Deering, Christopher J. *Committees in Congress.* Washington, D.C.: Congressional Quarterly, 1984.

Vogler, David J. *The Politics of Congress,* 4th ed. Boston: Allyn & Bacon, 1983.

Case History "Superfund" 1980, 1985

Part II: The Congress

On June 13, 1979, President Jimmy Carter sent to Congress a proposal to establish a $1.69 billion "Superfund" to deal with the problems of oil and chemical spills, and the cleanup of abandoned hazardous waste dump sites. In the Senate, the bill (S 1341) went to the Environment and Public Works Subcommittee on Environmental Pollution, which scheduled hearings within the week. In the House, because the bill (HR 4571) dealt with both oil and hazardous substances, it fell under the jurisdictions of three committees: the Public Works and Merchant Marine committees (both of which deal with oil legislation), and the Commerce Committee (which had jurisdiction over hazardous wastes). This multijurisdictional problem was the first of many roadblocks that would affect, and ultimately defeat, the president's proposal.

We have emphasized throughout this chapter, however, that Congress has the ability, if it chooses to exercise it, to exert considerable leadership in its own right. To be sure, that leadership potential is often linked to the presidency—especially if Congress and the presidency are controlled by the same political party. This linkage often means that congressional and presidential powers complement one another rather than bring about conflict. In the case of oil spill and hazardous waste legislation, Congress was actually "out in front of" the president.

By the time Carter's proposal reached Congress, both houses were already considering Superfund legislation, and the extent of the ongoing machinations in various committees virtually assured that Congress would continue to debate its own bills. At least four bills had already been introduced, each designed by committee and subcommittee chairpersons to limit jurisdiction to their own committees, and to deny jurisdiction to "rival" committees.

The bills embodying the Carter proposals, S 1341 and HR 4571, were both shelved in committee for the remainder of the legislative session.

By mid-1980, the media had given considerable attention to hazardous waste disposal. Communities across the country that had been victimized by past improper and unsafe disposal practices continued to suffer the consequences—and public opinion polls showed a dramatic increase in the importance the American people accorded this problem. An ABC News-Louis Harris Poll on July 8, 1980, found that an amazing 86 percent of the public favored "giving the problem of toxic chemical dumps and spills a very high priority for federal action." Congress, while not ready to accept Carter's proposal, was, nonetheless, grappling with the issue.

The principal Superfund bill in the House, HR 7020, was being considered by the Commerce Subcommittee on Transportation. Originally proposed by its chairperson, James J. Florio (D.-N.J.), in the previous session as HR 5790, the bill had a stormy history—but a history that demonstrates the collegial nature of Congress. Florio had proposed the bill the previous year as a $1.3 billion measure that would deal only with the cleanup of hazardous waste sites, not oil or chemical spills. This exemption ensured that only Fiorio's committee would have jurisdiction over the bill. But Fiorio had failed to consult with the members of his subcommittee before proposing and pushing the bill, which they perceived as heavy-handedness. As a result, the subcommittee "stonewalled" its chairperson and refused to permit the bill to be brought up for a vote. By early 1980 Florio had mended his fences and was working closely with the members of his subcommittee. The old bill had been scaled down and replaced with a compromise version, HR 7020, also written by Florio, which the subcommittee was willing to consider. Florio reported: "We have put together something that will get more support. I'm confident that we will get it out of full committee by May 15, and pass a bill this year."

HR 7020 provided for a $600 million fund for the cleanup of hazardous waste dumps. It was reported out of the subcommittee favorably on April 30 and was passed by the full committee by a vote of twenty-one to three on May 13—just two days before the deadline predicted by Florio several months earlier. The importance of the May 15 deadline was related not to the Superfund bill but to the congressional budget process. Under the provisions of the Budget Act, May 15 is the deadline for reporting bills out of committee (not subcommittee) that require funding authorization during the current congressional session. Unless the deadline is met, authorization is not forthcoming. Thus, HR 7020, as well as one of its "rival" bills that dealt with oil and chemical spills (HR 85), awaited floor action. But other roadblocks remained.

On May 8, Al Ullman (D.-Ore.), chairperson of the House Ways and Means Committee, asserted his committee's jurisdiction over both HR 7020 and HR 85 on the grounds that Ways and Means had authority over not only all legislation that contains tax revenue provisions but "revenue measures generally." Proponents of the legislation saw this move by Ullman as the death knell of Superfund in the 96th Congress—under the assumption that the bills would be bogged down for the remainder of the session in the Ways and Means Committee. But because both bills would impose considerable revenue-producing fees on the oil and chemical industries, Speaker O'Neill yielded and, on May 20, granted Ullman a thirty-day referral.

The Ways and Means Committee surprised both Congress-watchers and lobbyists (about whom we will have more to say shortly): on June 13—one week under the deadline—it approved HR 85. The Ways and Means Committee, however, has the ability to amend bills that it considers, just like any other substantive committee of the House. Among the changes to HR 85 proposed by the committee was an increase in the amount of money available to the oil and chemical spill fund, from $300 million to $750 million over a five-year period.

In a similar move, the committee approved HR 7020 on June 18—this time increasing the amount of money available to the fund to clean up hazardous dump sites from the $600 million approved by the Commerce Committee to $1.2 billion. In addition, the Ways and Means Committee increased the percentage of the fund that would be provided by a tax on industry. The Commerce Committee version of HR 7020 had provided for a fifty-fifty split, half the cost borne by industry and the other half by the federal government from general revenues; Ways and Means increased industry's contribution to 75 percent.

After Ways and Means Committee passage, the bills were still not ready for floor action; each had first to be granted a rule by the Rules Committee. For this reason the Ways and Means Committee held conferences with all committees that had previously handled the bills to get their concurrence on the latest version of each prior to Rules

Committee consideration. This maneuver helped to ensure the granting of a rule that would be acceptable to all the committees concerned and to reduce the probability that a displeased committee chairman would oppose the bill on the floor.

With the Ways and Means, Rules, and all substantive committees that had dealt with the legislation in agreement, HR 85 and HR 7020 were ready for floor action—but the lobbyists had been busy. At each successive stage of the development of HR 85 and HR 7020, environmental groups, federal agencies, oil and chemical companies, residents living near and affected by hazardous waste dumps, members of Congress, state and local officials, and a host of private citizens lobbied members of the House incessantly regarding various provisions of these bills. No matter how this legislation was written, someone somewhere would be dramatically affected by the outcome—whether the bill passed or failed to pass.

As HR 85 and HR 7020 had moved through successive stages of consideration by the various House committees that held jurisdiction over them, the lobbying by both sides had intensified. In the end compromises considerably weakened the provisions proposed in the original versions. Most observers agree that industry lobbyists won more than they lost during these compromise sessions. The Chemical Manufacturers' Association (CMA) representative called the final product "a constructive compromise" and "a substantial improvement" over the earlier version proposed by Florio. Marchant Wentworth of Environmental Action, however, noted: "Industry got what they wanted. The bill is a mere shadow of its former self." Similarly, Swep Davis, the Environmental Protection Agency's Associate Administrator for Water and Waste Management, commented: "If I were the industry, I'd go out and have a party." Rep. Jim Santini (D.-Nev.) suggested that the bill should be called "Superfraud" rather than "Superfund" because of the hoax it would perpetrate on the American people.

By the middle of September, the House was prepared to debate both bills on the floor, and the compromises that had been written into each bill, along with the popular sentiment for passage of some kind of legislation dealing with the likes of Love Canal, indicated that passage, although difficult, might be possible. In fact, the House approved both measures by overwhelming majorities—HR 85 on September 19 (288 –11) and HR 7020 on September 23 (351 –23). The House vote was so uneven for several reasons: no one wanted to go on record against dealing with the hazardous waste problem, and the CMA, previously having opposed HR 7020 as it had been voted out of the Ways and Means Committee, reversed its stand. What happened can be explained, in part, by constituent pressure on House members. In larger part it was a reflection of the industry's (and the members') doubts that a law could be passed during that session of Congress. Congress was expected to go into election recess on October 2, and even if there was a lame-duck session it was unlikely that the Senate would be able to pass its more extensive Superfund bill and even more unlikely that there would be enough time to come up with a compromise bill if the Senate bill did pass. As a result many members of the House who might otherwise have opposed either HR 85 or HR 7020 voted for passage.

While the House bills had been undergoing considerable weakening in the long compromise process through final passage, a measure that had originated in two Senate Environment and Public Works subcommittees had been moving slowly through the Senate. The Bill (S 1480) had been sponsored by Edmund S. Muskie (D.-Me.), chairperson of the Environmental Pollution Subcommittee, and John C. Culver (D.-Iowa), chairperson of the Resources Protection Subcommittee. S 1480, unlike either of its House counterparts, covered any release into the environment (i.e., into any "media"—not just water) of virtually any toxic substance, including nuclear wastes. The precedent-setting bill would have estalished a $500 million annual fund (based on industry fees) and would have compensated victims, permitted them to sue in federal court, and liberalized rules of evidence that would be admissible in such cases.

The Senate bill drew the concentrated opposition of industry lobbyists, who considered it completely unacceptable. One CMA official noted that the only way industry could accept S 1480 was if the Senate eliminated everything in the bill after the "Whereas." Industry representatives complained that the bill would be inflationary, that it would negate the effects of all previous environmental legislation (because it did not rely on previously specified minimum allowable quantities of substances released into the environment), and that the victim compensation provision would bleed industry dry. Environmental groups countered that because industry had benefited from the past practices of unsafe disposal through lower costs and higher profits, it should bear the burden of the environmental cleanup.

Another concern of industry lobbyists was that the "joint and several liability" provision of the House version of Superfund was missing from S 1480 as originally proposed. The "joint and several" provision, which has its origins in personal injury lawsuits, had previously rarely applied to environmental legislation; if applied to hazardous waste legislation, it would mean that anyone along the disposal chain (producer, transporter, owner or operator of the disposal site, and so on) could be held equally responsible for the damage caused. The government would collect the entire cleanup cost from any one of the responsible parties (a so-called "deep pocket"), who would then have to go to court to "fight it out among themselves" to see how much of the cost would be borne by each. Administration spokesmen began to lobby the Senate to have the "joint and several" liability provision included in S 1480.

By May 22, 1980, both subcommittees had favorably reported out S 1480, sending the measure to the full Environment and Public Works Committee, which began hearings on June 4. Although the subcommittees had made several changes in S 1480 (for example, increased the size of the fund to $800 million per year, with $100 million from general revenues rather than being solely industry based), most of the stickier issues had been left unresolved. The Environment Committee, under the chairmanship of Jennings Randolph (D.-W. Va.), held six working sessions on the bill. Among the more far-reaching compromises were the introduction of the strict joint and several liability provision, the determination of the size of the fund ($4.1 billion—with $510 million from the taxpayers), the inclusion of a list of forty-five substances with specified taxing rates (65 percent of the industry's contribution to the fund would be provided by taxes on petrochemicals; 20 percent, inorganic compounds; and 15 percent, petroleum), and the separation of natural-resource damage from personal injury in the area of victim compensation.

The bill itself was far too "radical" for industry's liking. Thus, by June 27, when the Environment Committee voted ten to one to send the bill to the floor of the Senate, industry pulled out all the stops in the initiation of a nationwide lobbying effort to defeat S 1480. As one Shell Oil lobbyist put it, "We are opposing it with everything we've got."

Chemical companies wrote to their shareholders, characterizing the bill as "overkill" and a "radical rewriting of all environmental legislation." More than 40,000 shareholders of Monsanto alone sent letters to the Senate. Curtis Moore, minority counsel for the Senate Environment Committee, stated, "This campaign is much more sophisticated, much more effective than a postcard campaign." Its effectiveness stemmed in part from the type of person writing the letters; engineers, attorneys, architects—that is, professionals who are accustomed to influencing policy.

Senators who favored S 1480 began to fight back. On July 11, twenty-five senators (an unusually high number) signed a letter addressed to Majority Leader Robert Byrd (D.-W. Va.) and Minority Leader Howard Baker (R.-Tenn.) urging them to schedule floor action on the bill. But just as HR 7020 and HR 85 had been referred to the Ways and Means Committee in the House because of revenue implications, the Senate Finance Committee, under Russell B. Long (D.-La.), insisted that it had jurisdiction over S 1480.

Senate-watchers widely believed that the referral of S 1480 to Finance would kill the bill. For one thing, Long had received over $25,000 during the preceding three years in campaign contributions from chemical-industry political action committees—and he was facing a primary election on September 13. But Long was also under pressure from constituents to favor the bill. Several then-recent incidents in Louisiana involving chemical and toxic substances had caused considerable concern in that state, as Long was being forcefully reminded. Bending to these pressures, he announced on August 22 that he was confident that a bill would pass during that session of Congress and that he expected "to help pass the bill." However, after holding hearings on September 11 on those portions of the bill that imposed new taxes, the Finance Committee was still not ready to report the bill back to the Senate. Although Long had earlier predicted passage, he did nothing to move the bill forward. When Congress recessed in early October for the upcoming elections, S 1480 was still bottled up in the Finance Committee. One Senate staffer mused, "We might have made it, if the bill could have been brought to the floor before the elections. Now, I just don't know."

In a book dealing with the politics, as well as the structure of the federal government, it should not be surprising that the 1980 presidential and congressional elections had a dramatic effect on the outcome of the Superfund proposals. By the time Congress reconvened in lame-duck session, the entire fabric of national politics had been substantially altered. Reagan had captured the White House and, for the first time in decades, the Republican party controlled a majority in the Senate. This meant that in the new Congress that would take its seat in January there would be split-party control, and that the Senate would likely be allied closely with the White House against the Democratic-controlled House of Representatives. Although Reagan had not taken a stand on the Superfund issue, industry representatives felt confident that any Superfund measure proposed by his administration would be "better" (from their point of view) than either the House-passed HR 7020 and HR 85 or the still unpassed S 1480. In short, industry wanted all action on Superfund postponed until the new Congress was seated. Republican leaders in the Senate concurred. Baker, who would become the majority leader in the new Senate, said he favored some kind of Superfund legislation but thought the new Congress could do a "better job" on the bill.

"Politics" had also altered some of the key players in the move to pass Superfund. Neither Muskie nor Culver (the originators of S 1480) would be in the new Congress. Muskie had given up his seat earlier to become secretary of state under Carter, and Culver was defeated in his bid for reelection. When Muskie left the Senate, Randolph had taken his place as chairperson of the Senate Environment Committee. The ranking Republican on the committee was Robert Stafford (R.-Vt.), who was slated to take over the chair. Both Stafford and Randolph were convinced that the only chance of getting a meaningful Superfund law on the books lay with the lame-duck Congress. Neither believed that the new Congress would be able to produce anything even remotely acceptable to those with environmental concerns because the influence of industry would be much expanded with Republican control of the White House and the Senate. What had begun as a Muskie-Culver proposal now depended on the success of a Randolph-Stafford compromise. On November 14 a $2.7 billion compromise was worked out. Stafford regretted the need to compromise but agreed to eliminate some of the more controversial liability and compensation provisions in the hope of getting the bill to the floor of the Senate, where he believed there would be sufficient votes to pass it.

80   The Finance Committee, however, still had S 1480 bottled up. Bowing to intense pressure from the senators who had worked out the compromise, the committee reported the bill to the floor, but without recommendation. Supporters of the compromise believed they had enough votes for passage. On November 20 Majority Leader Byrd tried to call up the bill, but Baker objected, arguing that the compromise was unacceptable to his side of the aisle. Byrd withdrew the bill from the floor so that proponents would have further opportunity to effect an acceptable compromise.

    Later that day, Baker joined in the negotiations on the compromise version and announced that he predicted a "favorable outcome" by the end of the session. The consessions made by proponents had been significant. One of the most important was the removal of coverage for medical costs incurred because of exposure to toxic and hazardous materials that had been released into the environment. Only state and local governments could be compensated from the fund, and then only for the loss of natural resources, such as lakes or timberland. Chemical-company liability provisions were further weakened, and the direct jurisdiction of federal courts in cases of victim suits against chemical companies was stripped from the bill. By the time Byrd called the bill up to the floor on November 24, Stafford was ready with the new compromise.

89   The bill that was called up to the floor, however, was the version that had been sent over from the House (HR 7020). Stafford moved to have the contents of HR 7020 replaced with the compromise version he and the other senators had worked out. The compromise had been successful enough to avoid even a last-minute threat by Jesse Helms to filibuster the bill, and the Senate accepted the new-compromise version of HR 7020 as a substitute for the House-passed measure by a vote of seventy-eight to nine. This vote substituted the language of the compromise for the language of the bill that had been passed by the House, so that the new HR 7020 was now ready for a final vote in the

Senate. Given the size of the vote to substitute, the bill passed by a simple voice vote.

By November 24, then, the House and Senate had passed widely differing versions of HR 7020. In fact, earlier in the month eight House members had written to Senators Byrd and Baker urging them to push for acceptance in the Senate of the original House versions of both HR 7020 and HR 85 so that the need for the lengthy conference committee procedure could be avoided. The House was not even back from its election recess and would not reconvene until December 1. With adjournment scheduled for December 5, it was highly improbable that a compromise could be worked out in conference and passed by both houses before the end of the session.

The Democratic leadership in the House began to lobby House members to accept the Senate version of HR 7020, but there were considerable obstacles to overcome. For acceptance, the language of the Senate-passed HR 7020 would have to be substituted for the language of the HR 7020 previously passed by the House and voted on "under suspension of the rules." In these circumstances, a minimum of 246 votes is required for passage. But the Senate version did not include funds for responding to oil spills, a provision that had been included in the House-passed HR 85. As a result, House members led by Edward R. Madigan (R.-Ill.) were pushing to amend the bill to include such a provision and send it back to the Senate.

Representative Florio led the fight to have the House accept the Senate version. He persuaded Speaker O'Neill to schedule the bill for consideration on December 3—but O'Neill pulled it from the schedule on the afternoon of December 2 because it did not look as if proponents would be able to muster the necessary 246 votes to assure passage. Madigan had been arguing persuasively that the House should not accept a bill that did not cover oil. Senators Stafford and Randolph, fearing that Madigan would carry the day in the House, sent a letter to Florio cautioning against returning the bill to the Senate. The Senate majority leader had already told Florio that if the bill were returned, Byrd would not call it up for consideration because of the likelihood of a filibuster. Stafford and Randolph argued that "only the frailest, moment-to-moment coalition" had allowed the Senate to pass its bill; in fact, it fell apart right after passage, and "it would now be impossible to pass the bill again, even unchanged."

Negotiations between Florio and Madigan broke down, and the House leadership decided to risk calling the bill up for consideration under suspension of the rules. The debate would take place on the floor of the House. Madigan, still incensed that the oil provisions had been excluded from the Senate version declared: "We have been left at a take-it-or-leave-it situation, and I rise to recommend to the House that we leave it." But others disagreed. Bob Eckhardt (D.-Pa.) asserted that "unless we move on swell of tide to deal with the question of hazardous waste today, it is not that we will do it three months from now, it may be that we will not do it for seven years from now." John LaFalce (D.-N.Y.), in whose district the infamous Love Canal is located, continued the argument: "Mr. Speaker, it is Wednesday night, December 3. We adjourn on December 5, this Friday. The time is now, or not maybe later. The time is now or never."

The time was now. On the evening of December 3, 1980—less than forty-eight hours before adjournment—the House passed a "new" HR 7020. Its language was identical to the language of the version of HR 7020 that had passed the Senate on November 24. The Comprehensive Environmental Response, Compensation and Liability Act of 1980 (CERCLA) was on its way to the desk of Jimmy Carter. Carter signed the bill on December 11. The country finally had a Superfund law.

The role of Congress in its lawmaking function does not stop with the passage of legislation. Laws are expanded, limited, or even nullified in subsequent sessions in response to the nation's experience with their implementation. Unlike many other laws, CERCLA had a termination date, September 1985, when the taxing authority to put money into the Superfund would expire if Congress did not reauthorize the act. As we noted in the case study section of the presidency chapter, Congress, anticipating the 1985 date, included in the 1980 law a requirement that the president deliver an evaluation of the Superfund program to Congress in December 1984.

In early January 1984, anticipating the president's State of the Union address, Representative Florio released to the press an internal EPA report that put the eventual cost of Superfund cleanup between $8 and $16 billion. Using this leverage, Florio again engineered the development of a Superfund bill—with an $11 billion price tag over five years. As he had neglected to do four years earlier, Florio did not seek the support of his subcommittee, which "stonewalled" the bill. The subcommittee substituted a much weaker bill, and Florio was forced to adjourn the subcommittee markup session or the new, weaker bill would have passed.

Eventually Florio mended his fences and the subcommittee voted out a strong bill, but Superfund reauthorization proponents lost valuable weeks in 1984. Proposed legislation did not pass through the full Commerce Committee until mid-June, leaving little time for the House Ways and Means Committee to consider the bill's monetary aspects. Proponents continued to push diligently, and the House, on the eve of its recess prior to the Republican National Convention in August, passed a Superfund reauthorization bill 323–33.

In the interim the Senate Environment and Public Works Committee, chaired by Stafford, was working toward a Superfund bill that would restore many of the elements that had been "compromised-out" of the 1980 legislation. Stafford, too, was unable to expand the authorities of the law greatly, but dramatically increased funding levels of Superfund; a $7.5 billion package went to the Senate Finance Committee on September 13, 1984, by a committee vote of seventeen to one. Unlike Long, who was forced to report out the original Superfund bill in 1980, Robert Dole (R.-Kan.), the new chairperson, successfully rebuffed pressures and Superfund reauthorization died in the 98th Congress. Essentially, in 1980 President Carter wanted the Democratic-controlled Senate to pass the proposal; in 1984 President Reagan wanted the Republican-controlled Senate to let it die.

But the groundwork had been laid. Much of the technical assistance provided by the professional EPA staff in working with the congressional staff during 1984 had been developed in support of the agency's Section 301 studies, the complete evaluation of the Superfund program that the act mandated for transmittal to the Congress in December 1984. As a result, when the administration, knowing Superfund's popularity, early in 1985 finally proposed its own Superfund reauthorization for $5.3 billion over five years, Congress was much quicker to act.

One big difference between 1984 and 1985 was the "necessity" of the administration's support for reauthorization in 1985. The tax that supported the program was due to expire in September 1985, so the reauthorization bill had to pass in 1985 or the popular program would end. During 1984 the administration was accused by Congress of "stonewalling"—even by members of the president's own party. During 1985, however, the cooperation between the administration and Congress was considerably better. The administration did not want its critics to accuse it of trying to kill Superfund. The result was the passage of a considerably expanded Superfund law in 1985.

Chapter 3

The Federal Judiciary

The federal judiciary has an important role in the political process, but it operates in conjunction with the other branches of government.

Congress, as we have seen, is not entirely independent of the executive branch, for the president is indeed the chief legislator. Similarly, the president is not entirely independent of the legislative branch; his programs require legislative approval, his treaties and many personnel nominations need senatorial confirmation, and his activities in executing the laws are under constant surveillance and oversight by Congress. The federal judiciary also is not entirely independent of the other branches of government. All federal judges are nominated by the president and then confirmed by the Senate. The jurisdiction (what kind of cases may be handled) of the judiciary, as well as its size and the remuneration of judges, is determined in part by Congress. Federal judges are not elected and often try to portray themselves as "above politics," but the judicial branch of our national government is very much a part of the political process.

This chapter deals with the federal judiciary, which has the Supreme Court of the United States at its pinnacle. The chapter does not describe the fifty systems of state courts that combine with the federal system to give the United States a dual system of courts. State court systems deal primarily with the enforcement of state and local laws and include a state's highest court, usually called a state supreme court, to which appeals from lower courts (for example, municipal, county, and magisterial courts) are directed. Of the more than ten million cases tried annually in the United States, most are tried in state courts and involve state and local laws. Judges in these state courts are recruited by various means, including election. They are required in all cases to apply national law if a question involving national law or the Constitution arises, even if national law contradicts a state constitution or state law.

Constitutional Prerogatives

There are two types of federal courts—judicial and administrative.[1] As table 3-1 summarizes, judicial courts are established under the judiciary article of the Constitution and include the Supreme Court, courts of appeals, and

---

[1]Many authors dealing with these two types of courts label what we call judicial courts *constitutional courts* and what we call administrative courts *legislative courts*. To minimize confusion, this chapter uses the accurately descriptive labels *judicial* and *administrative*.

Table 3-1
Judicial and Administrative Courts

	Judicial	Administrative
Authority for:	Art. III—Judicial article	Art. I—Legislative article
Functions of:	Judicial	Judicial, quasi-judicial, administrative
Advisory Opinions?	No	Yes
Tenure of Judges:	Life	At discretion of Congress
Examples:	Supreme Court Courts of appeals District courts	Court of Military Appeals Territorial courts Tax Court

Judicial courts decide only cases based on existing law.

Administrative courts perform whatever services Congress assigns them.

district courts. Administrative courts are created by Congress under its power "to constitute Tribunals inferior to the Supreme Court" (Article I, Section 8), which is granted in the legislative article, and include the Tax Court, territorial courts, and the Court of Military Appeals. Whereas the judicial courts are limited to deciding cases and controversies, the administrative courts perform quasi-judicial and administrative tasks as well. Administrative courts are often asked to provide advisory opinions—for example, rulings on the legitimacy of possible government actions in the absence of an actual case or controversy. Judicial courts cannot render such rulings. In addition, the judges on administrative courts may be removed by simple majority vote of Congress for any reason. In contrast, judges on judicial courts have lifetime tenure, subject only to impeachment.

Constitutional Authorization

The Constitution established the Supreme Court; Congress set up all the lower courts.

Judicial courts. The Constitution states simply in Article III, Section 1 that "the judicial Power of the United States, shall be vested in one Supreme Court and in such inferior Courts as the Congress may from time to time ordain and establish." Thus, there must be a Supreme Court, but the structure of the rest of the judiciary is determined by Congress and is therefore beyond the control of the judiciary. Yet, although the Supreme Court cannot control the lower courts' structure, it dramatically influences the politics of those courts. For instance, when the chief justice addresses a group such as the American Bar Association (ABA), the media give his remarks wide circulation, and they are likely to influence judicial actions even at the local level.

The Judiciary Act of 1789 established thirteen district courts, each with a single judge, and three circuit courts, each consisting of two judges: one from the Supreme Court and one from a district court. At that time the district courts handled mainly admiralty and maritime cases, and the circuit courts functioned as the basic trial courts. Over time Congress adopted a three-tiered system, with the district courts acting as the basic courts from which almost all federal cases originate. Cases are appealed from a district court to a circuit court of appeals and finally to the Supreme Court. This three-stage system has remained in effect and is shown in figure 3-1. However, as the nation has expanded, the number of district courts has grown to ninety-four and the

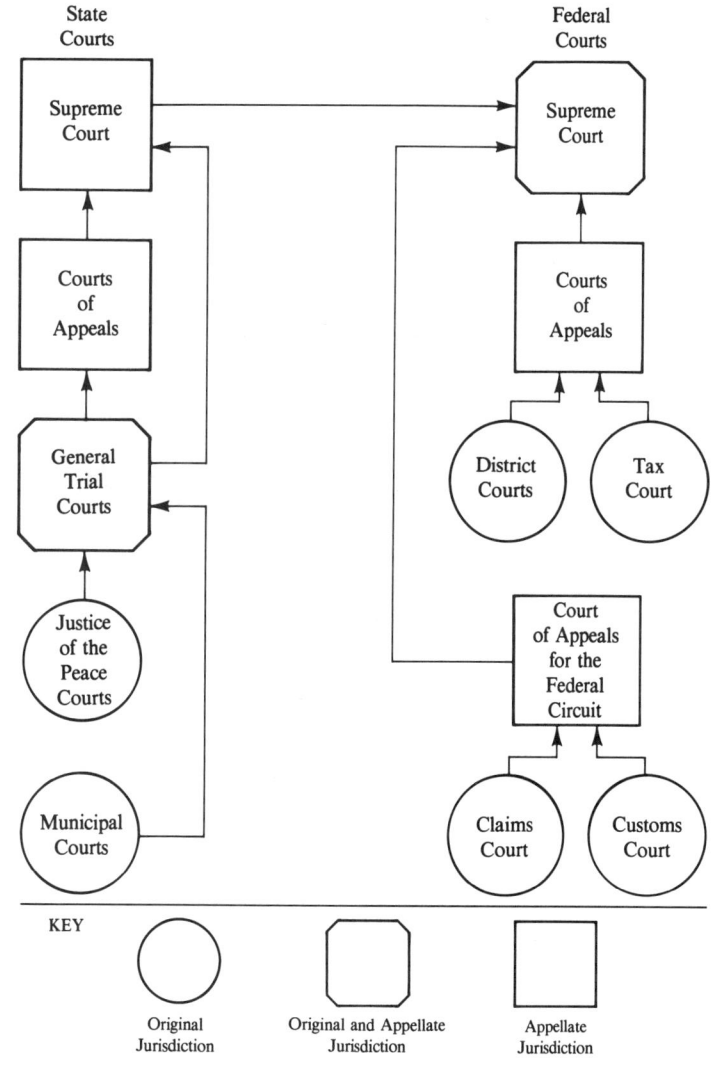

Figure 3-1. United States judicial systems. On occasion the Supreme Court hears a case appealed directly from a lower state court. This may happen if a federal question is involved and the litigant is denied by a state the opportunity to appeal to a higher state court. (The structure of state court systems may vary.)

number of circuit courts of appeals, with their own full-time judges, has reached twelve.

Tenure. The Constitution states that "the judges, both of the supreme and inferior Courts, shall hold their Offices during good Behavior," a provision of lifetime tenure. This constitutional guarantee protects judges on judicial courts from hostile majorities, a security unknown to either legislators or the president, who must face the voters periodically. Judges are not selected by the citizens and, once in office, they can be removed only by time-consuming, multistaged, and very rarely used impeachment proceedings in Congress. The only Supreme Court justice ever to have been impeached was Associate Justice Samuel Chase in 1804, and he was acquitted by the Senate and remained on the bench. Many Americans may be angered by Supreme Court decisions, but they are powerless to remove offending justices. This constitutional provision has enabled the Supreme Court to make decisions, unpopular at the time they were made, defending the rights of speech, fair trial, and the equal protection of the laws when applied to deviant minorities.

All federal judges in the judicial courts have lifetime tenure.

Administrative courts. Administrative courts come and go at the will of Congress. They are set up to remove some of the workload from the crowded judicial courts as well as to deal more efficiently with specialized needs. For example, the United States Court of Military Appeals is an administrative court that handles appeals of courts-martial involving military personnel. The United States Court of International Trade, known before 1980 as the United States Customs Court, was an administrative court until Congress made it a judicial court in 1956. The four territorial courts (Guam, Puerto Rico, the Virgin Islands, and the Mariana Islands) are administrative, as is the relatively new (1969) United States Tax Court, which had been an administrative agency under the Internal Revenue Service. Although Congress has the constitutional authority to establish many administrative courts empowered to hear cases in many areas, it has not chosen to make extensive use of administrative courts except in the area of military justice. Hence, this chapter's main focus is on the politics and structures of judicial courts.

Congress has not made extensive use of specialized administrative courts.

Congressional Limitations

Original jurisdiction and appellate jurisdiction. Congress has the means to limit the powers of the judiciary. With administrative courts Congress can change jurisdictions, fire judges, and even abolish any administrative court. With judicial courts Congress can take cases out of the hands of the courts and can limit their size and number, but it cannot replace judges who have incurred its wrath. In the case of the Supreme Court, the Constitution provides that the Court shall have original jurisdiction (the right to hear a case directly—not on appeal) only in rare cases involving ambassadors and those

The Supreme Court has little original jurisdiction.

in which a state is the litigant. Cases in which a state is a party generally involve interstate questions such as water rights (for example, a dam in one state reduces the flow of water into a downriver state), which are often settled out of court. In the entire history of the Supreme Court there have been fewer than 150 instances when the Court has exercised original jurisdiction. Thus, most cases handled by the Supreme Court involve its appellate jurisdiction (cases heard on appeal). In all other cases (not involving an ambassador or a state), the Constitution provides that "the supreme Court shall have appellate Jurisdiction, both as to law and Fact, with such Exceptions and under such Regulations as the Congress shall make."

Congress has the authority to limit the appellate jurisdiction of the federal courts but has rarely done so.

If the Supreme Court greatly angers Congress, the legislature can deny the Court its usual appellate jurisdiction. In fact, after the Civil War, Congress refused to permit the Supreme Court to review any of the Reconstruction laws. In recent years some members of Congress have tried to strip the federal courts of their jurisdiction over cases involving school prayer, abortion, and busing. In 1979 the Senate actually passed a bill taking away the courts' jurisdiction over school prayer cases, and in 1981 the Senate approved a bill prohibiting the federal courts from mandating busing as a remedy for segregated schools. Both of these bills died in the House of Representatives, and so the federal courts do continue to hear cases in these controversial areas. This legislative activity did, however, remind the Court that justices cannot totally ignore the political climate in the country or the desires of Congress, for the latter has the constitutional prerogative to take cases out of the hands of the judiciary.

In response to an unpopular Court decision, Congress can initiate the process of amending the Constitution.

Constitutional amendments. Congress in conjunction with state legislatures also has the constitutional prerogative to overrule the Supreme Court by amending the Constitution. Two-thirds of each house of Congress can endorse a proposed amendment, which then must be ratified by three-fourths of the states. The Eleventh, Fourteenth, Sixteenth, and Twenty-sixth Amendments reversed specific Supreme Court rulings. The Sixteenth Amendment, for example, ratified in 1913, was a response to the Court's ruling that a progressive income tax was unconstitutional (*Pollock* v. *Farmers' Loan and Trust Company,* 158 U.S. 601 [1895]). Similarly, the Twenty-sixth Amendment, ratified in 1971, was in response to the Court's ruling that Congress lacked the authority to mandate that states permit eighteen-year-olds to vote in state and local elections.

Congress can create new courts and increase the number of judges on existing courts, including the Supreme Court.

Size of the judiciary. Control over the size of the judiciary, including the number of justices of the Supreme Court, is also vested in Congress. Because of the provision that justices have lifetime tenure, Congress cannot penalize the Supreme Court by reducing its size; reduction can be accomplished only by Congress's specifying that vacancies, when they occur, will not be filled until the Court reaches the desired smaller size.

There is no provision prohibiting Congress from immediately increasing the size of the Court. This was the plan favored by Franklin D. Roosevelt in 1937 in his scheme to increase the size of the Court to enable him to add members sympathetic to his views. Roosevelt's proposal would have given the president the right to appoint an additional justice for every justice on the Court aged seventy or older. The plan would have expanded the Court to fifteen members and likely would have changed the many five-to-four decisions against New Deal legislation into ten-to-five decisions validating Roosevelt's programs. While the plan was being heatedly debated in Congress, the Court reversed its stand and began to validate New Deal legislation. Justice Owen Roberts had switched his voting habits, thereby turning five-to-four votes voiding New Deal legislation into five-to-four votes sustaining the laws. Roosevelt's bill died in Congress, a surprising loss for a president who had just won the biggest landslide in modern U.S. electoral history—a clear demonstration of the prestige held by the Supreme Court of the United States.

The Supreme Court has remained at nine judges since 1869 and is not likely to change.

In 1984 Justice William Rehnquist suggested that President Ronald Reagan might propose an increase in the number of Supreme Court justices so as to create a court more to the president's liking. Perhaps remembering Roosevelt's defeat, Reagan did not pick up on the idea.

Jurisdiction

The Constitution and statutes specify the types of cases that are handled by the federal judiciary. Besides the two areas of original jurisdiction of the Supreme Court, the federal courts have jurisdiction over cases involving federal crimes (for example, crossing a state boundary with a stolen vehicle), claims against the United States (for example, a suit to recover for overpayment of taxes), suits between citizens of different states, any federal question (for example, a patent dispute), and any constitutional issue. In civil cases (those involving relations between individuals or organizations), unless at least $10,000 is involved, the case is decided by the state courts, which apply their own state laws. All criminal cases (those involving crimes against society, such as the hijacking of airplanes) involving federal laws may be tried by the federal courts. Cases involving constitutional questions often begin in the state courts, reach the highest state court, and then are appealed directly to the Supreme Court. Figure 3-1 clarifies the usual routes of appeal.

Criminal cases in the federal courts involve violations of federal laws.

Civil cases in the federal courts involve citizens of different states suing each other for at least $10,000.

A strong court system was not guaranteed by constitutional provision but rather has evolved from the lack of explicit limitations on judicial power.

Thus, Articles I and III spell out the constitutional prerogatives of the federal courts. Article III authorizes federal courts to hear cases involving national law and establishes the Supreme Court with little original jurisdiction but with a possibility for appellate jurisdiction to be determined by Congress. Article I grants Congress the authority to establish administrative courts whose main purpose is to facilitate the administration of government programs. These constitutional prerogatives do not seem to amount to a powerful court system, but the Constitution, while doing little to help the

Supreme Court develop into a very powerful institution, also does little to hinder its development. While the Constitution gives the Court few formal powers that it can develop, it also fails to provide a list of powers explicitly forbidden to the Court. In the absence of limitations on its powers, the Supreme Court has evolved into an essential part of the national government.

Judicial Leadership

The question whether the judicial branch should provide leadership in national affairs was never raised in the Constitutional Convention. Only with the assertion of strong judicial independence by Chief Justice John Marshall (1801-1835) was this leadership realized, and many succeeding Courts have continued the expansion of judicial power. Under Chief Justice Earl Warren (1954-1969), the Court reaffirmed judicial leadership by instigating massive social and political reform. The Court mandated legislative reapportionment, an end to school segregation, and an expansion of individual rights.

The Supreme Court can exercise leadership through three means: (1) judicial review; (2) the review of state and local statutes and practices; and (3) the interpretation of federal statutes. However, the mere performance of these judicial functions does not guarantee judicial leadership. If the Court is to lead, it must, like Congress, also provide representation, create and clarify issues, oversee government, legitimate government policy, and participate in policy making.

Judicial Review

Without the right of judicial review—the right to strike down presidential or congressional actions as at variance with the Constitution—the Supreme Court would be severely restricted in its power.

The Supreme Court would exert little judicial leadership were it not for its power of *judicial review,* the right to strike down executive and legislative actions it deems to be at variance with the Constitution. The Constitution does not explicitly provide the Court with the authority to void congressional acts; instead, the Court itself assumed this authority through an early interpretation of its powers by Chief Justice Marshall in 1803.

Marbury v. Madison. Thomas Jefferson discovered in 1801 that his predecessor as president, John Adams, had appointed several federal judges in the waning moments of the Federalist's tenure as president. Jefferson also discovered that the commissions (the formal notifications) for some of these jobs had not yet been delivered, including one to William Marbury, Adam's appointee as justice of the peace for the District of Columbia. Jefferson ordered his secretary of state, James Madison, not to deliver the commission to Marbury, thereby denying Marbury the position. In response, Marbury sued for his commission under a provision of the Judiciary Act of 1789 that gave the Supreme Court the authority to issue writs compelling the delivery of the

Judicial review developed out of politically shrewd Supreme Court decisions, not from an explicit constitutional grant.

commissions. The Supreme Court ruled in favor of Madison on the grounds that the section of the Judiciary Act giving the Supreme Court the authority to issue the type of writ in question was unconstitutional.

Thus, Marshall both avoided a confrontation with the executive branch (had he ordered Madison to act, Madison might have refused, thereby precipitating a constitutional crisis, which the Court, in 1803, might well have lost) and established the principle of judicial review. By establishing this principle without requiring any action on the part of the president or Congress, Marshall made it impossible for the other branches of government to deny the validity of the principle—a basis of the power of the Supreme Court—upon which he expounded. Marshall wrote,"The Constitution is superior to any act of the legislature ... a law repugnant to the Constitution is void" (*Marbury* v. *Madison*, 1 Cranch 137 [1803]).

Judicial review of acts of Congress. The Supreme Court has usually, especially in its early years, been reluctant to overturn acts of Congress. Although the principle was established with *Marbury* v. *Madison* in 1803, the second use of judicial review to overturn a federal statute occurred fifty-four years later with the *Dred Scott* decision, which hastened the outbreak of the Civil War. In sum, the Court overturned only seventy-six federal laws between 1789 and 1941, an average of one every two years. Of course, the Court's judgments of unconstitutionality have not been spread out evenly over the years but have occurred sporadically. The activism of the Hughes Court between 1934 and 1936, for example, which invalidated thirteen New Deal laws, so infuriated Franklin Roosevelt that he proposed his "court-packing" scheme.

The Supreme Court has used judicial review to overturn federal laws sparingly.

During the post-World War II era, the Court has been less reluctant to overturn federal acts, although the acts overturned have not generally been major laws. In sixteen years (1953-1968) the Warren Court overturned twenty-one laws or sections of laws dealing with a wide range of issues; a typical example is the section of the Nationality Act of 1940 that provided for the loss of U.S. citizenship as a penalty for voting in a foreign election. In *Afroyin* v. *Rusk* (387 U.S. 253 [1967]) the Court ruled that Congress lacked the authority to pass laws depriving individuals of citizenship without a hearing.

The chief justice often sets the tone for how active the Court will be.

The Burger Court, beginning in 1969, has been overturning acts of Congress at a rate of almost two per year, although the overturned sections have generally been minor or outdated. One exception is *Oregon* v. *Mitchell* (400 U.S. 112 [1970]), in which the Court ruled that the lowering of the voting age to eighteen for state and local elections violated the constitutional provision granting states powers over their own elections. Another exception is *Buckley* v. *Valeo* (424 U.S. 1 [1976]), in which the Court overturned some significant sections of the Federal Election Campaign Act concerning campaign financing. In 1982 the Court invalidated the bankruptcy court system that Congress had established four years earlier (*Northern Pipeline Construction Co. v. Marathon Pipe Line Co.* [458 U.S. 50]) and in 1983 the Court struck down a minor provision of immigration law (*Immigration and Naturalization Service* v. *Chadha* [77 L.Ed 2d 317]), but, by implication, suggested that the legislative-veto provisions of other federal laws would also be invalid. Although Congress continues to insert legislative vetoes (a device giving Congress the right to reject orders and regulations issued by the executive branch to implement legislation), the *Chadha* decision calls into question the constitutionality of any congressional use of legislative-veto provisions. The *Chadha* decision may give Congress some problems in its efforts to influence executive branch behavior, but neither *Chadha* nor other rulings of the Burger Court have challenged the direction of national policy. These cases are minor in comparison with key New Deal legislation overturned in the 1930s.

The importance of judicial review extends beyond the fact that the Court has actually overturned federal legislation, for it has a deterrent effect on Congress as well. Just as Congress sometimes modifies bills in anticipation of a presidential veto, the lawmakers themselves may modify legislation at times in anticipation of a Court ruling of unconstitutionality.

Judicial review includes the right to overturn executive acts, although the Court has rarely done so.

Judicial review of presidential actions. Although judicial review usually involves the constitutionality of acts of Congress, judicial review also includes determination of the constitutionality of acts of the president. In 1952, during the Korean War, President Harry Truman sought to seize and to operate steel plants that were threatened with a strike. He justified the actions under his authority as commander in chief. The Court ruled that the president's actions were unconstitutional because he had failed to follow procedures set down by Congress for the seizure of private property during an emergency (*Youngstown Sheet and Tube Company* v. *Sawyer,* 343 U.S. 579 [1952]). Thus, the Court exercised judicial review over a presidential action and found it unconstitutional.

More recent examples of the Court's overturning presidential actions are difficult to find because the Court so rarely has ruled that presidential actions conflict with statutes or the Constitution. One significant case is *Train* v. *City of New York* (420 U.S. 35 [1975]), in which the Court ruled that presidents must spend funds appropriated by Congress even if they dislike the programs for which the funds were appropriated. President Richard Nixon had impounded funds in an effort to kill programs he thought wasteful.

Review of State and Local Actions

The supremacy clause. The principle of judicial law refers, then, to the right of the Court to review the constitutionality of acts by the two other

Most of the controversy surrounding the Court has come from its decisions outlawing actions and laws of state and local governments.

branches of the national government. Yet, even before Marshall established the principle, the Supreme Court had the authority to consider (and did consider) the constitutionality of acts of state and local governments. Article IV states, "This Constitution, and the Laws of the United States which shall be made in Pursuance thereof; and all Treaties made, or which shall be made, under the Authority of the United States, shall be the supreme Law of the Land." This clause, which is called the *supremacy clause*, has enabled the Supreme Court from its inception to strike down any act by local or state governments at variance with federal laws or the Constitution.

That the Supreme Court's review of the constitutionality of state and local actions is a source of leadership is indisputable. The Court in its history has overturned more than 1,000 state and local practices. Although each of these cases dealt with a practice in a specified place, the principles laid down are applicable everywhere. For example, the decision that outlawed *de jure* school segregation[2] (*Brown* v. *Board of Education of Topeka, Kansas*, 347 U.S. 483 [1954]) was in regard to Topeka, Kansas, yet, the principle that de jure school segregation violates the Fourteenth Amendment automatically became applicable everywhere in the country. Thus, the Court with a single local decision may indeed set national policy.

Until the Fourteenth Amendment passed in 1869, the freedoms guaranteed in the Bill of Rights protected citizens only from violations by the federal government, not by state or local governments.

The Fourteenth Amendment. Passage of the Fourteenth Amendment in 1869 greatly expanded the scope of the Court's role in reviewing state and local laws. Previously the Court could not intervene in cases of alleged denials of freedoms guaranteed by the first ten amendments, the Bill of Rights. The Bill of Rights specifically bars Congress from intervening in certain areas—for example, *Congress* "shall make no law respecting an establishment of religion. . . ." However, the Bill of Rights does not say that *state* or *local governments* are prohibited from restricting freedom of religion. This same distinction can be made for any of the rights enumerated in these ten amendments (speech, assembly, and so forth).

Thus, although the Court had found in 1833 (*Barron* v. *Baltimore*, 7 Peters 243) that a litigant had indeed been denied effective use of his property without just compensation (a violation of the Fifth Amendment if perpetrated by Congress), there was nothing the Court could do because the violation had been committed by a locality. Chief Justice Marshall stated that the Bill of Rights protected citizens from excesses by the national government but did not apply to the states.

By its statement that no state shall "deprive any person of life, liberty, or property, without due process of law; nor deny to any person within its jurisdiction the equal protection of the laws," the Fourteenth Amendment enables the Supreme Court to review the state and local denials of freedoms

---

[2] *De jure* segregation means segregation that is mandated by law, not merely a consequence of residential racial distribution.

Over time most of the guarantees in the Bill of Rights have been applied to state and local governments.

that are guaranteed by the Bill of Rights. But with passage of the Fourteenth Amendment, the Bill of Rights still did not become applicable automatically to the states. Instead, a process of selective incorporation took place by which the Court, over time, determined that individual elements of the Bill of Rights had become applicable to the states *through* the Fourteenth Amendment. The process began in 1925 when the Court first ruled that freedom of speech was a "liberty" protected not only from federal encroachment by the First Amendment but from state encroachment, as well, under the Fourteenth Amendment (*Gitlow* v. *New York,* 268 U.S. 652). Freedom of the press was covered in 1931 (*Near* v. *Minnesota,* 283 U.S. 697), followed the next year by the right to counsel in capital criminal cases[3] (*Powell* v. *Alabama,* 287 U.S. 45). In 1963 this right to counsel was expanded to include all criminal cases involving felony charges—that is, major crimes (*Gideon* v. *Wainwright,* 372 U.S. 335)— and it was further extended in 1971 to include all imprisonable crimes (*Argersinger* v. *Hamlin,* 407 U.S. 25). The other elements of the Bill of Rights (for example, freedom of religion and assembly, the right to remain silent to avoid self-incrimination) have similarly become applicable to the states through the Fourteenth Amendment. The only exception still outstanding is the Fifth Amendment's right to indictment by a grand jury for major crimes. (Although most states employ grand juries, trial without grand jury indictment is the practice in some states.)

Importance of state and local practice review. The court's review of state and local practices may well be its most important source of leadership. When Warren retired in early 1969 after sixteen years as chief justice, he remarked that his three most important cases were *Gideon* v. *Wainwright,* which expanded the right of the accused to fair trial; *Brown* v. *Board of Education,* which helped to create the civil rights movement; and *Reynolds* v. *Sims,* which, by establishing the one-person, one-vote principle, stopped the overrepresentation of rural areas in state legislatures. None of these involved judicial review of federal legislation; all dealt with state or local actions.

The Warren Court of the 1950s and 1960s expanded civil rights and civil liberties by overturning many state and local practices.

Issues of state and local practices. Current areas of controversy for the Court usually involve its review of state and local practices. For example, the dispute over whether the Court has gone too far in protecting the rights of the accused arose from the 1966 ruling that involved this type of review. This was the well-known *Miranda* decision, in which the Court ruled that the convicted was entitled to a new trial because the confession that police used in court had been obtained without informing the accused that he had the right to remain silent (*Miranda* v. *Arizona,* 384 U.S. 436). The Court ruled that the defendant's statements cannot be used against him unless he was warned "prior to any questioning ... that he has a right to remain silent, that any statement he

---

[3]Cases involving a possible sentence of death.

The Burger Court of the 1970s and 1980s has been more reluctant to overturn state or local actions than was the Warren Court.

does make may be used against him, and that he has the right to the presence of an attorney, either retained or appointed." As a result, police, using a "Miranda card," now read suspects their rights at the time of arrest.[4]

Critics, who have argued that the Supreme Court has "tied the hands of the police," have been heartened by some Burger Court decisions weakening the *Miranda* decision. In 1971, for example, the Court ruled that statements made by a defendant who had not been given the Miranda warnings could still be used in court in order to discredit his testimony (*Harris* v. *New York*, 401 U.S. 222). In 1974 the Court ruled that the police could introduce in court evidence obtained from a defendant who had been given every Miranda warning except the information that he was entitled to free counsel if he could not afford to hire his own lawyer (*Michigan* v. *Tucker*, 417 U.S. 433). In 1975 the Court continued to chisel away at the *Miranda* decision by ruling that statements made to police after a defendant had asked to see a lawyer could still be used in court (*Oregon* v. *Hass*, 420 U.S. 714).

Conservatives have not always been pleased with Burger Court decisions, even in regard to the Miranda warning. In 1976 the Burger Court reinforced the *Miranda* decision by ruling that a defendant's exercise of the option to remain silent after being given Miranda warnings could not be held against him or her in court (*Doyle* v. *Ohio* and *Wood* v. *Ohio*, 426 U.S. 610). And, in 1977 the Court reversed a conviction when police led a defendant (later convicted again without the tainted evidence) to incriminate himself during a long car ride with no lawyer present (*Brewer* v. *Williams*, 430 U.S. 387). The Burger Court, though reluctant to expand the rights of the accused, has rarely turned back earlier reforms.

Another area of state and local practice in which the Court has involved itself is the emotional abortion issue. In 1973 the Court ruled that the Fourteenth Amendment guaranteed to women the right to choose to have abortions during the early months of pregnancy (*Roe* v. *Wade*, 410 U.S. 113; *Doe* v. *Bolton*, 410 U.S. 179). The decisions struck down the anti-abortion laws of forty-six states as unconstitutional interferences with individual rights. However, in 1977 the Court determined that states have the right to refuse to spend public funds to pay for elective abortions for women unable to pay themselves (*Maher* v. *Roe*, 432 U.S. 464). Thus, the Court guarantees a woman's right to choose to terminate a pregnancy during the first three months, but only if she has the money to afford the operation. This situation satisfies totally neither the "pro-choice" nor the "pro-life" advocates, but it demonstrates that the Court plays an important role in the making of public policy. Both groups intensified their lobbying and politicking in the wake of these decisions.

---

[4]The Court did not free Miranda; he merely received a new trial and was convicted again, even without the confession. Out on parole in 1976, Miranda was stabbed to death during a dispute in a bar. The police, using a "Miranda card," read the prime suspect his rights. So it goes.

Interpretation of Federal Statutes

Many Supreme Court decisions do not involve challenges to the constitutionality of legislation but are disputes over how legislation should be interpreted.

The Supreme Court exercises leadership through its judicial review of actions by the national government and through its review of state and local practices only when the constitutionality of a statute has been challenged in court. Both these sources of leadership involve overturning a law or practice on the basis of its unconstitutionality. The interpretation of laws, which is the third source of judicial leadership, differs from the first two in that it does not involve findings of unconstitutionality.

As a policy the Court tries to avoid considerations of unconstitutionality. Frequently, to avoid this question, the Court interprets a law in a manner that changes the intent of Congress or a state legislature but avoids a finding of unconstitutionality. In 1968, for example, the Court interpreted the Selective Service Act to mean that a draft board could not withdraw a divinity student's draft exemption because of participation in antiwar protest activities (*Oestereich* v. *Selective Service Board,* 393 U.S. 233). Thus, although the Court had made national policy by prohibiting draft boards from removing the exemptions of protesters, it had not ruled the Selective Service Act, or any of its sections, unconstitutional. Two years later the Court again altered national policy regarding the draft by ruling that individuals were entitled to the status of conscientious objector if their objections to war came from deeply held moral standards, even if these standards did not stem from religious beliefs (*Welsh* v. *United States,* 398 U.S. 333). Thus, although the Court was interpreting the Selective Service Act in a new way, thereby effectively changing it, it had again not ruled any parts of the act unconstitutional.

Functions of Leadership

The judicial branch is similar to Congress in that neither can speak with one voice (as can the president), but both are capable of real leadership. In chapter 2 we noted that if Congress performed five functions well, it would be providing leadership. The five functions were (1) representation, (2) creation and clarification of issues, (3) oversight of government, (4) legitimation of government policies, and (5) lawmaking. To a significant degree the Court is also capable of realizing these functions. To the degree that the Court is able to perform these same functions, it, too, is capable of real leadership.

Representation. The Court has often provided a forum where minority positions receive representation—representation often already denied by the other branches of government. Sometimes these minorities have been privileged; for example, in 1918, business leaders were overjoyed when the Court overturned state legislation limiting child labor (*Hammer* v. *Dagenhart,* 247 U.S. 251). In contrast, since World War II the Court has often represented the

The Court, somewhat protected from public opinion, often provides representation to unpopular minorities.

views of unpopular and/or underprivileged minorities, including those of draft protesters, persons accused of crimes, and black schoolchildren.

Issue creation and clarification. That the Court has often provided leadership by creating and clarifying issues cannot be denied. Perhaps the most significant example of this is the *Brown* v. *Board of Education* decision of 1954. Prior to that decision the problem of inferior, segregated education was not an important issue before Congress and state legislatures. Indeed, the forces of integration were so weak that legislative remedies were not even being seriously debated, especially in those Southern states where conditions for black youngsters were most wretched. The *Brown* decision helped America to face up to its problems of racial discrimination.

The Court has put significant issues, such as racial segregation, on the political agenda.

Oversight. Although the Court itself cannot conduct investigations, it can perform an oversight function in response to claims by litigants who believe that government's administration of programs is denying them their rights. In the draft case discussed above, for example, the Court in effect reviewed the government's administration of parts of the Selective Service Act and ordered the executive branch to modify its behavior in line with the Court's ruling.

The Court has reviewed the constitutionality of the implementation of government programs.

Legitimation of government policy. Just as governmental policy is legitimated by passing through the representational process in Congress, policy is also legitimated when it receives a "seal of approval" of constitutionality from the Supreme Court. Although the Court may seem to lead only when it is actively protecting the rights of citizens from government infringement, the Court is not unimportant when it endorses the constitutionality of an act of government. The judiciary does provide a third arena, in addition to the legislature and the executive, for political battle. The mere existence of this third arena, with its august judges and hallowed traditions, tends to increase popular respect for the government and the legitimacy of governmental policies.

By providing another forum for appealing government policies, the Court legitimates the entire policy process.

Policy making. The Court does not make laws in the same sense that Congress passes legislation. Yet, it does make policy through its decisions, and such policy has the force of law. Most often the Court does not make an entirely new policy but instead causes existing policies to be modified in accord with the Court's interpretations of the Constitution. Thus, the Warren Court decisions that expanded the rights of the accused did not initiate entirely new policies regarding relations between the police and the accused. The decisions did not call for any such "revolution" in police behavior, and even those changes that the Court did mandate were often ignored by the

The Court has forced significant modifications in government policies.

police.[5] Nevertheless, in the post-World War II period, no one can deny that the Court has had a major impact in changing national or state policies regarding legislative apportionment, the rights of the accused, abortion, and the civil rights of black Americans.

Judicial Activism versus Judicial Restraint

Its power to strike down laws as unconstitutional and to interpret statutes provides the Supreme Court the opportunity to lead. Still, the justices on the Court must personally decide that they want to lead, that the Court should exert strong leadership. Individuals who favor a strong leadership role for the Court support the philosophy of *judicial activism;* others who favor a more limited role for the Court favor a philosophy of *judicial restraint.*

Judicial activism involves the willingness of the Court both to accept controversial cases and then to find behavior by government officials—national, state, or local—to be unconstitutional. Thus, activism is not just a matter of the Court's willingness to disagree with other government institutions; it is primarily a matter of willingness even to accept cases. As discussed later in this chapter, in its area of appellate jurisdiction the Court is free to choose which cases it will hear. A Court dominated by a philosophy of judicial restraint will be reluctant to hear cases, much less rule against decisions made by elected officials.

Judicial activists want the Court to move quickly to stop violations of the Constitution.

One argument for judicial activism is that the justices are appointed for life tenure specifically to insulate them from public passions so that they will protect the liberties of minorities. This view holds that the powers of government are indeed limited by the Constitution and that it is the function of the courts to be very wary that the government is not infringing on citizens' rights. This was generally the philosophy of the Warren Court, a philosophy that enabled it to initiate changes beneficial to disadvantaged minorities.

Advocates of judicial restraint want the Court to be reluctant to overturn actions by national, state, or local governments unless severe and obvious violations of the Constitution are occurring.

Advocates of judicial restraint, in contrast, argue that the justices, not being directly elected, are least accountable to the people and therefore should be very reluctant to disallow the actions of elected officials. This view holds that governmental acts should be upheld unless they very clearly violate a specific clause of the Constitution. This point of view, by suggesting that the Supreme Court should almost always uphold governmental actions, relegates the Court to a position well short of leadership. The judicial restraint point of

---

[5]An example of noncompliance with a Supreme Court decision is the persistence of school prayers in the wake of the *Engel* v. *Vitale* decision (370 U.S. 421 [1962]), barring state-imposed prayers. A 1969 *New York Times* survey (March 26, p. 1) reported that 13 percent of schools nationally, including half of those in the South, continued to have some type of organized prayer or religious reading seven years after the decision banning such activity.

view has been advocated by Reagan, who has often criticized the federal courts as too willing to disallow the actions of state and local authorities.

Areas of Confusion

Loose and strict constructionism.

The debate between judicial activism and judicial restraint is sometimes confused with the debate between loose constructionism and strict constructionism. The constructionist debate has two dimensions. The first hinges on the interpretation of the Tenth Amendment: "The powers not delegated to the United States by the Constitution, nor prohibited by it to the States, are reserved to the States respectively, or to the people." Strict constructionists prefer a literal interpretation of this amendment, an interpretation that limits the powers of national government to those explicitly granted. Loose constructionists, in contrast, argue that the "elastic," or "necessary and proper," clause (Article I, Section 8) permits the national government broad powers to carry out the explicitly stated powers. Strict constructionists, who have been losing most court challenges in recent years, might argue, for example, that the national government does not have the power to force chemical manufacturers to keep records of hazardous waste disposals because the Constitution nowhere explicitly mentions hazardous waste control as a responsiblity of the national government. Loose constructionists would argue that control of hazardous waste disposal is a logical extension of the federal government's right to regulate interstate commerce.

The second dimension of the constructionist debate refers not to the powers of the national government but rather to the individual rights guaranteed in the Bill of Rights. In this debate, strict constructionists argue that the wording of the Bill of Rights must be taken literally. Strict constructionists say, for example, that the First Amendment statement that "Congress shall make no law . . . abridging the freedom of speech" means that Congress shall make *no* such law regardless of the circumstances. According to this strict interpretation, all speech is protected from congressional sanction regardless of whether the speech incites to riot, advocates violent overthrow of the government, or is racist or sexist in nature. Strict constructionists argue that Congress can punish individuals for actions (for example, rioting, discrimination, or attempting to overthrow the government by violence) but not for speech. Loose constructionists argue instead that, in the instance of speech, the government has the authority to protect itself and the citizenry by prohibiting incendiary remarks, such as in the face of a clear and present danger of irreparable harm.

Liberalism and conservatism.

The position of judicial activism argues for a Court that takes the lead in protecting minority rights, but such a position should not be assumed to be politically liberal or progressive. For several decades prior to 1937, the Supreme Court took an activist role in defense of a

---

Strict constructionists believe that the powers granted the federal government in the Constitution should be interpreted narrowly to limit what the federal government can do.

Loose constructionists are reluctant to limit the activities of Congress and the president.

Strict constructionists also believe that the federal government is tightly prohibited from limiting individual freedoms such as speech and religion.

Loose constructionists again are reluctant to limit Congress and the president if these elected officials believe that laws limiting civil liberties are warranted.

privileged minority—namely, big corporations. The Fourteenth Amendment provides that no state shall "deprive any person of life, liberty, or property, without due process of law." The Court interpreted a corporation as a "person" within the meaning of the Fourteenth Amendment and struck down a great deal of antitrust and child labor legislation as well as many other New Deal efforts.

In that era, the position of judicial restraint held by Justice Oliver Wendell Holmes, Jr., made him appear to be quite progressive. Holmes, although personally quite conservative and pro-laissez faire in his political views, believed that government should be permitted by the courts to pass whatever legislation it desired unless the legislation was obviously unconstitutional. For this view Holmes is remembered as "the great dissenter" by reason of his many disagreements with his activist colleagues on the Court who had overruled much legislation. It was not that Holmes considered the legislation to be wise but that he held to the judicial restraint position that the elected branches of government should be permitted a very wide range of activities. When legislatures are passing much progressive legislation, a Court that intervenes to strike down such legislation is activist and conservative. When legislatures are enacting reactionary legislation, say, segregation laws, a Court that intervenes to strike down such legislation is activist and progressive. Given this interpretation of judicial restraint, Holmes, a progressive member of the Taft Court of the 1920s, would have been a very conservative member of the Warren Court of the 1960s.

Linkage with the Political-Question Doctrine

The political-question doctrine holds that some issues are so tied to the other branches that the courts should not decide them.

Advocates of judicial restraint vigorously embrace the "political-question" doctrine, which holds that certain issues are political questions to be decided by the executive or legislative branches, not by the Court. In the case of *Luther* v. *Borden* (7 Howard 1 [1849]), Chief Justice Roger B. Taney was faced with a suit charging that the chartered government of Rhode Island was not the legitimate government because it so restricted voting rights that it violated the clause in Article IV, Section 4, guaranteeing to every state a republican form of government. In his decision Taney laid down the political question doctrine by stating that such a determination could be made only by the president and/or Congress.

Until the *Baker* v. *Carr* (369 U.S. 186 [1962]) decision of the Warren Court, the political-question doctrine was applied to all cases of legislative apportionment. The Court refused to hear such cases on the grounds that they were "political questions," that plaintiffs from underapportioned areas should seek a remedy from the legislature, not from the courts. Of course, asking the residents of an underapportioned area to seek a remedy from a malapportioned legislature was similar to asking a rape victim to seek a remedy from the rapist. However, once the Court had ruled in 1962 that apportionment cases are justiciable (able to be decided by the courts), only two years elapsed before it ruled that both houses of all state legislatures must be apportioned on a one-person, one-vote formula. In *Reynolds* v. *Sims* (377 U.S. 533 [1964]), Chief Justice Warren ruled that "to the extent that a citizen's right to vote is debased, he is that much less a citizen." Any debasement of citizenship was indeed viewed with alarm by the activist Warren Court.

Judicial Recruitment
Appointment of Federal Judges

The president nominates and the Senate confirms judicial appointments.

The road to a federal judgeship, although not especially complicated, is strewn with possible pitfalls and rejection. The necessity of obtaining Senate approval of all presidential nominees for these positions is a primary source of such rejection. Congress determines not only the number of districts into which the federal judiciary shall be divided but also the number of justices within each district as well. There are currently 571 judges in the district courts of the United States and an additional 156 in the courts of appeals. Thus, approximately 725 judges determine the application of federal law in a population of over 250 million.

General criteria. Nowhere in the law is there a written requirement that the president must nominate only lawyers to be judges, but this custom has developed so strongly in this century that were the president to nominate a person who was not a lawyer, the outcry from the American Bar Association would be so great that the nominee would face almost certain rejection by the Senate. Although many county and local judges throughout the state systems are not lawyers, every recent federal judge has been a member of the bar at the time of nomination to the bench.

All recent judges have been lawyers.

Only the president, who must nominate, and the Senate, which must confirm, are formally involved in the recruitment of federal judges. Others, however, also play important roles. For instance, a deputy attorney general is usually instructed to prepare a list of potential nominees for the president.

Senatorial courtesy. In preparing the list, the attorney general's office will certainly learn the wishes of the senators from the president's own party from the state with the vacant judgeship. As we noted in chapter 2, the practice of senatorial courtesy applies to district court judges, so that any presidential nominee must be approved by the appropriate senators (if both senators from a state are of the president's party) or senator (if only one of a state's senators is of the president's party). In practice, senators from the state with the vacancy usually submit a list of four or five preferred individuals, from which the president chooses the new judge. If neither senator is of the president's party,

Senatorial courtesy is involved in district court appointments.

the deputy attorney general is not concerned with senatorial courtesy but instead consults with local or state party officials to identify prospective nominees.

Although presidents have often stated their intentions to find the "best man for the job" and have emphasized the nonpartisan nature of the work, a very substantial majority of the judges appointed in this century have been of the president's party. Among recent presidents, the only one to nominate even 10 percent of his judges from the other party was Gerald Ford, a Republican who made Democrats 21 percent of his judicial nominations.

Every president has made the great majority of appointments from among lawyers who share his party affiliation.

Nominees are chosen after consultation with relevant senators, state party officials, and the president's patronage adviser.

The American Bar Association ranks potential nominees.

Potential judges are identified through contacts with state party leaders, the attorney general's office, and, of course, relevant senators. A deputy attorney general then asks the FBI for a background investigation and members of the bar and judges in the affected area for their assessment of the potential nominee's professional competence and their opinion of whether he or she is likely to blend well with the other members of the court. The deputy attorney general also turns over the names of all serious potential nominees to the American Bar Association's Standing Committee on Federal Judiciary, which rates candidates as exceptionally well qualified, qualified, or *not qualified*. A low rating from the committee generally results in a decision by the president not to put that person's name in nomination. The Senate is unlikely to confirm a nominee who the ABA declares publicly is not qualified for a federal judgeship.

Senate action. Once a nomination is made it is considered by the Senate Judiciary Committee, which, after hearings, usually supports the president's choice—assuming, of course, that senatorial courtesy has been exercised. Action on the floor generally follows in the form of almost unanimous approval of the nominee. The president is then empowered to appoint his nominee and to grant the commission—that is, the authority to carry through the duties of the judgeship.

Appointment of Supreme Court Justices

The appointment procedure for Supreme Court justices is much more rigorous than for other judges because of the great nationwide political interest in the Supreme Court. While the senators from Maine are likely to care very little about who is going to be a district court judge in New Mexico, they are understandably concerned about nominees for the Supreme Court. Because senatorial courtesy does not apply to nominations for the Supreme Court, the president takes a much greater personal interest in the nomination. He very much wants to nominate individuals who, while on the Court, will support his position on issues, for he is well aware that the Court can make policy through its decisions.

Senatorial courtesy is not applicable to Supreme Court appointments.

Sometimes presidents miscalculate and later regret their appointments. Once a nominee is on the bench, however, a president cannot remove him or her. Conservative President Dwight D. Eisenhower reportedly described his appointment of Earl Warren as the worst decision of his presidency. Warren's record as governor of California evidenced little concern for civil rights, for example, those of Japanese Americans, but Chief Justice Warren consistently championed the causes of underprivileged minorities.

President Nixon's four appointees sometimes supported his conservative views but also frequently disagreed with his positions. What perhaps has been most surprising is the high level of activism of the Burger Court. In spite of Nixon's statements that his appointees would limit the role of the Court, the Court has not been reluctant to tackle issues and to rule government actions unconstitutional. On the emotional issue of abortion, three Nixon appointees (Burger, Blackmun, and Powell) voted with the Court's majority, which struck down state laws that had prohibited abortion in the early months of pregnancy (in opposition to Nixon's antiabortion stance). In the decision probably most resented by Nixon, his appointees voted unanimously that he had to turn over "Watergate tapes" to the special prosecutor.

The Senate's record. Only 20 percent of all presidential nominations for Supreme Court seats have been rejected by the Senate, but recent years have contributed substantially to this percentage. Nixon saw two nominees rejected: Clement F. Haynsworth, on the basis of conflicts of interest, and G. Harrold Carswell, because of a record of thorough insensitivity to black Americans. Although the rejection rate has not been substantial, the threat of rejection has caused presidents not to nominate controversial figures and sometimes to withdraw names of nominees once it became clear they were not likely to meet with Senate approval. In 1968, for example, the nomination of Justice Abe Fortas to be elevated to the vacant post of chief justice was withdrawn by Lyndon Johnson. The Senate expressed displeasure over Fortas's social activism, the "lame-duck" nature of the appointment (Johnson was soon to leave the White House), and the alleged element of "cronyism" (Fortas had long been a personal friend of the president).

The Senate scrutinizes Supreme Court nominees to the extent that historically one in five has been rejected.

The Judges
District Court and Appeals Court Judges

Supreme, district, and appeals court judges all have lifetime tenure.

Federal judges are predominantly middle-aged white men with substantial salaries and the exceptional job security of knowing that they can be removed only through impeachment.[6] This situation still has not satisfied at least a few

---

[6] In 1982 district court judges received $76,000 annual compensation; court of appeals judges, $80,400; associate justices of the Supreme Court, $100,600; and Chief Justice Burger, $104,700.

federal judges who have resigned in order to resume private law practices promising earnings well over $100,000 annually. No justice has ever resigned from the prestigious Supreme Court for financial reasons, although several have stepped down in response to the pressures of the position.

As table 3-2 shows, the record of the Carter administration in nominating black women and Hispanics to the lower federal courts stands out in contrast to that of other presidents. Jimmy Carter's impact in diversifying the federal judiciary was aided by the Omnibus Judgeship Act of 1978, which created 152 new judgeships to handle the ever-increasing federal court caseload. Carter nominated, and the Senate confirmed, 56 appointments to courts of appeals and 206 to district courts. Through 1984, Reagan had appointed 31 judges to courts of appeals and 130 district court judges.

The ninety-four United States district courts are staffed by approximately 575 judges who annually decide over 200,000 civil cases and 30,000 criminal cases. At this level, the judges are concerned primarily with the facts of the case, not with the interpretation of law and constitutionality. In contrast, the 156 judges of courts of appeals never hear new factual evidence; they depend on the records of the lower courts from which the appeals are made. Usually sitting in groups of three, appellate court judges rule on questions of judicial error and interpretation of law in cases appealed from the lower courts.

Until the Carter administration, the federal judiciary was almost entirely white and male.

District courts are concerned with the facts of cases; appeals courts are concerned with questions of judicial error and misinterpretation of law.

Table 3-2
Judicial Nominees

	U.S. Courts of Appeals		
	Women	Blacks	Hispanics
Johnson	3%	5%	Not available
Nixon	0	0	Not available
Ford	0	0	Not available
Carter	20	16	4%
Reagan (1981–1984)	9	3	3

	U.S. District Courts		
Johnson	2%	3%	3%
Nixon	1	3	1
Ford	2	6	2
Carter	14	14	7
Reagan (1981–1984)	9	1	5

Source: Congressional Quarterly Weekly Report, December 8, 1984, p. 3075.

Supreme Court Justices

The median age of the Supreme Court justices in 1986 was 77.

As table 3-3 illustrates, turnover among Supreme Court justices is not rapid. Most justices remain in office until declining health leads to a retirement decision. Each judge individually decides when the time is appropriate to resign. With two exceptions, all members of the Supreme Court have been white males. The only black justice, Thurgood Marshall, was appointed in 1967 by Lyndon Johnson, and the only female justice, Sandra Day O'Connor, was appointed in 1981 by Reagan.

The chief justice is nominated by the president for that specific office; he is not the most senior justice, nor is he or she chosen chief justice by the Court.

Warren Burger. The chief justice in 1986 was seventy-eight-year-old Warren Burger, who was appointed by Richard Nixon in 1969. Burger had been active in Republican politics before being appointed to a court of appeals by Eisenhower in 1956. His record as a judge on the appellate court was marked by judicial restraint and an anti-civil libertarian attitude toward the accused. As chief justice, Burger chairs the Friday conferences of the Court at which, meeting with only the justices present, the Court discusses and decides cases. Burger also has the responsibility, when he decides with the majority, of assigning to a particular justice the writing of the majority opinion. When the chief justice is in the minority, the most senior justice in the majority assigns the writing of the majority opinion.

William J. Brennan. William J. Brennan, in 1986 both the oldest (seventy-nine) and the most senior member of the Court, received a "recess appointment" from Eisenhower in 1956. When a vacancy occurs in a judgeship at any

Table 3-3
Justices of the Supreme Court

1985 Justices	Appointed by	Age[a]
Warren Burger	Nixon	78
William Brennan	Eisenhower	79
Byron White	Kennedy	68
Thurgood Marshall	Johnson	77
Harry Blackmun	Nixon	77
Lewis Powell	Nixon	78
William Rehnquist	Nixon	61
John Paul Stevens	Ford	69
Sandra Day O'Connor	Reagan	55

[a]Ages as of January 1, 1986.

If a vacancy occurs while the Senate is in recess, the president can name a temporary appointee who is eligible to be nominated for a permanent judgeship when the Senate reconvenes.

level while the Senate is in recess, Article II, Section 2 applies: "The President shall have Power to fill up all Vacancies that may happen during the Recess of the Senate, by granting Commissions which shall expire at the End of their [Congress's] next Session." Thus, Brennan first took office without Senate confirmation. When Congress reconvened, the president had forty days in which to submit Brennan's name (or a replacement) for the permanent appointment, which Brennan received early in 1957. A member of the Supreme Court of New Jersey at the time of his appointment, Brennan held the traditional "Catholic" seat on the Court. A holdover from the Warren Court, he is a leader of the liberal bloc.

Byron R. White. The only appointee of John F. Kennedy was Byron R. White, who in 1986 was sixty-eight years of age. White ran the Citizens for Kennedy organization in the 1960 presidential campaign. He was rewarded with an appointment as deputy attorney general and, in 1962, an appointment to the Supreme Court. In keeping with his emphasis on vigor, Kennedy appointed a lawyer who, as "Whizzer" White, had led the National Football League in ground gaining in 1938 and whom Kennedy first met in the Navy during World War II. White has been a swing voter, sometimes siding with the liberal bloc of Brennan and Marshall and sometimes with the conservative bloc of Burger, Rehnquist, Powell, and O'Connor.

Although nominees often have experience as judges in lower federal courts or state courts, judicial experience is not required for nomination to the Court.

Thurgood Marshall. The only Johnson appointee remaining on the Court in 1986 was seventy-seven-year-old Thurgood Marshall, who, as a lawyer for the Legal Defense and Education Fund of the NAACP, argued and won the famous *Brown* v. *Board of Education* (347 U.S. 483 [1954]) case, which outlawed *de jure* racial segregation in schools. Marshall was solicitor general of the United States from August 1965 until his appointment to the Court in 1967. A strong believer in a liberal activism, Marshall often finds himself with Brennan and one or two other justices in writing dissenting opinions.

A liberal bloc of judges dominated the Warren Court; conservative judges have usually formed majorities on the Burger Court.

Harry Blackmun. Besides Chief Justice Burger, Nixon made three other appointments to the Supreme Court. Harry Blackmun (seventy-seven), a childhood friend of Burger's, was an Eisenhower appointee to the court of appeals. Appointed to the Supreme Court in 1970, Blackmun has become more liberal, often siding with Brennan and Marshall. In selecting Blackmun, a Methodist, Nixon broke with the tradition of maintaining a "Jewish seat" on the Court. Since the appointment of Louis Brandeis in 1916, who held the seat for twenty-three years, the Court had always included one Jewish justice until Abe Fortas's resignation in 1969.

Lewis F. Powell and William H. Rehnquist. Both Lewis F. Powell (seventy-eight) and William H. Rehnquist (sixty-one), the two last Nixon appointees, have espoused judicial restraint on the bench. Both were nominated in wake of the Haynsworth and Carswell fiascoes and were rapidly confirmed in 1971. Powell, formerly president of the American Bar Association, became the first justice from Virginia since 1841. Rehnquist, the most conservative justice, was working as an assistant attorney general in the Justice Department's Office of Legal Counsel at the time of his nomination.

John Paul Stevens. John Paul Stevens, sixty-nine years of age in 1986 and the only Ford appointee, joined Burger, Stewart, and Blackmun as former court of appeals judges on the Supreme Court. In 1975 Stevens replaced William O. Douglas, who had served on the Court for thirty-six years, longer than any justice in the nation's history. Douglas's record of unusually strong advocacy for civil liberties and environmentalism so angered his conservative detractors that at one time Ford, then Republican House minority leader, called for Douglas's impeachment. Steven's moderate record has been by no means as controversial as that of Douglas, but Stevens has been respected for his well-drafted, scholarly opinions.

When a Supreme Court vacancy occurs, many influential persons, including senators and even associate justices, lobby the president's advisers to have their favorite nominated to the Court.

Until President Reagan appointed Sandra Day O'Connor in 1981, the Court had been an all-male institution.

Sandra Day O'Connor. In a previous edition of this book we predicted that Carter would nominate a woman to serve on the Supreme Court. We were wrong about which president would appoint the first woman to the Court (Carter made no Supreme Court appointments) but right that the Court's days as an all-male institution were numbered. In 1981 Reagan nominated, and the Senate confirmed, fifty-five-year-old Sandra Day O'Connor as an associate justice of the Supreme court. An Arizona appeals court judge at the time of her nomination, O'Connor was boosted for the nomination by influential Sen. Barry Goldwater (R.-Ariz.) as well as by Associate Justice Rehnquist, a Stanford Law School classmate. They were able to convince the Reagan administration that O'Connor would become the type of justice Reagan envisioned. On the Court, she has voted consistently with the conservative bloc.

The ages of the justices (in 1986 five justices over seventy-five) and the health problems of several suggest that Reagan is likely to have the opportunity to select additional nominees to the Court. Reagan may have the opportunity to influence public policy through his judicial appointments well after the conclusion of his own period in public office. This is especially true if liberal justices Brennan and Marshall retire and are replaced by conservative Reagan nominees.

How Judges Decide

Knowing who judges are and how they think is important because judges do not "objectively" apply the law as a concrete entity that can be "correctly'" ascertained through study. Instead, they make policy through their interpretations and decisions, which necessarily involve their own personal policy

Judges interpret laws on the basis of their own values and what they think is best for America.

preferences. As Justice Felix Frankfurter wrote, "The meaning of 'due process' and the content of terms like 'liberty' are not revealed by the Constitution. It is the justices who make the meaning. They read into the neutral language of the Constitution their own economic and social views. . . . Let us face the fact that [the] justices of the Supreme Court are the molders of policy rather than the impersonal vehicles of revealed truth."[7]

Discretion in judicial behavior is found primarily at the level of the Supreme Court, for district court judges are usually more concerned with the facts of a case (and appellate court judges with judges' errors) than with the interpretation of law. Only after the facts of a case are clear (for example, that a police officer really did arrest and question a suspect without informing him of his constitutional rights) and a subsequent question of the interpretation of a law or the validity of a law arises does a case reach the Supreme Court. District courts and courts of appeals will almost never decide a case by ruling that a law is unconstitutional.

The myth of "the law." Although Supreme Court justices do indeed make decisions on the basis of their own social views, legal tradition insists that justices in general not admit to doing so. Instead, they give the impression that they make decisions by applying the "correct" statute or the "correct" constitutional provision with proper reasoning. They justify rulings on the basis of *stare decisis*, which means "to stand by what has been decided" (commonly called *precedent*); they search for a previous case involving similar principles. Because there are invariably several precedents to support the plaintiff and the defendant, justices choose the precedent they wish to find applicable to the facts of the case.

Judicial decisions list relevant precedents to explain why they are interpreting the law as they are.

With the availability of so many precedents in the Supreme Court's many years of cases, the Court rarely finds it necessary to overrule one of its own decisions. This gives constitutional law a logical continuity supportive of the myth that there is "the law," which has an existence independent of what the justices say it is. This myth, that the "law" exists before judicial decisions, which merely "speak the law," helps to legitimate judicial actions.

The Court tries to create an aura of solemn professionalism to enhance respect for the Court and its decisions.

If the judicial function is purely passive in that it simply tells us what "the law" is, judicial decisions become more than the opinions and values of common mortals. They become professional statements of reality, similar to a medical doctor's diagnosis of an individual's disease. And, again similar to the medical profession, the legal profession has developed its own jargon, which helps to obscure its dealings. Any group of practitioners that wishes to legitimate its actions can do so most effectively by claiming professional status. Because part of being professional involves possession of specialized expertise, the professional can argue that his or her actions or decisions may be properly evaluated only by other professionals having the same expertise.

---

[7]Felix Frankfurter, "The Supreme Court and the Public," *Forum* 83 (June 1930): 332-334.

Thus, many judges claim that their decisions are objective, value-free, professional determinations of reality ("the law") and, as such, are beyond criticism except by other professionals. Because many laypeople also accept this notion of professional objectivity, the decisions of judges, including Supreme Court justices, are usually respected—further legitimizing Court decisions.

The Operation of the Court System

Only a minute proportion of federal cases reaches the Supreme Court.

The focus of most of this chapter has been on the Supreme Court, the ultimate arbiter of federal cases and controversies and the locus of important policy changes. Yet, only a very small percentage of the thousands of federal cases involve questions of constitutional law of sufficient importance to reach the Supreme Court. Each year the Court is asked to hear approximately 4,000 cases; it declines all but about 150 of the requests. The vast majority of cases are resolved without involving the Court—either in the lower judicial courts, which include the district courts, courts of appeals, and special judicial courts (figure 3-1, page 107), or in the administrative courts.

Lower Judicial Courts

Courts of appeals. The courts of appeals, the tribunal immediately below the Supreme Court, are asked to hear over 27,000 cases annually. All of these come up on appeal from the district courts, territorial courts, Tax Court, or independent regulatory commissions. For example, in 1973 District Court Judge John Sirica ruled that President Nixon had to turn over nine "Watergate tapes" to the court for scrutiny (*United States* v. *Mitchell et al.*, 377 F. Supp. 1326 [1974]). Nixon appealed with an argument based on the separation of powers between government branches. A court of appeals rejected this argument (*Nixon* v. *Sirica*, 487 F. 2d 700), and Nixon chose not to appeal the decision to the Supreme Court. He turned over the tapes to Sirica.

To handle the vastly increased workload of federal cases, Congress created many new judgeships in 1978.

Most federal cases are civil in origin (based on diversity of state residence), not criminal.

District courts. The bulk of the work of the federal judiciary is handled by the district courts, which have only original jurisdiction. The approximately 976 judges of these courts handle all violations of federal laws, as well as civil actions arising under the Constitution, laws, or treaties of the United States and cases involving citizens of different states. The last category is handled by state courts unless at least $10,000 is claimed. However, in cases involving citizens of different states even if over $10,000 is involved, the state courts may still handle the case if the litigants agree. The district courts also handle admiralty and maritime cases, as well as any other that Congress prescribes.

Each case is handled by a single judge sitting with a jury unless the litigants agree to a nonjury trial. In the vast majority of cases, the final determination occurs at the district court level because most losers find themselves without a sufficiently good case or the funds for an appeal.

The Federal Judiciary

The offices of U.S. marshals and attorneys have traditionally been patronage positions.

In addition to the judge, significant officers at the district level are the United States marshal and United States attorney. The former has the responsibility to make arrests, guard prisoners, and serve court orders; the latter is the prosecutor for the government in criminal cases. Both serve under the authority of the attorney general and are appointed by the president with Senate approval. Traditionally these positions, one for each of the ninety-five district courts, have been patronage positions.

Special judicial courts. Special judicial courts differ from district courts in that the special courts adjudicate cases in specified substantive areas. The special courts, which were administrative courts until they were converted by Congress, do not have general jurisdiction.

The Court of International Trade hears disputes only when citizens claim the government is not properly implementing customs law.

The largest of the three most major special courts is the *Court of International Trade,* whose nine members (no more than five of whom may be members of the same political party) each receive $76,000 annually. This court hears civil cases arising from claims that rulings and appraisals by customs officials are in error. The judges sit in panels of three in various ports of entry.

The Court of Appeals for the Federal Circuit provides an opportunity for citizens to appeal patent, claims, and customs decisions.

The *Court of Appeals for the Federal Circuit* has only appellate jurisdiction over decisions made in the Court of International Trade, the patent office, the tariff commission, and the Court of Claims. The court has twelve members, who each receive $80,400 annually. Like all judges in judicial (as distinct from administrative) courts, they can be removed only by impeachment.

Individuals who believe that the federal government has wronged them can sue in the Court of Claims.

The *Court of Claims,* founded in 1855, adjudicates citizens' suits for damages against the federal government. Individuals who believe the government has reneged on contract obligations, taken their property without just compensation, or caused personal injury (through the negligent behavior of a government employee) must sue in this court rather than in a general-purpose court. The court has five members, each compensated at $67,800 annually, and is assisted by eleven commissioners who investigate the validity of claims.

Administrative Courts

The three major administrative courts are the Tax Court, the territorial courts, and the Court of Military Appeals.

Tax Court. The sixteen members of the *Tax Court* are appointed to twelve-year terms by the president with the consent of the Senate. Each compensated at $70,300 per year, the judges respond to taxpayer claims that the Internal Revenue Service has misinterpreted the tax code in a specific application to the plaintiff. Thus the Commissioner of Internal Revenue is always the defendant in these cases.

Territorial courts. The *territorial* courts differ widely in their authority, for each is tailored to local customs and needs. In Puerto Rico, for example, the court has jurisdiction over only questions of national law, because Puerto Rico has separate local courts. In other jurisdictions the courts handle local disputes as well. The judges of these courts, appointed by the president and confirmed by the Senate, serve eight-year terms except in Puerto Rico, where the judges have lifetime tenure.

Court of Military Appeals. The *Court of Military Appeals* has an unusual record in that in over half the cases it hears it overturns the verdict of the court-martial. The court is composed of three civilian judges and is the final appellate tribunal in court-martial cases. It was established in 1950 as part of the revision of the Uniform Code of Military Justice, the first major overhaul of the system of military justice in 150 years. Its three judges are appointed for fifteen-year terms by the president with Senate confirmation. At its discretion the Court of Military Appeals is authorized to review decisions of courts-martial involving prison sentences of more than one year and/or bad-conduct discharges. The court is required to review any decision considered suspect by the judge advocate general as well as all decisions that involve generals or admirals or the imposition of the death sentence.

Military personnel accused of misbehavior while on duty are subject to court-martial procedures, not trial in the regular judicial courts.

The role of this court is not inconsequential because over two million Americans are subject to military justice. The court has in fact had a substantial impact in that it has effected the application of most of the Bill of Rights to courts-martial. In 1967, for example, it ruled that the "Miranda procedures," by which a suspect is read his or her rights at the time of arrest, apply to military justice as well as civilian justice (*United States* v. *Tempia*, 16 USCMA 629). In 1969 the disparity in rights afforded military personnel in comparison with those of civilians was further reduced by a Supreme Court ruling that, during peacetime, service personnel would be tried in civilian courts for offenses committed while off duty or on leave (*O'Callahan* v. *Parker*, 395 U.S. 258). Continuing the trend toward affording military defendants the same rights as civilian defendants, in 1980 Carter ordered courts-martial to use the same rules of evidence applied in federal criminal trials.

Over time the Court of Military Appeals has been applying to military hearings the same standards of judicial process as used in other federal courts.

Supreme Court Procedures

Jurisdiction. The Supreme Court, as noted earlier in this chapter, has two types of jurisdiction, original and appellate. Most cases that the Court decides involve appellate jurisdiction; that is, they are appealed to the Supreme Court by the loser in a lower court or a state court of last resort. The lower federal court is usually a court of appeals because cases may be appealed directly to the Supreme Court from a district court only in special, rare circumstances (for example, a decision holding an act of Congress unconstitutional) and because cases from the special-purpose courts are rarely reviewed by the Supreme Court. Cases from a state court of last resort (usually called the state supreme court) are appealed directly to the Supreme Court if the loser feels that a substantial question of federal law or the Constitution is involved.

The Supreme Court rarely hears a case under its own original jurisdiction.

The Federal Judiciary

The writ of certiorari. An appeal to the Supreme Court to hear a case is no guarantee that the Court will agree to take the case; four justices must vote to place the case on the docket before it can be heard. Only questions of substantial social and/or legal importance are granted writs of *certiorari* (a Latin term meaning "made more certain") and called up; the other 95 percent of petitions for *certiorari* are denied, usually without explanation. Besides rejecting cases that are too minor in subject matter for the Court's time, justices sometimes refuse to hear cases because of the sensitivity of the issues involved. Often this involves the "political-question" doctrine discussed earlier in this chapter.

The Court decides which cases it will hear on appeal.

The Court accepts only a small percentage of the cases appealed to it.

The Supreme Court refused to rule on the constitutionality of the Vietnam War, although it had been presented with several cases challenging the war's legality. Although we cannot know the reasoning of the nine justices, several historians have suggested that their refusal was based on political reality. Had the Court ruled the war unconstitutional and demanded the immediate withdrawal of all U.S. troops from Vietnam, the president might simply have refused to obey. Such an action by any president would throw the nation into a constitutional crisis accompanied by massive chaos and bewilderment. The ultimate outcome would be uncertain, but Supreme Court justices are well aware that, in any confrontation with the other branches of government, all the money and all the guns are in hands other than theirs. The Court does not operate in a political vacuum.

Amicus curiae briefs. Another indication of the political nature of the Supreme Court is the use of *amicus curiae* briefs in a substantial number of cases. Such briefs are rarely used in lower courts. An *amicus curiae* brief ("friend of the court" in Latin) is a document presented to a court in support of the arguments of one of the parties in a case. The brief of an *amicus curiae* attempts to bolster the position of a litigant by providing additional legal argumentation and by demonstrating organizational or interest-group support. *Amicus curiae* briefs are a means by which interest groups and other political organizations communicate their views on issues to the Court. Those that submit such briefs are usually groups, either governmental (for example, the city of New York or the state of Mississippi) or organizational (for example, the American Civil Liberties Union, Liberty Lobby, NAACP, or Friends of Animals).

In most Supreme Court cases several amicus curiae *briefs are filed.*

The Supreme Court in session. The Supreme Court of the United States is in session from October through June in the District of Columbia's 1935 replica of the Greek Temple of Diana at Ephesus. Monday through Thursday the justices hear cases from 10 A.M. to 2:30 P.M.—one of Washington's fascinating free exhibitions. With rare exceptions, a lawyer is permitted one-half hour to state a client's case, although some of this time is used by the justices posing questions and asking for clarifications. On Fridays the justices meet alone (the Friday conference) to decide on applications for *certiorari* and

Four days a week the justices listen to oral arguments on cases; on Fridays the justices meet together alone to discuss their decisions.

to determine the results of cases already heard. At the Friday conference the chief justice gives his position (on each case) first, followed by the other justices in order of seniority. The final vote is taken in the opposite order, from the newest justice through the chief justice. After that vote, the chief justice assigns the author of the opinion if the chief justice is a member of the majority; otherwise, the most senior member of the majority decides who will write the majority opinion. Justices may, of course, submit concurring or dissenting opinions either individually or in combination.

Conclusion

In comparison with most of the world, the U.S. court system is independent and powerful.

The American judicial system is quite different from those in most nations of the world in that it functions with greater independence from the parties in power in the executive and congressional branches. Throughout most of the world, it is unlikely that a court would rule an act of the ruling party or coalition to be unconstitutional. It is even less likely that, were such a ruling of unconstitutionality made, the ruling would be respected and the orders of the court followed by the executive or legislative branch.

The Supreme Court operates in a political world; it can provide leadership in many ways, but it cannot stray too far from public opinion for too long.

The Supreme Court exhibits an immense potential for exercising political power, but the actualization of that potential is determined by the "climate" in which the Court operates. The justices are acutely aware that the area of jurisdiction open to them is determined by Congress. In addition, we have already documented the persuasive powers inherent in the office of the president regarding presidential-congressional relations. If the Court digresses too far or too consistently from the interpretation of "reality" ("the law") as it is viewed by Congress and/or the president, legislative pressure to remove the relevant cases from the Court's jurisdiction inevitably results. Thus, the parameters within which the Court is free to act are set by the president and Congress, yet these parameters are of such a width that the Court may, provided it is willing and politically astute, assume a role of effective leadership.

Selected Additional Readings

The authors found the following works to be most helpful in the preparation of this chapter and recommend them to students who want additional information on the judiciary:

Abraham, Henry J. *The Judiciary,* 6th ed. Boston: Allyn & Bacon, 1983.

Ball, Howard. *Court and Politics: The Federal Judicial System.* Englewood Cliffs, N.J.: Prentice-Hall, 1980.

Baum, Lawrence. *The Supreme Court,* 2d ed. Washington, D.C.: Congressional Quarterly, 1985.

Congressional Quarterly. *The Supreme Court,* 3rd ed. Washington, D.C.: Congressional Quarterly, 1983.

Jacob, Herbert. *Justice in America: Courts, Lawyers, and the Judicial Process,* 4th ed. Boston: Little, Brown, 1984.

Case History: "Superfund" 1980, 1985

Part III: The Courts

106-107

We noted in the text that the court system in the United States both is hierarchically arranged and consists of multiple layers. Thus, despite the importance and complexity of the Comprehensive Environmental Response, Compensation and Liability Act of 1980 (CERCLA), no case based on this statute reached the Supreme Court during the original act's existence. A case related to the possible interpretation that the law permits the government to hold any party "strictly, jointly and severally" liable may eventually reach the Court, but by 1985 no such case was introduced into the Court system. In this end-of-chapter segment of the Superfund case history we will outline the nature of cases likely to be brought and examine those cases that have been raised in the lower courts.

The first case to be brought to federal court under CERCLA was filed in the U.S. District Court of New Jersey (**Lesniak et al.** v. **United States et al.**) soon after President Jimmy Carter signed the legislation. Section 114 (c) of the law states:

> Except as provided in this Act, no person may be required to contribute to any fund, the purpose of which is to pay compensation for claims for any cost of responses or damages or claims which may be compensated under this title. Nothing in this section shall preclude any State from using general revenues for such a fund or from imposing a tax or fee upon any person or upon any substance in order to finance the purchase or prepositioning of hazardous substance response equipment or other preparations.

This section of the law is commonly known as the "preemption" provision, because it preempts the states from establishing a tax, or fee, on any "person" (a legal term that includes corporations) for the same purposes (i.e., to cover the same cleanup operations) as those that are covered by the federal tax on petroleum and chemical companies. This is a very complex way of saying that no one may be taxed twice for the same purpose. A companion lawsuit was filed in the U.S. District Court for the District of Columbia by the State of New Jersey, but that suit was dismissed by the court because New Jersey could not point to an existing case that was affected by the preemption provision.

Several states, however, had already passed fee-based hazardous substance response programs similar to Superfund. The purpose of the Lesniak suit was to clarify the relationship between those state provisions and CERCLA. The plaintiffs in the Lesniak case sought a judgment from the court that Congress did not intend Section 114 (c) of CERCLA to apply to any state fee-based funds that were to be used for the following purposes:

1. To finance the administrative costs of a state fund
2. To finance the purchase or prepositioning of hazardous substance response equipment and other preparations for responding to releases within a state
3. To finance the cleanup of oil spills
4. To pay the required state contribution to cleanup actions financed by the Superfund Response Fund
5. To pay third-party damage claims
6. To "advance" funds for cleanup actions eligible for coverage by the Superfund Response Fund if the state has received a commitment of reimbursement from the Superfund Response Fund and makes its own expenditure in the expectation that the commitment will be honored
7. To pay for cleanup actions that in theory could be paid by Superfund but in practice will not be paid because of funding limitations

Lesniak et al. argued that none of the seven "purposes" outlined above were covered by CERCLA; that is, the Hazardous Response Trust Fund established by the act could not be used to pay for any of these costs. The court set January 25, 1982, as the hearing date for the Lesniak case.

On January 23, just two days before the hearing date, EPA Administrator Anne Gorsuch approved an out-of-court settlement that admitted the correctness of all seven points raised in the Lesniak case. Thus, even though the case never reached the hearing stage, the court served a valuable function in the policy-making process. Because the court accepted the Lesniak suit, it "forced" the executive branch to clarify CERCLA by having EPA admit that the seven functions listed in the suit were not at odds with the preemption provision of Section 114 (c). As a result, more states passed hazardous waste fee-based legislation that was modeled after the fee system represented in the Lesniak suit. This out-of-court settlement helped to preserve, at the state level, a potentially powerful mechanism to fund state participation in the Superfund program and to permit the states to respond to those hazardous substance releases into the environment that the federal government either could not or would not clean up. The way the law was **structured** had been clarified in the courts. That clarification was expanded in 1985 when Congress reauthorized CERCLA and specifically removed the preemption clause from the law.

The second case brought to the federal court system is much more complex, because it deals with the **politics** of the executive branch, rather than the structure of the law itself. Section 105 of CERCLA holds:

> Within one hundred and eighty days after the enactment of this Act, the President shall, after notice and opportunity for public comments, revise and republish the national contigency plan for the removal of oil and hazardous substances, originally prepared and published pursuant to Section 311 of the Federal Water Pollution Control Act, to reflect and effectuate the responsibilities and powers created by this Act.

The National Contingency Plan (NCP) was the "blueprint" used by the federal government and the states in cleaning up oil spilled into the nation's surface waters. Congress was requiring the executive branch ("the President") to revise the NCP so that it would cover the release of virtually any toxic substance, pollutant, or contaminant into the environment. Further, the NCP was, according to Section 105 of CERCLA, to be revised and republished to provide national guidelines to the thirteen federal agencies and the states—all of which play a role in the cleanup of hazardous waste sites and chemical spills—by June 9, 1981 (180 days after Carter signed the bill into law).

As the section of the case study that deals with the president's role makes clear, the NCP is central to the implementation of CERCLA. We note there, too, that Carter assigned a central role to the Council on Environmental Quality in the NCP's revision, whereas President Ronald Reagan rescinded the Carter decision and gave a central role to the Environmental Protection Agency. Actually, as we shall see in the case study at the end of the chapter on bureaucracy, EPA had been very active in the preparation of the NCP from the very beginning. What had really changed with the inauguration of Ronald Reagan was the philosophy of the top management of those federal agencies charged with protecting the environment. Industry was to have a much greater influence over the policies of the Reagan administration than it had exerted during the Carter years.

Through the latter half of 1980 and the first several months of 1981, bureaucrats from EPA worked closely with the other federal agencies that make up the National Response Team (NRT) to draft a revision of the NCP that would be acceptable to the entire federal establishment. This was, however, the period of transition from one administration to another and, therefore, a period of flux in the federal government. Such a large and complex organization as the federal establishment is not "turned around" overnight—it takes months (often years) for an incoming president to shape even the highest echelons of the federal bureaucracy to his liking; indeed, some never succeed. From Reagan's inauguration through May 20, 1981, EPA was without an administrator. So, when Gorsuch took over as agency head, everything that had been accomplished on the NCP (and it was, at that point, virtually completed) was scrapped. The new administration would not have the NCP out in time to meet the congressionally mandated deadline.

Environmental groups, concerned that the lack of an NCP would mean the lack of effective cleanup, began to put pressure on the new administration. Letters requesting information on new deadlines for NCP publication and personal visits to EPA officials followed, but by September 1981 the NCP was still not ready. In fact, Section 105 of CERCLA specifies that the NCP should be revised and republished only "after notice and opportunity for public comments." This terminology means that EPA could not simply "publish" the document in "final form." The agency was required to inform the public, beforehand, of what would be proposed as the final version. Thus, before a document like the NCP could be "binding"—i.e., have the force of law—it first must be printed in the **Federal Register** so that the public would have the opportunity to comment on the proposed provisions. By September 1981, the NCP had not even been proposed in the **Federal Register**—EPA was in violation of Section 105 of CERCLA.

On September 3, 1981, the Environmental Defense Fund (EDF), a Washington, D.C.-based environmental group, brought suit in the District Court for the District of Columbia for "injunctive relief" ordering EPA to revise and republish the NCP by February 1, 1982. The court ordered EPA to respond to the EDF suit within sixty days (by November 3, 1981). This schedule is indicative of the slow pace at which the court system operates. The sixty-day time frame was the period within which EPA was required by the court to **respond** to EDF's complaint. If there was no response, "judgment by default" would be taken against EPA, and the court would mandate the publication of the NCP on February 1, 1982. As usually occurs in court cases, the defendant (EPA) took the full sixty days to respond to the EDF complaint. The agency's response was followed by an "amended complaint" filed by EDF on November 19 and, again, EPA had additional time to respond to the amended complaint. This process of complaint, followed by response, followed by an amended complaint and subsequent response is yet another delaying tactic often used in the court system. So long as the court permits both plaintiffs and defendants to continue the argument, the court is unable to issue an opinion.

Finally, on February 12, 1982, eleven days after the date on which the EDF suit had requested final NCP publication, U.S. District Judge John H. Pratt issued his ruling. Drawing arguments from an earlier case that he used as precedent—**Association of American Railroads** v. **Costle**, 562 F.2d 1310 (D.C. Cir. 1977)—Pratt found for the plaintiffs, **EDF** *et al.* In his opinion, he explained that the statutory timetable noted in CERCLA evidenced congressional concern that the NCP be issued expeditiously and that the "defendants have ignored the intent expressed in the statute." He "brushed aside as diversionary" many of EPA's arguments concerning the court's authority to grant relief to the plaintiffs, and simply noted:

> In view of the Congressional intent clearly manifested in the statute, we think it appropriate that a court-ordered publication schedule (for the NCP) now be established. . . . We conclude that the defendants have unlawfully failed to discharge their statutory and non-discretionary duties to revise and republish the supplemental National Contigency Plan required under (CERCLA).

As a result, the judge ordered EPA to propose the NCP in the **Federal Register** no later than 30 days after the date of his ruling—i.e., by March 12, 1982. He further ordered that the public comment period be limited to thirty additional days and that the final version of the NCP be published within ninety days from the date of his ruling. On Friday, March 12, 1982, EPA Administrator Gorsuch announced the proposed National Contingency Plan. It was published, on that date, as required, in the **Federal Register**. Nine months later than the congressional deadline for finalization, the NCP had at last been proposed for public comment. Yet, even as plans for proposal were underway, EPA was requesting that the Department of Justice file a motion for reconsideration with the district court. The agency would be unable to meet the other two deadlines imposed by the court, but at least the plan was before the public. It would not have come out as quickly as it did were it not for the intervention of the federal courts.

Court cases like preemption or failure to meet a congressionally established deadline are not likely to reach the Supreme Court. There is little in this type of case to warrant the attention of the highest court in the federal system. But the possibility does exist that a CERCLA-based case may yet be heard by the Supreme Court. Such a case, if it comes, is likely to revolve around the question of "strict, joint and several liability." In the end-of-chapter segment of this case study in which we dealt with the actions of Congress, we noted that the provision for joint and several liability had been included in some of the bills that had been considered. The inclusion of such a provision would mean that government could collect all the money it spends in cleaning up a site from a single responsible party, forcing that responsible party to take other responsible parties to court to recover that portion of its damages for which others could be held liable. It would not, therefore, be necessary for the government to determine **how much** of the responsibility for a given release into the environment of a hazardous substance could be attributed to a particular party. If that party contributed to the release, that party could be held accountable for all the damage that was done.

If such a case is brought to the courts, the government will first have to attempt to hold someone liable in this way. If this occurs, the courts will have to decide the case on the basis of CERCLA's "legislative history." The legislative history of an act includes all the comments made by members of Congress during debate on the legislation. It is the legislative history that is used to attempt to determine "legislative intent"—just as Judge Pratt did in the EDF case.

The legislative history on this question is interesting because it supports both sides of the argument. Although the earliest version of S 1480 did not contain a provision for strict, joint and several liability, we noted in the Congress chapter that the administration was able to persuade the Senate committee to add the provision, which was in the House version of the bill. However, in the compromises that preceded passage, the Senate accepted the following definition: " 'Liable' or 'liability' under this title shall be construed to be the standard of liability which obtains under Section 311 of the Federal Water Pollution Control Act" (CERCLA Section 101 (32)).

Thus, the type of liability (whether strict, joint and several or not) is to be determined by the standards applied in the Clean Water Act. Opponents of joint and several liability argued on the floor (and therefore it is a part of the legislative history) that, in the absence of specific language granting joint and several liability, there was none. However, supported by statements from the Department of Justice and the Coast Guard (which administers the Clean Water Act Section 311 fund), proponents of joint and several liability argue that common law and the Clean Water Act provide for this type of liability under certain circumstances. The affidavit of Alan S. Parker, Assistant Attorney General, Office of Legislative Affairs, entered into the **Congressional Record** (and therefore into the legislative history) by Rep. James Florio (D.-N.J.) during floor debate, argues: "It is the Department's view that common law provides for joint and several liability where the act or omission of two or more persons results in an indivisible injury. It is also our view that where the actions of two or more persons, otherwise liable under FWPCA, combine to cause the release of oil or hazardous substance, those persons are jointly and severally liable for clean-up costs under Section 311."

Thus, the legislative history does contain some support for both sides of the argument. It will be up to the courts in future years to determine which side will win. Given the millions of dollars involved in the cleanup of every single hazardous waste site, the stakes are extremely high. When the stakes are this high, the Supreme Court is likely to get the case. But the executive branch will have to bring the case to court. The Court has no power to rule in the absence of a case. If the bureaucracy never attempts to hold a responsible party jointly and severally liable, the standard of liability, by default, will fall short of what **might** be possible.

In the next end-of-chapter segment of the case study, we will look more closely at the bureaucracy and at the pressures brought to bear on it.

Chapter 4

The Federal Bureaucracy

No treatment of the operations and functions of the federal government's established institutions would be complete without devoting considerable attention to the "fourth branch." Although it was not specifically established by the Constitution, the Founders assumed that some type of administrative structure would evolve and that it would be officially under the control of the president. We have already noted that such control is necessarily incomplete, that the president must persuade bureaucrats to do what he wants just as he tries to persuade members of Congress. The bureaucracy is very much an important political force independent of the president.

The bureaucracy is the one political structure that exercises the most direct and pervasive influence over the life of the average American citizen. Yet it remains the least understood and most maligned arm of the national government. Its development and proliferation not only exemplify the interrelated nature of governmental institutions but also account for the continued interdependence among the three constitutionally established branches of government. To speak of the impact of the president, Congress, or the courts without reference to the bureaucracy is an exercise in futility.

Characteristics of Bureaucratization

Organizations are bureaucracies to the extent that they have a division of labor, hierarchical structure, and fixed framework of rules.

In the late nineteenth century, the German sociologist Max Weber analyzed the elements by which bureaucracies have come to be identified. According to the Weberian model, organizations are to be judged "bureaucratic" to the degree that they exhibit the fundamental characteristics of (1) a division of labor, (2) a hierarchical structure, and (3) a fixed framework of rules. A division of labor means that the bureaucracy is organized so that different employees have different functions to perform according to areas of specialization. In the State Department, for example, some employees work at the East Asian desk while others work at the Latin American desk; the employees are specialists, not generalists.

A hierarchical structure means that authority flows from the top down, with inferiors reporting to and receiving instructions from superiors. A bureaucracy has clearly defined levels with employees at lower levels responsible to employees at higher levels. Because there are almost invariably more employees at lower levels, the organization chart of a bureaucracy resembles the familiar pyramid. On top is one individual, the secretary of state in the case of the State Department.

A fixed framework of rules means that the activities of employees are governed by preestablished formal rules and regulations. Decisions in a Weberian bureaucracy are made by applying the appropriate rule to any given situation. Every employee must apply the same rule in the same way to every situation in which the rule is deemed applicable. Discretion in rule application must, therefore, be studiously avoided. Advancement or promotion in such hierarchical structures is determined by the employee's competence in memorizing and applying the formal rules.

Most large U.S. organizations attempt to realize the Weberian bureaucratic ideal.

Of course, no organization realizes these three characteristics (division of labor, hierarchy, and fixed rules) in their entirety, but few organizations fail to display at least a modicum of bureaucratization. Theoretically the end result of this combination of specialization, hierarchy, and formal rules and regulations is the efficient implementation of government policies. At times this happens. At other times one encounters delay, confusion, waste, and rigidity.

The Organization of the Federal Bureaucracy

The federal bureaucracy has a variety of types of organizations.

The federal bureaucracy comprises almost three million civilian employees who work for hundreds of departments, agencies, bureaus, commissions, interagency committees, citizen advisory groups, and presidential committees, commissions, and task forces. Our aim in this chapter is not to provide an encyclopedic listing of federal agencies; the *United States Government Manual* does that in more than 900 pages. Instead, we will describe the four main elements of the bureaucracy (cabinet departments, independent regulatory commissions, independent executive agencies, and government corporations), explain their similarities and their differences, and show how these elements of the bureaucracy interact with and are affected by the other three branches with which we have dealt.

The Cabinet Departments

Heads of departments form the president's cabinet.

The thirteen cabinet-level departments are the largest bureaucratic structures within the federal government. Each department is headed by a secretary (the attorney general in the case of the Justice Department) who holds cabinet rank and presidential appointment with senatorial consent. Immediately below the secretary each department begins its own unique proliferation of under secretaries, deputy under secretaries, assistant secretaries, executive secretaries, and bureau chiefs, ad infinitum. Figure 4-1 shows the organization of the Department of the Treasury, which, although it is unique (in that no other department is organized in exactly the same way), is representative of the type of organizational structure in all the departments.

Cabinet development. Cabinet-level, or executive, departments date from 1789, when George Washington appointed secretaries of war, state, and treasury. An attorney general also has held cabinet rank from that time, but he did not receive a department until 1870. The Department of the Navy was added in 1798, which precipitated a series of conflicts with the War Department that continued until the two were merged (together with the Air Force) in 1949. Subsequent conflicts between the services have been viewed as "intradepartmental" and are therefore, theoretically, more easily resolved.

The early departments dealt mostly with foreign affairs.

The postmaster general was admitted to the cabinet in 1829, although his department (established as an independent agency of the national government in 1792) did not receive cabinet-level recognition until 1872—a status that they both lost in 1971 when the post office was reorganized as a governmental corporation. By the middle of the nineteenth century one other department (Interior) had been added, which yielded a cabinet of five departments (War, State, Treasury, Navy, and Interior) and seven officers (secretaries of each department plus the attorney general and postmaster general).

By World War I departments responsive to farm, business, and labor interests had been added to the cabinet.

Drastic alterations in the American economy toward the end of the nineteenth century prompted congressional response in the form of new cabinet posts. Thus, in 1889 the Department of Agriculture (under a commissioner since 1862) was elevated to cabinet rank as Congress responded to the demands of the nation's farmers. Pressures emanating from business and industry prompted the inclusion of a Department of Commerce and Labor in 1903, which was quickly split into two departments ten years later in recognition of the different needs being served. President Lyndon Johnson proposed that, for the sake of efficiency, the Departments of Labor and Commerce be recombined into one department, as they had been during Theodore Roosevelt's presidency. This proposal quickly died in Congress because business interests feared that the combined department would be controlled by labor, and labor interests feared that the new department would be controlled by business.

In the post-World War II era, agencies have been elevated to department status to demonstrate the nation's commitment to health, education, energy, transportation, housing, and urban needs.

As governmental concerns and involvements have broadened since World War II, Congress has responded by creating new cabinet positions. The Department of Health, Education and Welfare (established in 1953) combined a number of formerly independent agencies in order to better coordinate their operations and to indicate a national commitment to help provide all Americans with adequate human services. In 1979 this department was split into two departments: Health and Human Services, and Education. Interests favoring increased federal support for education were successful in their push for the creation of a new department focused solely on education.

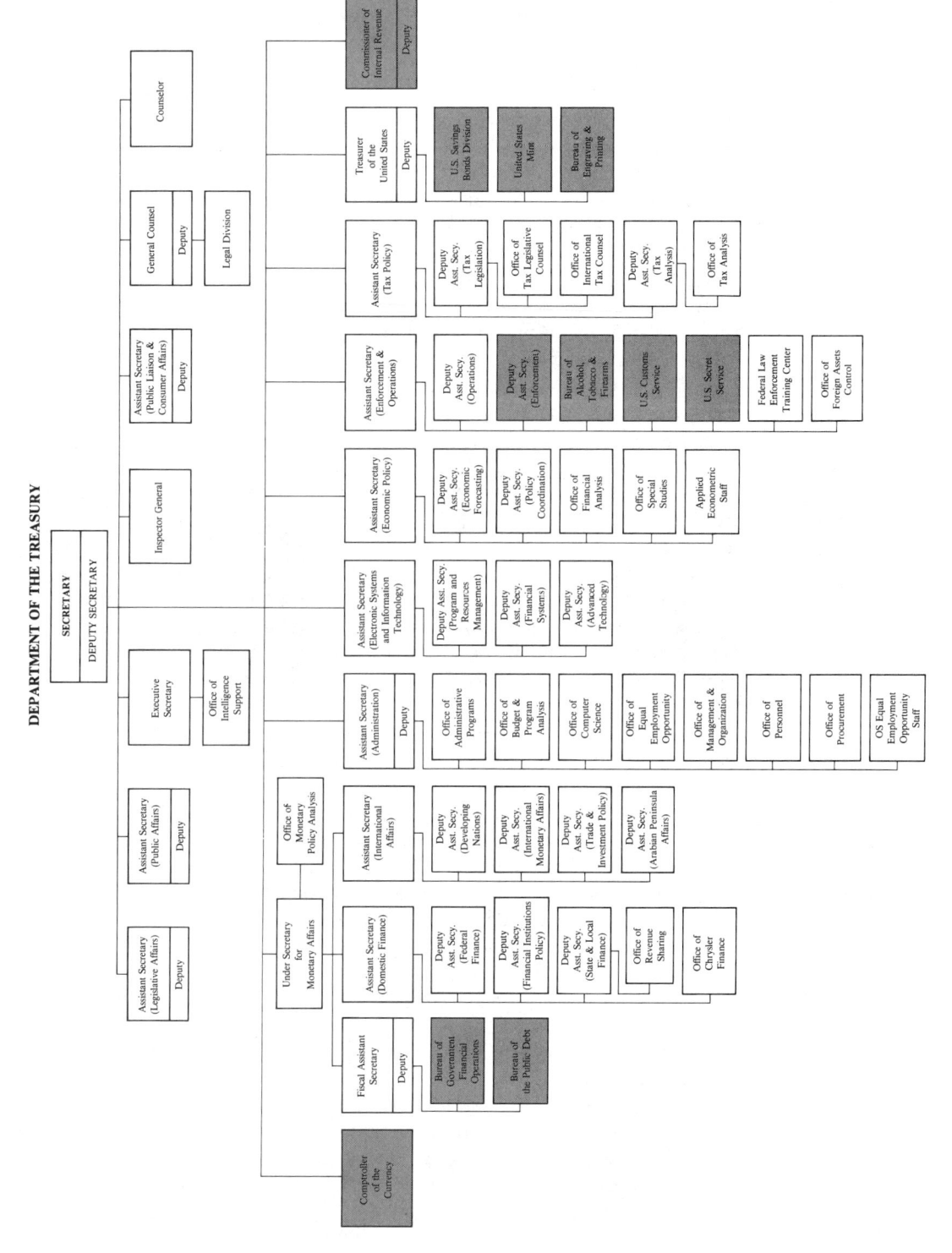

DEPARTMENT OF THE TREASURY

Figure 4-1.

Proponents of federal aid to education felt that having "their own department" would aid their efforts. In contrast, President Ronald Reagan campaigned to abolish the new Department of Education as part of his efforts to reduce federal involvement in education. Supporters of the department, however, were able to thwart Reagan's efforts.

In the 1960s urban problems came to the forefront, which resulted in the creation of a Department of Housing and Urban Development (1965) and a Department of Transportation (1966). By the mid-1970s Americans were concerned, justifiably, with problems of energy and the allocation of increasingly scarce natural resources. Congress again responded to both public and presidential pressure and created the Department of Energy in 1977. The creation of this department is an excellent illustration of a congressional response to extracongressional pressures. It also demonstrates how previously existing federal agencies can become established as cabinet-level departments.

After President Jimmy Carter had proposed to Congress on March 1, 1977, the creation of a new cabinet department to deal with energy concerns, Congress for three months held hearings on and debated the wisdom of such a department. In the end the president received the authorization to proceed, but with some modification of his original proposal. The newly created Department of Energy consolidated all powers previously wielded by the Federal Power Commission (FPC), the Federal Energy Administration (FEA), and the Energy Research and Development Administration (ERDA), as well as the powers of various energy programs scattered throughout the bureaucracy. The most important alteration from the original proposal was the refusal of Congress to accede to the president's wish that the secretary of the new department be granted the power, previously held by the FPC, to set the price of natural gas. Congress, responding to lobbying pressures from American companies, vested that and similar economic powers not in the new secretary but in an independent regulatory commission within the new department. This important alteration of the president's proposal demonstrated that the process by which departments are created, merged, split, and disbanded results from congressional response to pressures. Congress has the final word on the establishment of cabinet-level departments.

Characteristics of cabinet members. In selecting cabinet members, presidents generally proceed quite cautiously, for they realize that cabinet members are key actors in implementing the administration's policies. Cabinet members differ from the leaders of Congress in both age and background. While the seniority system ensures that many leaders of Congress will be well beyond the standard retirement age of sixty-five, the cabinet member over sixty-five is a rarity. Although the members of the Reagan cabinet were somewhat older than recent cabinet members at the time of their appointments to office, they are still younger as a group than the leaders of Congress.

Cabinet members resemble corporate executives more than do congressional leaders.

The Federal Bureaucracy   **147**

In background, cabinet members tend to be of urban origin, with careers in business or law, a combination that often ensures their residence in large metropolises. One often finds, too, that several members of the same cabinet have headed large, prestigious law firms or corporations. (In the Reagan administration, for example, Secretary Samuel R. Pierce, Jr., left a prosperous position in a prestigious law firm to enter government service, and Secretaries George Schultz and Caspar Weinberger resigned leadership positions in one of the nation's largest corporations). The background in corporate law, big business, and metropolitan residence distinguishes the cabinet from the leadership of Congress.

What cabinet members do have in common with congressional leaders is that both are almost certain to be white males. The first successful attempt to open the cabinet to blacks and women was that of the Carter administration, which included a black secretary of housing and urban development (HUD), Patricia Harris, and the first female secretary of commerce, Juanita Kreps. In the second Reagan administration, two women were appointed to head cabinet departments—Margaret Heckler at Health and Human Services, and Elizabeth Dole at Transportation—while Samuel Pierce at Housing and Urban Development is the sole black cabinet officer.

Most cabinet members stay in office for the full four-year presidential term.

A total turnover among cabinet members usually occurs at the election of a new president, for he customarily replaces all his predecessor's appointees. Most presidents then retain their appointees for the full presidential term, with a minimal number of resignations and new appointments. The major exception was Richard Nixon, who, during his five and a half years in office, had thirty-one cabinet appointees. Ulysses S. Grant, whose administration was also scandal-ridden, ran a close second to Nixon, with twenty-six appointees in eight years. Franklin Roosevelt, in contrast, named only twenty-five cabinet members during his thirteen-year tenure in office. The president with the fewest cabinet appointees is John Adams, who had six appointees covering the five cabinet positions during his one term in office.

Cabinet members often have extensive previous government experience.

The sheer number of cabinet appointments by any president should not necessarily be construed to mean that different individuals are constantly being brought into the upper echelons of the bureaucracy. Often the same individuals will have served in previous administrations in varying capacities. In the Reagan cabinet, Secretaries Pierce, Shultz, and Weinberger all served under previous presidents, although Pierce had not formerly been a department secretary. Cabinet members sometimes even move from position to position under the same president. At the beginning of his second administration, Reagan moved Edwin Meese, John Herrington, and James Baker out of the White House into cabinet posts: Meese as attorney general, Herrington as secretary of the Department of Energy (replacing Donald Hodel, who became secretary of the Department of the Interior), and Baker as secretary of the treasury (replacing Donald Regan who moved into the White House as chief of staff).

Autonomy of units within departments. The organization of each cabinet department reflects its particular historical development in response to governmental and nongovernmental pressures. Thus, the Federal Bureau of Investigation, while a Justice Department agency under the titular authority of the attorney general, is actually controlled by the director of the FBI and operates with a degree of autonomy that certainly violates the Weberian characteristics of bureaucratic organization.

Under its founder and first director, J. Edgar Hoover, the FBI developed such a positive image among most Americans that Hoover was able to operate independently of the wishes of the attorney general (Hoover's superior in the Justice Department). Although the attorney general has always possessed the formal authority to fire the director of the FBI, Hoover's popularity made such a firing politically impractical. Presidents John Kennedy and Lyndon Johnson clearly would have preferred a director of the FBI who would have more vigorously enforced civil rights laws than did Hoover, but they both believed that the political costs of removing Hoover were too great.

Several factors combined to reduce the power of the FBI director after Hoover's death in 1972. His successors have lacked the personal prestige and national image that Hoover enjoyed, and the bureau was tainted by improprieties connected both with Hoover's autocratic rule and with the Watergate affair. As a result, Congress moved to insulate the director from political pressures that might emanate from the White House, while simultaneously minimizing the possibility that the director would wield concentrated, autocratic control within the bureau. By the Crime Control Act of 1976, Congress prescribed a single, ten-year term of office for the director. William Webster, appointed by Carter and confirmed by the Senate in 1978, will serve as FBI director through 1987. So, although Webster is formally under the attorney general, the FBI director cannot be replaced except "for cause." Because what constitutes adequate "cause" for removing the FBI director is unclear, Webster has great autonomy to run his bureau as he sees fit. Such a situation is at variance with the standards of a true Weberian bureaucracy.

Another agency within a cabinet-level department with a great deal of independence from the secretary of the department is the Secret Service (figure 4-1). Established in 1865 to combat the counterfeiting of U.S. currency, the Secret Service was given the added responsibility of protecting the president's life after the assassination of William McKinley in 1901. From that time on, the relationship between the Secret Service and the hierarchical organization of the Treasury Department gradually changed. Because of their close association with the White House staff, Secret Service agents have engaged in matters of little or no concern to the Treasury, without the knowledge of the assistant secretary to whom they are supposedly responsible. Thus, during the Nixon presidency, agents of the Secret Service tapped the phones of the president's brother, operated an elaborate secret taping system in the White House, and opened the White House safe of E. Howard Hunt

---

Although the FBI is formally under the attorney general, the agency has used its sensitive function to gain much independence within the Department of Justice.

The proximity of the Secret Service to the president has promoted its independence within the Treasury Department.

after the Watergate burglary. These acts were committed without the knowledge or approval of the secretary of the treasury.

Independent Regulatory Commissions

Independent regulatory commissions set rules in areas of business and commerce.

The president appoints commission members with the approval of the Senate, but, once they are appointed, cannot remove them.

Organization of regulatory commissions. Independent regulatory commissions differ from cabinet departments in very fundamental aspects of operation and function (table 4-1). The commissions are headed by five or seven members (with the exception of the Interstate Commerce Commission, which has eleven) appointed on a bipartisan basis by the president, with the approval of the Senate, for a specified number of years. Appointments are staggered to reduce the possibility of any president's attempting to "stack" commissions. Each commission has been created by act of Congress for the express purpose of regulating a specific economic interest.

Development of the ICC: the regulatory commission prototype. The Interstate Commerce Commission (ICC) was the first attempt of Congress to establish a regulatory commission (figure 4-2). Such a commission would

Table 4-1
Comparative Characteristics of the Federal Bureaucracy

	Cabinet Departments	Independent Executive Agencies	Independent Regulatory Commissions	Government Corporations
Head:	Cabinet secretary	Administrator or commission	Multimember board or commission	Boards or commissions
Appointment:	Presidential, with Senate Approval	Presidential (some with Senate approval)	Presidential, bipartisan with Senate approval	Presidential (some with Senate approval)
Term of Office:	President's discretion	Presidential discretion (or specified[a])	Specific, staggered	President's discretion
Removal:	President	President (or for cause only[a])	For cause only	President[b]
Role:	General administration	Specialized programs	Economic regulation	Business enterprises
Functions:	Administrative Quasi-judicial Quasi-legislative	Administrative—all Quasi-judicial—some Quasi-legislative—some	Administrative Quasi-judicial Quasi-legislative	Administrative

[a]Only those independent executive agencies to which quasi-judicial and/or quasi-legislative authority has been specifically granted by Congress have members who can be removed only for cause and who have specified terms of office.
[b]Some corporations have boards whose members serve a fixed term. They can be removed only for cause.

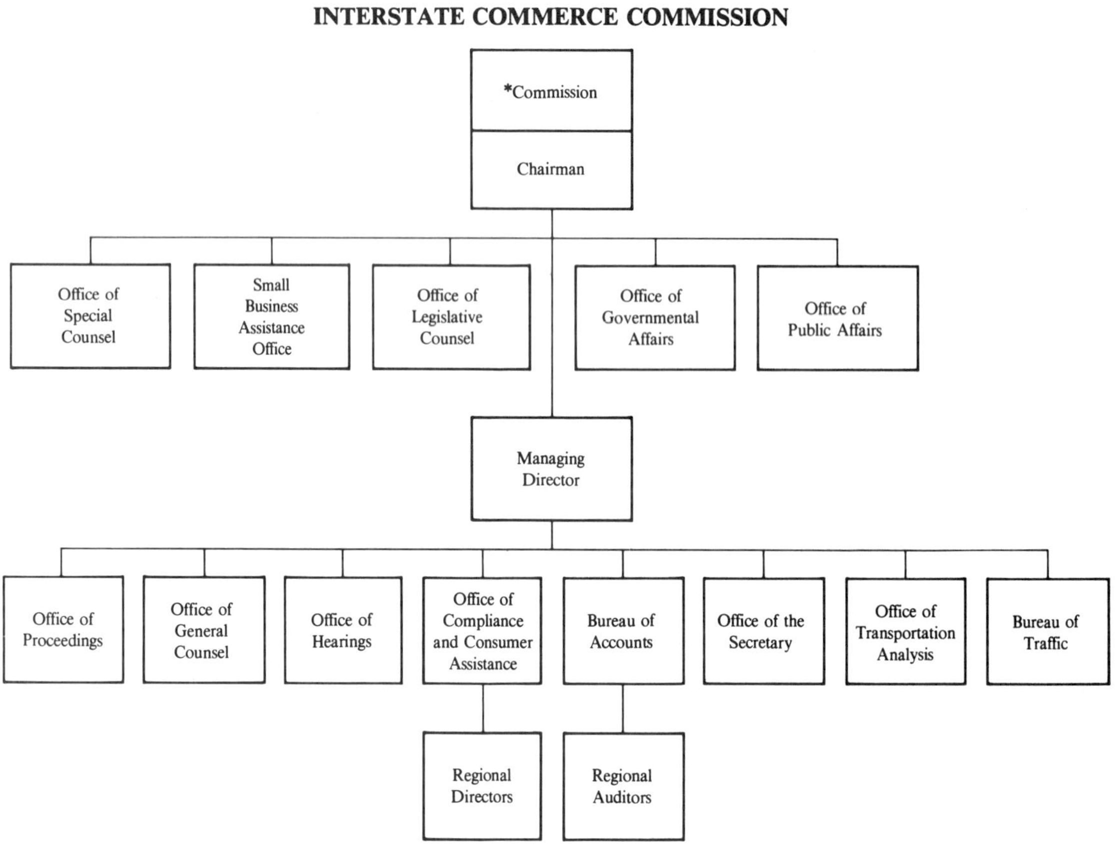

INTERSTATE COMMERCE COMMISSION

*In deciding most proceedings, the Commission is divided into two divisions of general jurisdiction, each comprised of three Commissioners. Rulemakings and significant adjudications are decided by the entire Commission.

Figure 4-2. Sample independent regulatory commission: Interstate Commerce Commission.

> *Independent regulatory commissions both set rules and adjudicate disputes arising from those rules.*

have to combine the necessary degree of expertise, continuity, quasi-legislative and quasi-judicial powers, and immunity from governmental and nongovernmental interests in order to function effectively in the economic sphere. Quasi-legislative and quasi-judicial authority can be best understood as authority granted by Congress to an agency to advance specific regulations under the terms of the broad powers conferred on the agency and to adjudicate disputes arising out of the enforcement of those regulations. The "broad power" to be conferred on the ICC was the authority to regulate all interstate surface transportation and would eventually be expanded to include trains, buses, interstate waterway and coastal shipping, freight forwarders, oil pipelines, and express companies. The ICC's quasi-legislative authority permits it to design regulations for these industries that will have the effect of law, while its quasi-judicial authority permits it to adjudicate disputes arising from its own regulations.

Created by the 1887 Act to Regulate Commerce, the ICC was the response of Congress to a Supreme Court ruling the previous year (*Wabash, St. Louis, and Pacific Railroad* v. *Illinois,* U.S. 557 [1886]) that had prohibited state regulation of interstate commerce. Agrarian interests, especially in the Midwest, were being openly exploited by railroad magnates who charged exorbitant and discriminatory rates for the shipment of farm products.

Originally under the jurisdiction of the secretary of the interior, the ICC gained administrative independence within two years of its creation—a process that has been mirrored in the development of subsequent commissions. It was not until 1920 that the ICC realized the fullness of its regulatory powers. Several acts of Congress (most notably the Hepburn Act of 1906) removed judicial interference as an effective tool of the railroads in blocking ICC regulatory decisions. The railroads were finally, so it seemed, to be subject to government regulation. But the meaning of *regulation* was about to undergo significant changes—changes predicted in 1892 by Attorney General Richard S. Olney:

> The [ICC] as its functions have now been limited by the Courts, is, or can be made of great use to the railroads. It satisfies the popular clamor for a government supervision of railroads, at the same time that the supervision is almost entirely nominal. Further, the older such a Commission gets to be, the more inclined it will be found to be to take the business and railroad view of things. It thus becomes a sort of barrier between the railroad corporations and the people and a sort of protection against hasty and crude legislation hostile to railroad interests.[1]

Independent regulatory commissions sometimes have been "captured" by the industries they are supposed to be regulating; when this happens, regulations are used to stifle competition, rather than to promote fair competition and consumer interests.

Regulation as protection from competition. Most regulatory commissions have followed this same pattern, each eventually coming under the control of the very interests it had been designed to regulate. Commission members are often drawn from the regulated interests, under the justification of expertise; and the commission subsequently takes the regulated interests under its wing to "protect" them from the development of strong economic environments hostile to their profits. *Regulation* has thus become *protection.*

This tendency was evident in the battle between the Ford administration and the trucking industry. In announcing his proposed deregulation legislation, Gerald Ford said, "It is now clear that this patchwork regulatory structure has not kept pace with changes in the industry and the economy. We have permitted regulation designed in theory to protect the public interest to become in practice the protection of special industry interests." At issue was whether the ICC should continue to issue "certificates of convenience and necessity" by which individual carriers are granted exclusive operating rights for specified interstate trucking routes. These certificates, issued by the ICC at no cost to the truckers, have become so valuable that one bankrupt New York City trucking firm netted almost $21 million in July 1976 by selling its

---

[1]James M. Smith and Paul L. Murphy, eds. *Liberty and Justice* (New York: Knopf, 1958), pp. 292-293.

Industries that have control over an independent regulatory commission oppose deregulation because such industries would then have to compete with new businesses and with one another.

certificates to other companies at public auction. The trucking industry lobbied so heavily against the proposed deregulation that the legislation remained bottled up in congressional committees until Ford was out of office. Carter, who had campaigned with promises to eliminate regulations that restricted competition to public detriment, proposed legislation similar to Ford's to deregulate the trucking industry. Congress did pass the Motor Carrier Act of 1980, which facilitated the entrance of new companies into the industry, promoted competition, and reduced the power of the ICC in the trucking area. Critics charged, however, that industry lobbyists had been successful in watering down the bill so that many regulations inimical to the public interest remain. Reagan, who campaigned in 1980 against government regulations in general, proclaimed during his campaign that he would not support any further deregulation of the trucking industry. Pleased with his position, the Teamsters Union was one of only two national unions to endorse Reagan for the presidency.[2]

Throughout all the controversy over efforts to deregulate the trucking industry, one constant element has been the preference of the large trucking firms and their union for the ICC regulations. What this means is that even though a president might wish to deregulate a particular industry, such action may be extremely difficult because, among other reasons, the "regulated" interests enjoy their "regulations."

Regulatory commissions as decision makers. Encouraged by its early experience with the ICC, Congress responded to subsequent political pressures from various segments of the economy by establishing additional independent commissions (table 4-2). These commissions exert tremendous power over the operation of the U.S. economy, most notably in their ability not only to administer but to legislate and adjudicate as well. The courts are constitutionally limited (Article III) from initiating actions against the bureaucracy, including the regulatory commissions, and can intervene only after suit has been filed by a third party. Thus, the regulatory commissions administer broad congressional legislation in specific areas (thereby, themselves, making policy) and subsequently adjudicate disputes arising from their own decisions.

Decisions made by independent regulatory commissions can rarely be challenged in the courts.

One example of the breadth of power exerted by the regulatory commissions is the Federal Communications Commission. The FCC determines what proportion of "prime-time" television must be of local origin as opposed to network programs, what proportion of air time must be "public-interest" broadcasting, and even how strong a station's transmitter is permitted to be. A station that is out of favor with the FCC may find its request for license renewal rejected by the FCC. Thus, it is not surprising that in 1973, after FCC Chairperson Dean Burch, responding to White House pressures, spoke out against radio talk shows with sexual topics, several of these shows shifted

[2]The other union to endorse Reagan was the Professional Air Traffic Controllers Organization. This union died after Reagan fired all of its members who engaged in an illegal strike.

Table 4-2
Principal Independent Regulatory Commissions

Commission	Date of Creation	Number of Members	Term (in Years)	Principal Tasks
Interstate Commerce Commission (ICC)	1887	11	7	To regulate railroads and carriers
Federal Reserve Board	1913	7	14	To regulate banking practices
Federal Trade Commission (FTC)	1914	5	7	To regulate industry by protecting consumers from unfair business practices
Federal Communications Commission (FCC)	1934	7	7	To license and regulate all radio and TV frequencies and establish telephone and telegraph rates
Securities and Exchange Commission (SEC)	1934	5	5	To supervise all security and financial markets, including brokerages and stock market
National Labor Relations Board (NLRB)	1935	5	5	To rectify unfair labor practices annd designate appropriate bargaining units
Nuclear Regulatory Commission (NRC)	1974	5	5	To license and regulate the uses of nuclear energy, protecting the public health and safety and the environment

overnight from discussing sex to debating football. These stations became "wholesome" in fear that the FCC would otherwise find a reason to reject their request for license renewal.

Regulations sometimes have been used to harass businesses well beyond the intentions of a commission's enabling legislation.

Regulation as harassment. Thus, *regulation* can come to mean political harassment rather than protection. In this case, the regulatory commission, in effect, lost some of its independence to the White House, thereby opening up the possibility of harassment of regulated interests. As Clay Whitehead, head of the Nixon White House Office of Telecommunications Policy, proclaimed: "Station managers and network officials who fail to correct imbalance or consistent bias from the networks—or who acquiesce by silence—can only be considered willing participants, to be held fully accountable . . . at license-renewal time."[3] Because the FCC, not the White House Office of Telecommunications Policy, rules on license renewals, Whitehead could not have made this statement if the FCC were truly independent.

[3] *New York Times,* December 19, 1972, p. 1. © 1972 by The New York Times Company. Reprinted by permission.

Regulation as consumer protection. Thus far in this chapter we have considered regulations as industry efforts to control competition or as harassment by ideologically motivated bureaucrats. This is an incomplete characterization of what the independent regulatory commissions do. Although critics have complained that the Nuclear Regulatory Commission (NRC) is too dependent on nuclear industry sources for its information, on more than a few occasions the NRC has refused to grant licenses to nuclear power-generating plants because NRC inspectors found evidence that safety precautions at these plants were insufficient. What plant owners then called "harassment" and "overregulation," environmental groups called "good decisions in the public interest." One can cite similar examples for each of the independent regulatory commissions, from citizens saved from stock swindlers by the Securities and Exchange Commission to consumers protected from unscrupulous sales techniques by the Federal Trade Commission. It is all too easy to dwell on the mistakes and problems of these commissions and other bureaucracies while neglecting their contributions to our quality of life.

> *When independent regulatory commissions are active in protecting consumer interests, the commissions may come under harsh attack by industries accustomed to regulations as protection from competition.*

On January 1, 1985, the only independent regulatory commission ever to "go out of business," the Civil Aeronautics Board (CAB), ceased to exist. The CAB had been established in 1938 to supervise and license all airline routes and rates. In 1978, responding to air-carrier pressures for deregulation, Congress passed a law setting the schedule for eventual deregulation. The act contained the provision by which the CAB would cease to exist in 1985. It is significant, however, that Congress chose to deal with the question again, in 1984—not in terms of deregulation or for the purpose of retaining the CAB but because Congress had failed to provide in 1979 for the preservation of the consumer-protection function of the board. As a result, on September 20, 1984, Congress transferred the CAB's consumer-protection function to the Department of Transportation, thereby preserving that function while still disbanding the board.

The Federal Reserve Board. One independent regulatory commission that has been the target of much congressional criticism is the Federal Reserve Board. When Congress set up "the Fed" in 1913, the legislative intent was to provide a body with sufficient independence so that it could pursue its functions free of short-range political pressures. The seven members of the Board of Governors are appointed by the president with Senate confirmation for fourteen-year terms, staggered so that a term expires every two years. The chair is appointed from among the seven governors for a four-year term.

> *The Board of Governors of the Federal Reserve System sets monetary policy; members are appointed by the president with Senate confirmation but cannot be removed during their 14-year terms.*

The Federal Reserve Board sets policy for the twelve regional federal reserve banks and the 6,000 member banks of the Federal Reserve System. The board determines the buying and selling of government securities, the amount of money each member bank must keep on hand as reserves, and the interest charged to banks that borrow from the Federal Reserve System to cover short-term needs. These policies have a great impact on the supply of money in the economy. An increased money supply lowers interest rates, makes borrowing easier, and spurs the economy, but may have inflationary consequences. A decreased money supply has the opposite effects: tougher borrowing, higher interest rates, economic slowdowns, but reduced inflation. By functioning as a national bank, the Federal Reserve System controls monetary policy. Every president tries to promote healthy economic needs. The independence of "the Fed" limits the president to attempts at persuasion; he cannot order the board to do anything, nor can he fire recalcitrant members. The power to set economic policy is dispersed in our national government and requires cooperation for coherence to emerge.

Independent Executive Agencies

Organization of independent executive agencies.

Independent executive agencies form a third and no less important element of the federal bureaucracy. Table 4-3 illustrates the size and diversity of some of the major independent executive agencies. The heads of these agencies (some of which are directed by multimember boards) are presidential appointees whose appointments may require Senate approval. Each independent executive agency is responsible for a specialized area of jurisdiction, and within that area it may exercise quasi-legislative and/or quasi-judicial functions. The agencies are independent of cabinet departments and report directly to the president. They were set up outside the departments, either because their subject matter did not fit well within any of the departments (for example, the case of the National Aeronautics and Space Administration), or because Congress and the president thought that independence from established departments would engender fresh approaches to policy problems. Independent agencies are not necessarily smaller than cabinet departments: only the Department of Defense and the United States Postal Service (reorganized as a government corporation in 1971) have more employees than the Veterans Administration.

Independent executive agencies perform services for specific groups, such as veterans (by the Veterans Administration), or have special areas of responsibility (such as the Environmental Protection Agency).

Diversified functions of independent executive agencies.

Unlike regulatory commissions, independent executive agencies are not designed to deal primarily with economic regulations but rather to perform some specific service or administrative function. These functions are diverse in purpose and range from assisting small groups (as does the Farm Credit Administration) to performing special functions for large government departments (as does the General Services Administration). To fulfill these functions, it is often necessary for the agencies to have regional offices scattered throughout the country (figure 4-3). For administrative purposes, the United States has been divided into ten regions, with the principal city in each region serving as the headquarters for the entire area. Most government bureaucracies whose duties include a wide range of services to be dispensed outside Washington, D.C., operate on the same ten-region plan. Thus, the organization charts of both the Environ-

The larger independent executive agencies have regional offices similar to those of departments.

Table 4-3
Selected Major Independent Executive Agencies

Agency	Employees (in 1982)	Principal Tasks
ACTION	583	To mobilize volunteers for service in VISTA (in the U.S.) and in the Peace Corps (in developing countries)
Environmental Protection Agency	12,273	To protect and enhance the environment
General Services Administration	30,397	To manage government property and records
National Aeronautics and Space Administration	22,563	To conduct research on flight within and outside the earth's atmosphere
National Foundation on the Arts and Humanities	267	To support progress in the arts and humanities
National Science Foundation	1,344	To support scientific research, including social science efforts, that can lead to improvements in the quality of life
Panama Canal Commission	8,329	To coordinate operation of the Panama Canal with the Republic of Panama
Small Business Administration	4,975	To aid the interests of small business
Smithsonian Institution	4,317	To preserve for study and reference items of scientific, cultural, or historical interest
Veterans Administration	235,982	To provide social services to veterans and their dependents

mental Protection Agency and a cabinet department such as the Department of Health and Human Services indicate regional offices in the same ten cities.

As with regulatory commissions, the actual degree of agency independence is a result of historical development, as well as the conditions under which Congress established the agency. All independent agencies develop a degree of independence from congressional and presidential control that is consistent with the influence of the organizations they serve. The Veterans Administration, for example, often works with the American Legion and the Veterans of Foreign Wars in publicizing the programs and services that the VA offers to veterans. Any efforts by the president or Congress to curtail the services of the VA would incite the veterans' interest groups to furious lobbying efforts. Indeed, the president and Congress both know they must tread lightly when dealing with budgetary allocations for the VA. Thus, this particular executive agency has attained a significant degree of independence from congressional and presidential control.

Of course, the independence of these agencies does not negate the oversight function of Congress. During the first Reagan Administration, congressional investigators became convinced that the Administrator of the

The Federal Bureaucracy

U.S. ENVIRONMENTAL PROTECTION AGENCY

ADMINISTRATOR / **DEPUTY ADMINISTRATOR**

STAFF OFFICES
- Administrative Law Judges
- Civil Rights
- Small & Disadvantaged Business Utilization
- Science Advisory Board

- Associate Administrator for International Activities
- Associate Administrator for Regional Operations

Assistant Administrator for Administration & Resources Mgmt.
- Office of Administration
- Office of Administration RTP, NC
- Office of Administration Cincinnati, OH
- Office of the Comptroller
- Office of Human Resources Management
- Office of Information Resources Management

Assistant Administrator for Enforcement & Compliance Monitoring

General Counsel

Assistant Administrator for Policy, Planning & Evaluation
- Office of Policy Analysis
- Office of Standards & Regulations
- Office of Management Systems & Evaluation

Assistant Administrator for External Affairs
- Office of Intergovernmental Liaison
- Office of Congressional Liaison
- Office of Public Affairs
- Office of Federal Activities

Inspector General
- Office of Audit
- Office of Investigations
- Office of Mgmt. & Technical Assessment

Assistant Administrator for Water
- Office of Water Enforcement and Permits
- Office of Water Regulations and Standards
- Office of Water Program Operations
- Office of Drinking Water
- Office of Ground Water Protection

Assistant Administrator for Solid Waste & Emergency Response
- Office of Solid Waste
- Office of Emergency & Remed. Response
- Office of Waste Programs Enforcement

Assistant Administrator for Air & Radiation
- Office of Air Quality Planning & Standards
- Office of Mobile Sources
- Office of Radiation Programs

Assistant Administrator for Pesticides & Toxic Substances
- Office of Pesticide Programs
- Office of Toxic Substances

Assistant Administrator for Research & Development
- Office of Monitoring Systems & Qual. Assur.
- Office of Env. Engineering & Technology
- Office of Env. Processes & Effects Research
- Office of Health Research
- Office of Research Program Mgmt.
- Office of Exploratory Research
- Office of Health & Environmental Research

| Region 1 Boston | Region 2 New York | Region 3 Philadelphia | Region 4 Atlanta | Region 5 Chicago | Region 6 Dallas | Region 7 Kansas City | Region 8 Denver | Region 9 San Francisco | Region 10 Seattle |

Figure 4-3.

Environmental Protection Agency, Anne M. Gorsuch, was failing to perform her mandated functions of enforcing the nation's environmental laws. In fact, one of her Assistant Administrators, Rita Lavelle, ultimately served time in prison for perjury connected with the case. By the time it was over, after almost two years of often acrimonious struggle between Congress and the executive, at least twenty-five high-level Reagan appointees had resigned or been dismissed from the EPA and William Ruckelshaus, the agency's first administrator under Nixon in 1970, returned to Washington to accept Gorsuch's post.

Government Corporations

Government corporations are the newest addition to the bureaucratic maze, dating from the early 1930s. These corporations are actually quasi-business enterprises established by act of Congress to accomplish specific, primarily economic tasks either in specified localities or across the nation. The Federal Deposit Insurance Corporation, for example, monitors funds and protects deposits in banks across the country, while the Tennessee Valley Authority operates in only a specified area, the massive Tennessee Valley, to provide electrical power and other services for economic development and recreation. Another government corporation with responsibilities for economic development in a specified area is the Saint Lawrence Seaway Development Corporation. Such corporations were originally semiautonomous, but the Government Corporation Control Act of 1945 placed them more directly under the control of Congress and the president.

Government corporations generally are headed by boards or commissions appointed by the president. In some instances, in an effort to isolate the boards of government corporations from political pressure, Congress has mandated bipartisan membership, removal by the president only for cause, and long terms of service. Similar to private businesses, government corporations can borrow money and undertake specific projects without congressional approval.

One of the newest government corporations is the United States Postal Service, which was a cabinet department until 1971. The Postal Service employs more than 650,000 people to perform a communication function absolutely vital to the nation's economy. The controversy that has engulfed the Postal Service in recent years is at least partly a result of its status as a government corporation. On the one hand, private business has actually entered into competition with the Postal Service and has taken over many of its money-making operations. (United Parcel Service, for example, has taken over much of the Postal Service's package-delivery business. Yet, while private enterprise would be more than happy to assume the lucrative New York-Chicago-Los Angeles type of mail run, no private business has offered to deliver mail to rural Alaska at any price; this remains the responsibility of

Government corporations are nonprofit entities that perform infrastructural tasks such as postal services.

the Postal Service.) On the other hand, Congress continues to keep a wary eye on this government corporation because many rural congressional constituencies feel threatened by the Postal Service's moves to decrease the number of rural post offices, employees, and delivery days in order to increase cost effectiveness. As a quasi-business enterprise, then, the Postal Service can neither compete effectively with private enterprise nor depend entirely on government subsidy.

The Bureaucrats
Developing a Civil Service

The spoils system. In response to an ambassadorial appointment by President Andrew Jackson in 1832, Senator William Learned Marcy of New York admitted: "To the victor belong the spoils." Such was, indeed, the tendency in the federal government from its inception. Washington was convinced that the best and most influential men in the colonies should and would be drafted for service in the new national structure, a process he ensured by naming former colleagues of the Constitutional Convention to his cabinet.

When Thomas Jefferson, who had resigned from Washington's cabinet in protest over Alexander Hamilton's economic policies, succeeded to the presidency, cabinet posts were given to Democratic Republicans rather than to Federalists. It is interesting to note that Albert Gallatin, whom Jefferson chose as Hamilton's successor as secretary of the treasury, continued the policies of his predecessor virtually unchanged. This lack of policy change was understandably facilitated by the presence, barely a decade old, of a bureaucratic structure (the Treasury Department), accustomed to the implementation of certain policies and therefore reluctant to enforce new policies.

Until 1883 all federal jobs were filled under the patronage system.

Creation and expansion of the civil service. Bureaucratic structures have become increasingly important as the patronage that originally governed the entire system has given way to the civil service. The first commission to investigate the possibility of establishing such a service was set up in 1871 by Grant, who, ironically, had one of the most corrupt administrations in the history of the presidency. The reluctance of Congress to appropriate the needed funds for such a project aborted it in 1875. Six years later the assassination of a president highlighted the need for a civil service: on July 2, 1881, Charles J. Guiteau, after a vain attempt to procure the post of ambassador to Austria or consul to Paris, shot and killed President James Garfield.

The Garfield and Chester Arthur ticket of 1880 had united a reform president and a vice-presidential candidate of antireform, or "Stalwart," persuasion in order to balance the Republican platform. But Guiteau's cry as he assassinated Garfield ("I am a Stalwart and now Arthur is president") spelled the end of his own life and that of the "spoils system" itself. Arthur, to the dismay of his Stalwart friends and in light of aroused public opinion in the aftermath of the assassination, endorsed and signed into law the Civil Service Reform Act of 1883 (known as the Pendleton Act). This first congressional attempt to replace the spoils system provided for 10 percent of the federal bureaucracy to be chosen on the basis of merit as determined by competitive examination. Since then the figures have been reversed, civil service positions now accounting for over 90 percent of the bureaucracy's personnel. Hiring by competitive examination usually involves a written test, even though similar positions in industry would not. Examiners must sometimes strain to create an appropriate examination for a particular position, as demonstrated by the following questions designed for elevator operator applicants:

> Now the vast majority of federal jobs fall under civil service regulations.

1. A sign inside your car states that no smoking is allowed. A passenger carrying a lighted cigarette enters your car. You should say (A) "Read that sign and then put your cigarette out." (B) "Peruse the announcement, sir, and then extinguish your cigarette." (C) "Smoking not permitted." (D) "No, smoking, please."

2. A sudden stop in an elevator is undesirable mainly because it (A) wrecks the mechanism (B) is not allowed (C) may lead to the loss of his job by the operator (D) discommodes and may injure passengers.[4]

Personnel

Remaining appointive positions. We have noted that fewer than 10 percent of all federal jobs are currently outside the civil service system. The appointive positions that remain in force can be roughly divided into three categories:

1. *Appointive policy-making positions.* These account for approximately 600 direct presidential appointments. These officials often are granted considerable latitude by the White House when they, in turn, appoint several hundred additional subordinates. All these positions, which are theoretically superior to the career civil servant positions, form the main component at the top of the bureaucratic hierarchy.

> The president is entitled to appoint primarily administrators at the highest levels of the bureaucracy.

2. *Independent regulatory commissioners.* These number several dozen members appointed by the president, but their set terms of office and concomitant independence effectively remove them, once in office, from presidential control.

3. *Lower-level nonpolicy patronage positions.* These are similar to the appointive positions mentioned in (1) except that they are non-policy-making positions, such as secretarial assistants to the policy makers. The logic behind this type of appointment is that the policy maker should be free to appoint people who can be trusted to handle sensitive matters. In practice, many of the people who hold these non-policy-making positions exert considerable influence on policy. Similar non-policy-making positions are available for patron-

---

[4]Sample questions taken from David R. Turner, *Civil Service Handbook: How to Get a Civil Service Job* (New York: Arco, 1972), pp. 30-31. The correct answer to each question is *D*.

The Federal Bureaucracy   161

age appointments by senators and local party leaders. The number of positions in this category was drastically reduced in 1971 with the reorganization of the Post Office Department by the United States Postal Service Act. In accord with the provisions of the act, most of these positions became career-merit, rather than senatorial-patronage, in nature.

Distribution of personnel. The distribution of civil service personnel across the bureaucracy demonstrates the relative size of the various elements in the federal structure. Over 35 percent of all civil service personnel are employed by the Department of Defense (counting civilian employees only), with the Postal Service following with 23 percent of the total, and the Veterans Administration employing about 7 percent. The remaining third of civil service personnel are distributed throughout the rest of the bureaucracy.

The Defense Department employs by far the largest number of civilian government employees.

The federal bureaucracy, with its 2.8 million civilian workers, is undoubtedly large. We must note, however, that only 18 percent of government employees work for the national government; the other 82 percent work in state or local government bureaucracies. Similarly, most money is spent on the state and local levels rather than by the federal government. Although some political candidates may be given to railing at "big government in Washington," the vast preponderance of the "government" we experience is at the state or local level, delivered by state or local bureaucrats.

Of all government employees, most work for state or local governments, not the national government.

For that matter, most of the people who work for "the government in Washington" do their work outside the nation's capital and the metropolitan Washington area. Only 11 percent of federal employees work in the Washington area; the rest work in the ten regional headquarters of federal activities and thousands of district offices.

Only 11 percent of federal employees work in the Washington area.

Representative bureaucracy? Federal bureaucrats are similar to the American population as a whole, although more differences appear when we focus on only the high civil servants. In 1978, 44 percent of federal employees in the general schedule (GS) pay system were women and 13 percent were blacks, so that women were slightly underrepresented in the bureaucracy and blacks well represented (12 percent of the general population is black). However, when we disaggregate the bureaucracy by hierarchical level, minorities and women are overrepresented in the lowest grades and underrepresented in the supergrades. Table 4-4 presents the starting salary levels and sample occupations of the eighteen GS levels. Three-quarters of the bureaucrats making up to $16,000 a year are women; only four out of every 100 bureaucrats making $60,000 a year are women. Similarly, blacks and other minorities are commonly found in the lowest-paying jobs and rarely spotted in the supergrade positions. This situation reflects the placement of minorities and women in large private bureaucracies, in which one finds fewer and fewer minorities and women the higher one climbs the corporate ladder. In fact, the record of the federal government in promoting nondiscriminatory hiring and promotion policies is better than that of the private sector. Further, trends in

The federal bureaucracy resembles private corporate bureaucracies in its underrepresentation of minorities and women in higher positions.

Table 4-4
Starting Salaries, United States Government, Effective October 1, 1985

Grade (with Sample Occupation)	Starting Salary
GS-18 (Top career official)	$84,157[a]
GS-17 (Supervisory Professional)	71,840[a]
GS-16 (Supervisory Professional)	61,296
GS-15 (Senior analyst)	52,262
GS-14 (Chief accountant)	44,430
GS-13 (Personnel director)	37,599
GS-12 (Accountant, experienced)	31,619
GS-11 (Buyer)	26,381
GS-10 (Engineering technician)	24,011
GS-9 (Secretary, experienced)	21,804
GS-8 (Accountant, beginning)	19,740
GS-7 (Engineer, beginning)	17,824
GS-6 (Secretary, beginning)	16,040
GS-5 (Junior draftsman)	14,390
GS-4 (General stenographer)	12,862
GS-3 (Typist, experienced)	11,458
GS-2 (Keypunch operator, beginning)	10,501
GS-1 (File clerk, beginning)	9,339

[a] In most cases the maximum salary payable is $68,700.

the past fifteen years are toward a lessening of racial and gender-based discrimination. Among supergrade bureaucrats, 4.2 percent were women in 1978, up from a mere 1.4 percent in 1970. In 1978, 4.5 percent of supergrade bureaucrats were members of minority groups, up from 3.7 percent in 1972. Similar trends are found, particularly among women, for the other GS levels requiring professional or administrative skills.

The higher-level civil servants, the ones with the most policy-making discretion, do not differ greatly from other Americans with similar educations. Their parents were likely to be richer than the parents of a general sample of Americans, but in this relatively upper-status background the higher civil service does not differ from similarly trained administrators and professionals employed in the private sector. There is no evidence, for example, that scientists who work for the Environmental Protection Agency have different social backgrounds than scientists employed by private sector industries or universities.

Politicians are sometimes given to depicting the federal bureaucracy as a bunch of ideologues out of step in their thinking with the American people. This is simply wrong, for surveys show federal bureaucrats to be diverse in their thinking, just as are the American people. There is a slight tendency for bureaucrats to be more liberal than the American populace as a whole, but the differences are minor. To predict the attitudes of bureaucrats, the mission of the agency that employs them is the key factor. Civil servants rarely disapprove of their agencies' missions. For example, an employee of the Department of Education is likely to favor more federal aid to education programs, and a Defense Department employee is likely to want increased defense spending. Where a bureaucrat's office sits is a good predictor of where that bureaucrat stands on issues, at least those relevant to his or her agency.

Finally, we will consider how bureaucrats leave office. Because civil service rules restrict firings for political reasons, the bureaucracy has developed the reputation of being a large, stagnant mass whose members leave only to retire. Although civil servants leave their jobs at only half the rate of employees in the private sector, there is still an annual turnover of over 20 percent. During the 1970s there were 600,000 or so annual departures, only 15 percent of which were retirements. One-third of departures were employees who simply quit, presumably to seek employment elsewhere. Another third, over 200,000 annually, were fired. Ten percent were RIFed; a "reduction in force" in their agency eliminated their positions. The remaining 8 percent were suspended without pay. During the Reagan administration RIFs increased as the administration sought to reduce federal involvement in domestic policy areas.

Leadership and Limitations

A consideration of the leadership and limitations of this mazelike national bureaucracy must take into account three separate areas of influence. The first area concerns the interrelatedness of the bureaucracy with the executive, legislative, and judicial branches; how do these governmental institutions affect and determine bureaucratic leadership? Second, what are the effects on the bureaucracy of extragovernmental sources of influence? And, finally, what are the bureaucracy's internal limitations on its own powers?

Governmental Influences on the Bureaucracy

Relations between bureaucracies and the president. Several of the president's powers mentioned in the first chapter directly affect his relations with the bureaucracy. Those powers we considered under presidential leadership are particularly important. The president's willingness to use his powers of persuasion to threaten and cajole, to plead and bargain may be aimed as much at a bureaucrat as at an elected official. Presidential favors are prestigious regardless of the object of the president's attention. The tactic of presidential pressure is, of course, particularly effective when applied to presidential appointees (as seen in table 4-1), many of whom are subject to dismissal at the president's discretion. However, every president also attempts to influence the bureaucrats over whom he does not have dismissal authority. These bureaucrats can make it extremely difficult for a new administration even to acquaint itself with the workings of the bureaucratic maze.

The president's persuasive task with bureaucrats is similar to his persuasive task with Congress: he cannot command effectively; he must persuade.

In fact, it is never easy, even with the support of the bureaucrats, for a new president to discover exactly how the bureaucracy operates; without their support, it is virtually impossible. As one White House staff aide during Nixon's years expressed it, "President Nixon doesn't run the bureaucracy; the civil service and the unions do. It took him three years to find out what was going on in the bureaucracy. And God forbid if any President is defeated after the first term, because then the bureaucracy has another three years to play games with the next President."[5]

We do not mean to suggest, however, that the president is impotent in dealing with the bureaucracy. Both directly and indirectly, through congressional allies, the president exerts great influence over the bureaucracy. This influence is greater when he wants to stop bureaucrats from doing what he does not want than when he wants reluctant bureaucrats to follow his lead.

White House involvement in budgeting, reorganizing the bureaucracy, promotions, and modifying regulations may be used to persuade agencies to implement programs as the president desires.

First, the president, together with Congress, dictates the annual budget. An agency in the president's favor is likely to receive increased funding, while an agency that has incurred the president's wrath can expect a sharp cut or even elimination. For example, the Legal Services Corporation (LSC) provides assistance to poor citizens in civil disputes, a federal activity Reagan has long disliked. Every year Reagan proposes cutting off all funding to the LSC, thereby effectively firing all of its employees by eliminating the agency. Although allies in Congress save the LSC from extinction, it has survived with sharply reduced funding.

Second, under his executive or administrative authority, the president can reorganize departments. If he believes that a particular policy is not being effectively administered by a certain bureau in a department, he can shift the responsibility for administering that policy to a different bureau. The use or threatened use of such reorganizations helps the president to persuade the bureaucracy to do what he wants.

Third, the president and his high-level political appointees have more control over personnel policies with civil servants than one would expect in a strict Weberian bureaucracy. Promotions are supposed to be entirely by merit, but especially at the highest grades, civil servants who enthusiastically

---

[5]Quoted in Richard P. Nathan, "The Administrative Presidency," *The Public Interest*, no. 44 (Summer 1976), p. 44.

endorse the president's policies may be found to have more "merit" than employees with reservations about the wisdom of the president's ideas. Civil servants at the lower grade levels cannot be fired, except for cause, but they may be harassed at times into choosing other employment. A GS-12, for example, who has taken a public position with which the administration does not agree might be given few or no responsibilities and denied any real promotion potential. Rather than "stagnate" at that level, doing nothing, the dissatisfied employee may choose to resign.

For members of the civil service at the supergrade level (GS-15 and above) who have elected to enter the Senior Executive Service (SES), the extent of control exercised over their positions by the political level is even more extensive. Any career civil servant who wishes to advance to the highest managerial levels in the government must enter the SES, but in doing so may lose a good deal of security. An SES civil servant with close family ties in Virginia and a new home there may be given a transfer to the bureau's office in Seattle. The SES career bureaucrat has only two choices: accept the transfer, or resign from the government. Not every president or cabinet secretary has made frequent use of such distasteful methods, but bureaucrats know that if they become too obnoxious to their political bosses, the result is an increased probability that such methods will be applied.

Fourth, the president can change regulations to clarify how legislation is to be implemented. For example, if the president believes that the bureaucracy has been too quick to provide black-lung benefits to former miners with respiratory problems, he can require additional authentication of each applicant's case. This would reduce the bureaucracy's efficiency in processing claims but realize the president's purpose.

Congress's involvement in the budgetary process is its key resource in attempting to influence behavior in the bureaucracy.

Relations between bureaucracies and Congress. Congress, like the president, relies most heavily on the appropriation process to limit the power of bureaucracy. Congressional "power of the purse" is a formidable weapon rendered even more imposing by the long tenure of powerful appropriations subcommittee chairpersons. In that their tenure often outlasts that of any president, these members of Congress are in a position to exercise an elephantine memory for the activities of executive departments and agencies. Agency representatives must appear before Congress annually to justify their budget requests, at which time they are often questioned on the entire range of the agency's activities.

The mere fact that a program's budget request has cleared the OMB and been included in the president's budget proposal to Congress is no guarantee that the program will receive the requested amount or, for that matter, any money at all. Carter's amnesty program serves as an illustration. The administration had lobbied against and defeated a move in Congress to reject the amnesty program, but many of its provisions were inoperable without federal funds. Despite the president's victory, Congress, when it passed the 1978 budget, refused to grant any funds for the operation of the amnesty program.

Conversely, the deletion of a given program's budget request from the president's proposal to Congress carries no assurance that the program is dead. The above-mentioned effort by Reagan to kill the Legal Services Corporation is an example of a congressional rescue of a program marked for extinction by the president. A bureaucracy's relationship with Congress is as important as its relationship with the president. Either may be a determining factor in how much (or, indeed, whether) money will be available for a given program.

Monetary considerations also play a part in the congressionally controlled General Accounting Office (GAO) and the Office of the Comptroller General. The GAO acts as the congressional "watchdog" of the Treasury. The head of GAO, the comptroller general, is appointed with the consent of the Senate and may be removed only with the consent of both houses of Congress. All government expenditures must be authorized by the GAO and bear the signature of the comptroller general. For the bureaucrat it may be a long, arduous road from the OMB, through Congress, to the GAO—a road on which more than one program has been robbed of every cent.

The GAO also uses this "watchdog" authority over the manner in which the Treasury's dollars are spent to evaluate entire federal programs for Congress. At the request of any member of Congress, the GAO may enter virtually *any* area of operation of a federal department or agency and conduct an investigation. This investigative function is often augmented by the physical presence, in the same building that houses the department or agency, of full-time GAO investigators.

Aside from strictly monetary and investigative considerations, Congress also retains the option of program authorization and amendment. Consequently, bureaucrats not only seek to appease powerful congressional leaders but actively court their favor. Congress has increasingly granted broad authorization to the bureaucracy to pursue its programs, but such programs can be changed or even eliminated through a "reduction in force"—called a "RIF"—(the wholesale elimination of job positions) by Congress at any time. The wise bureaucrat must balance this against both the desires of the agency or department he or she represents and those of the president—a feat of no mean proportion.

Members of Congress, on an individual basis, also seek to influence bureaucratic activities through public exposure. Efforts by members of Congress to influence the implementation of the Superfund legislation by the Environmental Protection Agency, discussed in the case study in this book, often involved public prodding. Failing to persuade EPA officials in private communications, members tried to build public political pressure to force EPA to act.

Congressional-bureaucratic relations are not a one-way street involving

In performing oversight activities, Congress may elicit public pressure on an agency.

The bureaucracy employs lobbyists to advance its positions on Capitol Hill.

Congress trying to get bureaus to do what it wants. The bureaucracy employs hundreds of lobbyists, who cannot legally be called lobbyists, to provide "informational" assistance to Congress. Lobbyists for the bureaucracy, regardless of what they are called, behave similarly to private interest-group lobbyists in working to persuade Congress to pass legislation favorable to their interests. The Department of Defense, for example, has one of the largest lobbying staffs in Washington. Daily it sends dozens of officers from the Pentagon to the Capitol to advance the interests of the military. Members in key positions with records of enthusiastic support for Pentagon spending proposals are likely to be rewarded with the placement of military installations in their districts. Other agencies have fewer resources with which to reward their congressional supporters. Other agencies also have greater difficulty maintaining support for their programs in Congress.

Relations between bureaucracies and the courts. The courts, too, retain some degree of control over the activities of the bureaucracy. We have already noted that Congress has the constitutional prerogative to establish judicial authority in the lower courts, and the Supreme Court has ruled that this same congressional authorization of the right to adjudicate is extendable to the independent regulatory commissions and other agencies established by congressional mandate. Thus, the courts may not intervene or accept appeals from the quasi-judicial proceedings of the bureaucracy.

The courts rarely accept challenges of administrative decisions.

If a suit disputing the authority of a bureaucracy is filed by a third party, the court must first determine the "delegation of congressional intent" (whether Congress had the power to delegate this authority to the department or agency). Once the delegation of congressional intent has been granted, the court is then limited to a determination of the question of *ultra vires* (beyond legal power)—that is, whether the agency is operating within the confines of the legislation in question. To rule *ultra vires,* however, the court must point to congressionally enumerated limitations of power in the statute that the agency has violated. Given the broad delegation of authority that Congress usually imparts to the bureaucracy, such rulings are increasingly rare. Thus, except in questions of constitutionality, the bureaucracy is relatively free from external judicial review.

Although the courts rarely question actions by the bureaucracy, judges have been more willing to hear suits claiming that the bureaucracy has failed to act as mandated by law. An example of this type of involvement appeared in the case study at the end of chapter 3. In that case, an environmental group, joined by the states of New Jersey and Connecticut, sued the Environmental Protection Agency because EPA had failed to promulgate regulations within the time frame specified by Congress. This type of suit is often brought against bureaucracies to prod an administration into acting in an area in which it has a mandate to act but, for policy reasons, is reluctant to do so.

Extragovernmental Influences on the Bureaucracy

Effectiveness of interest groups. The second general area of influence on both bureaucratic leadership and the limitation of bureaucratic power is the entire interest-group structure around which the bureaucracy is organized. We have already seen that the personnel who serve in the "four branches" of the federal government are drawn disproportionately from the upper socioeconomic strata of the society. Further, because society's resources are not randomly distributed throughout the population but, rather, concentrated in the same strata from which these personnel are recruited, the influences brought to bear on the bureaucracy reflect "the business or upper-class bias of the pressure system."[6] Admittedly, some exceptions to this general rule do exist, but the interests of consumers and of the disadvantaged in American society (for example, the poor, migrants, the aged, women, and blacks) generally find weak representation in the pressure system.

In order for pressure to be effectively exerted at any point in the political process, the interest-seeking representation must exert organization, concentration, and the necessary financial or political resources to have its voice heard. Without money or votes, an interest group is unlikely to be effective. In general, the more diversified interest groups are less effective than the more specialized ones, which are able to focus their energies. Thus, the Chamber of Commerce of the United States exerts less influence than the American Medical Association (AMA), given the latter's ability to concentrate its considerable resources on specific legislation.

Specialized interest groups may be very effective, but this efficacy is usually limited to the interest group's area of specialization. The American Legion, for example, is a very influential interest organization when it is lobbying for veterans' benefits. Leaders of the Veterans Administration and of the veterans' affairs committees of Congress pay careful attention to Legion statements on the needs of veterans and often modify policies on the basis of Legion lobbying efforts. However, when the Legion moves outside its area of specialization to urge that certain policies be adopted in the realm of foreign relations or internal security, its recommendations receive little serious attention.

Interest groups as allies of the bureaucracy. The relationship between the American Legion and the Veterans Administration does involve an interest group influencing the bureaucracy, but it also indicates a bureaucracy working closely with the group to advance their common interests. After all, the VA wants to serve veterans, the same goal that the American Legion has. Often bureaucrats in the Veterans Administration work closely with lobbyists from the leading veterans' organizations to work out a common strategy to

---

[6]E.E. Schattschneider, *The Semi-Sovereign People* (New York: Holt, Rinehart & Winston, 1960), p. 31.

Upper-class and upper-middle-class interests are more effective than those groups working for responsiveness to the needs of disadvantaged people.

Interest groups that focus their energies on particular subject areas are generally more effective than larger, more heterogeneous interest groups.

Agencies work as allies with interest groups that represent the clientele the agencies serve.

impress Congress and the president with the importance of funding programs for veterans. Increased funding pleases the bureaucrats because the agency expands (thereby expanding agency jobs, power, and prestige). Increased funding pleases the interest groups because their leaders can point with pride to their success at helping their members.

Our example of the VA working closely with veterans' lobbying groups is not intended to suggest uniqueness in the relationship. Instead, almost every agency has a clientele relationship with some interest group whose members are provided a service or "regulated" by the agency. Examples are numerous and obvious. Employees of the Department of Labor have their contacts with union lobbyists. Defense Department people work with lobbyists for weapons industries, what Dwight Eisenhower called the military-industrial complex. Environmental Protection Agency personnel work with environmental groups. These contacts continue, though sometimes clandestinely, if a new cabinet secretary or agency administrator is disdainful of the agency's traditional clientele groups. The bureaucrats know that most of them will still be working for the agency long after their bosses have been replaced.

Internal Influences on the Bureaucracy

Specialization and hierarchical inefficiency. Finally, we must consider the bureaucracy itself as a source of its own limitations, as well as its strengths. Within the hierarchical structure one must remember that specialization is the order of the day. In this case specialization ensures incomplete control of superiors over inferiors; bureaucratic "inferiors" are likely to possess a degree of expertise in a given area of specialization not equaled by the superiors. Thus, the idea that bureaucracies can be viewed as merely mechanical administrative bodies under the control of elected or appointed officials is illusory. Inherent specialization at each level of the bureaucratic structure results in each level establishing its own specific goals. These goals are established over the years in response to the particular political and administrative environment (congressional liaison, pressure group influence, and so forth) in which the specialization occurs. As a result, even lower-level career administrators have far more familiarity with the programs and policies of the department or agency in question than "transient" political appointees of the president could ever hope to gain. The "inferiors" in the hierarchical structure are therefore relatively free from interference by the appointed officials, and unless blatant controversies develop or the situation is publicly aired, the president may neither know nor act on the continued noncooperation and intransigence of the career administrator.

A consequence of hierarchy is specialized expertise and information, which gives lower-level bureaucrats substantial independence in implementing policies.

Institutional loyalty. Harold Seidman has characterized bureaucracies as affected by "deeply ingrained cultures and subcultures reflecting institutional history, ideology, values, symbols, folklore, professional biases, behavior

Agencies fight among themselves, as do offices within agencies, for power, prestige, and money.

patterns, heroes and enemies."[7] The strong feeling of institutional loyalty thus engendered can produce not only the refusal to submit to hierarchical authority but also fierce disputes over questions of jurisdiction with parallel bureaucratic structures in other agencies. Entire bureaucratic structures may, in fact, be so affected, resulting, for example, in little or no communication between the Department of Labor and the National Labor Relations Board or between the Department of Commerce and the Federal Trade Commission. Such lack of cooperation and reciprocity can only serve to increase the confusing nature of the bureaucratic maze.

Conclusion

Instances of poor service to individuals are inherent in bureaucratic organization.

It is easy, perhaps too easy, to write cynically of the bureaucracy. All of us have personal horror stories about our misfortunes dealing with public and private bureaucracies, including those at American universities and colleges. Sometimes our particular need does not match up well with relevant rules and regulations, so that what seems to be a simple problem with an obvious solution gets bogged down in red tape, generates exchanges with rude officials who seem insulted that our problem does not fit one of the ready categories, and never does result in the adoption of the obvious solution. Although well-managed and well-funded bureaucracies can reduce these types of problems, they can never be entirely eliminated, for the complexity of the human experience defies the creation of an appropriate rule for every circumstance.

One reason the federal bureaucracy is an easier target for criticism than private bureaucracies is that we, as individuals, can choose to avoid many private bureaucracies that have angered us. If employees of a restaurant treat us rudely, we can decide to avoid that restaurant. If we have bad experiences with the Internal Revenue Service or the Postal Service, what are we to do? We can (and should) complain to appropriate officials so that we are treated fairly, but we do not have the simple solution of going to a different Internal Revenue Service.

Much presidential and congressional time and effort are spent in attempting to control the bureaucracy.

The bureaucracy frustrates elected officials as well as individual citizens. We have tried to show that much of the dynamics of politics in Washington involves efforts by the White House and Congress to persuade entrenched bureaucrats to administer programs the way the president and Congress want them administered. The other side of the coin is that much politics involves the bureaucrats and their interest-group allies attempting to persuade the president and Congress to adopt policies favorable to the individual agencies. More than one president has concluded that dealing with *his* bureaucracy is similar to punching out a pillow: you get exhausted after exerting much energy, but after the struggle ends, the pillow returns to its original shape.

[7]Harold Seidman, *Politics, Position, and Power*, 2nd ed. (New York: Oxford University Press, 1975), pp. 98-99.

If there are these problems with the federal bureaucracy, why do we not try to get rid of it? At rallies in the 1960s and 1970s presidential candidate George Wallace suggested just such a dismantling (except for the Defense Department), to the wild cheers of his followers. With similar appeals in 1980, Ronald Reagan was elected to the presidency.

The bureaucracy survives and prospers because it alone is capable of accomplishing certain of our national goals.

The essential reason we have the bureaucracy is the desire of the American people that certain tasks be accomplished—tasks that only the federal government can perform. This is not to say that the bureaucracy is not in need of reform or that none of its activities is wasteful or that some of what it does could not be beneficially decentralized to the states and localities. What we are saying is that the American people want certain things done, things that only large-scale public bureaucracies can accomplish. Two examples of successful bureaucratic responses to public demands are the space program and Social Security.

The bureaucracy has at times performed impressively in accomplishing difficult tasks.

Americans want to be able to retire from their jobs before they die and to be free of devastating medical expenses in their senior years. The states and private pension arrangements are unable to provide such security in an equitable manner to all Americans who have worked throughout their lives. The Social Security Administration, through the system of employer and worker contributions to the old-age insurance and Medicare funds, has been able to send monthly checks to millions of senior citizens and to provide medical insurance. Although no one is saying the system is perfect, it has provided a means of living in dignity and security for millions of retired people. This is no mean accomplishment.

The second example of successful bureaucratic behavior is the placement of a man on the moon only ten years after America's space effort began on a serious level. Starting far behind the Soviets, the American space progam was able to surpass the Soviet effort in only a decade. This trip to the moon was celebrated, as it should have been, as a remarkable scientific and technological accomplishment. It was just as much a bureaucratic accomplishment, for the National Aeronautics and Space Administration was able to amass and organize the talent and material necessary to get the job done. With Congress, the president, and the bureaucracy in agreement on what was to be done, the policy was effectively implemented.

Selected Additional Readings

The authors found the following works to be most helpful in the preparation of this chapter and recommend them to students who want additional information on the federal bureaucracy:

Meier, Kenneth, *Politics and the Bureaucracy: Policymaking in the Fourth Branch of Government.* Monterey, Calif.: Brooks/Cole, 1979.

Nakamura, Robert T., and Smallwood, Frank. *The Politics of Policy Implementation.* New York: St. Martin's Press, 1980.

Nathan, Richard. *The Plot That Failed: Nixon and the Administrative Presidency.* New York: Wiley, 1975.

Seidman, Harold. *Politics, Position, and Power: The Dynamics of Federal Organization,* 3rd ed. New York: Oxford University Press, 1980.

Wilson, James. *The Politics of Regulation.* New York: Basic Books, 1980.

Case History: "Superfund" 1980, 1985

Part IV: The Bureaucracy

By the time President Jimmy Carter signed the Comprehensive Environmental Response, Compensation and Liability Act of 1980 (CERCLA) on December 11, the U.S. Environmental Protection Agency was already prepared to implement the legislation. EPA staff had written the initial Carter proposals for a Superfund designed to deal with the nation's hazardous waste sites, and the agency would become the primary source of implementation as well. In this fourth end-of-chapter segment of the Superfund case study, we will look at some of the preparatory work done by EPA to prepare for CERCLA passage in both 1980 and 1985, and examine the effects of the election of Ronald Reagan and interest-group lobbying on EPA in its subsequent implementation.

The version of the Superfund bill that had been presented to Congress by Carter had been developed at EPA by a task force under the direction of an assistant administrator. Ordinarily, this type of legislative preparation is the extent of a federal agency's involvement prior to passage of legislation. To be sure, top-level bureaucrats will testify before congressional committees reviewing the proposed legislation, but the department or agency, **as an organization,** does not usually proceed any further until the legislation is passed. There is no guarantee that Congress will enact the proposal at all, and even if it does, it is surely not going to pass the legislation in exactly the same form as it is proposed. Certainly Superfund falls into this latter category, for the Carter proposals never got past the committees to which they were originally referred.

However, in the summer of 1979, EPA was coming under severe criticism in Congress and the press for failure to implement some of its existing programs rapidly enough. Senior EPA staff reasoned that the public concern evidenced over abandoned hazardous waste sites like

Love Canal, combined with the magnitude of the problem and the size of the fund that was being considered to deal with it, required an unusual approach to the normal "waiting period" between bill proposal and legislative enactment.

By February 1980, EPA had formed a new office to plan for the implementation of Superfund. That office forced EPA to concentrate on issues likely to confront the agency when the bill passed. By the end of 1980, the Superfund organization in EPA, named the Office of Hazardous Emergency Response (OHER), had a virtual monopoly on the competence required to manage the huge hazardous waste cleanup program.

When Carter signed CERCLA into law on December 11, he was already a "lame-duck" president. Reagan, the president-elect, would bring a different philosophy to the White House—and to the rest of the federal establishment. For the first five months of the Reagan administration, EPA was without an administrator: Anne M. Gorsuch was not named to the post until May 20, 1981. During that interim period, OHER continued its activities, no longer in a preimplementation mode—now, with CERCLA a reality, the office was able to "flesh out" the decisions it had made earlier and focus its attentions on the specifics of implementing the law.

One such specific was the National Contingency Plan (NCP). The NCP had originally been written to provide for a federal response capability to the spill of oil or certain hazardous materials into the navigable waters of the United States. With the passage of CERCLA came the responsibility of revising and republishing the NCP to include multimedia responses involving any hazardous substance. However, with the passage of CERCLA, something else came to EPA: the lobbyists who had been working Congress trying to influence the legislation.

Now that the legislation had passed, environmental groups and industry representatives shifted their focus and tried to influence the specific regulations and policies by which the law would be implemented. The chemical industry had, in effect, "lost" the congressional battle. CERCLA had passed through Congress in the eleventh hour, but Congress does not implement the laws it passes; only the bureaucracy has that authority. The battle lines were drawn anew.

By mid-May 1981 virtually every program at EPA was at a standstill. The holdovers from the old administration were in no position to act, and the Reagan appointments had not yet been made. Nevertheless, OHER forged ahead with preparation of the NCP. However, CERCLA was still under the implementation authority of Carter's Executive Order 12286, and the new administration made it quite clear that it did not want the NCP promulgated (because it was such an important regulation) until after the Reagan team had taken over. Several times the NCP was on the verge of being published in the **Federal Register** but was always pulled back.

When the new administrator took office on May 20, she began the process of appointing her subordinates, who would be the upper-level managers in EPA. Barely a month later, she announced her choices for several key positions, and environmental groups were outraged. The agency, which had previously been viewed as the protector of the environment, was now looked on by many as a polluter's stonghold. Among the appointments that angered environmentalists were Frank A. Shepherd, associate administrator (formerly an attorney for large corporations), John E. Daniel, chief of staff (formerly with the American Paper Institute), Robert M. Perry, general counsel (formerly with Exxon), and Thornton W. Field, special assistant to the administrator (formerly an attorney for Adolph Coors Company). With these and other new senior staff members in place, the receptivity to industry pressure at the agency increased dramatically.

Several iterations of drafts of the NCP circulated through EPA during this period. In June, and again in October, the Chemical Manufacturers' Association (CMA) sent lengthy position papers to EPA outlining what it wanted to see in the upcoming NCP proposal. CMA's position on various policies was often incorporated in subsequent drafts of the NCP.

The influence of CMA and other industry-based groups became so blatant that Rep. Toby Moffett (D.-Conn.), chairperson of the House Government Operations subcommittee, summoned Administrator Gorsuch and Deputy Administrator John Hernandez to answer allegations that the latter's meetings with industry representatives were policy-making sessions. In six meetings held between June 19 and September 29, chemical industry representatives, but no environmental or public-interest groups, met with Hernandez to discuss issues that were then before the agency. It was clear, Moffett argued, that the industry "perceives this as unusual and delightful."

It was against this backdrop of perceived industry influence on the agency that the Environmental Defense Fund (EDF) filed its suit to compel EPA to propose the NCP in the **Federal Register.** EDF staffers reasoned that the longer the agency delayed, the more pervasive industry's influence would be.

OHER, which had now been renamed the Office of Emergency and Remedial Response (OERR), operated during this period on the basis of "interim guidance"—that is, policy decisions that were promulgated by OERR to implement the cleanup program in the absence of the NCP. Using a complex ranking system that identified the more dangerous hazardous waste sites around the country, OERR generated a list of 115 "interim priority sites" for Superfund to move against. "Movement" at these sites, however, did not necessarily mean "cleanup." Often the agency's attorneys, using a variety of legal mechanisms (notice letters, administrative orders, and so on), sought to compel private-party cleanup, rather than Superfund-financed cleanup. The advantage to the responsible party was less cost, but often more delay. It was not until mid-1982 that the program office (OERR) and the legal (enforcement) offices were able to move concurrently at many of the sites on the interim priority list.

Two kinds of program actions were authorized by CERCLA. One is the "emergency" action—a relatively short-lived action intended to prevent imminent human or environmental harm. Officially dubbed "removal" actions, these responses often resembled the classic oil-spill cleanup (as, for example, when a tanker truck overturns on the highway). The second type of action—termed "remedial"—is defined by CERCLA as being "consistent with a permanent remedy." It was in this area the OERR faced an enormous task. No one, government or private industry, had any experience in this type of action—providing a remedy for the environmental harm. The bureaucracy "learned as it went along." New technologies were developed and novel approaches were implemented. The planning process alone for remedial-action cleanup could take more than a year. The investigation to locate and identify the various hazardous materials at a site may take six to twelve months. A feasibility study is then required that consumes additional months. This, in turn, is followed by engineering designs, the selection of an appropriate design for the site, and, finally, construction of facilities needed to deal with the problem. The aim of CERCLA is not construction but the remediation of an environmental harm. If, for example, groundwater has been contaminated by leached toxic chemicals, a complex treatment system may have to be built to pump the contaminated water to the surface, treat it to remove the contaminants, and reinject the cleaned water into the aquifer. This "pumping and treating" may take twenty to thirty years at a single site in order to clean up the contamination.

The law required that the state in which the site exists must contribute to the cost of cleanup. In the early 1980s, with the cutback in many federal programs mandated by the Reagan administration, many states were unable to afford their share (10 percent of the cost if the site were privately owned, and 50 percent or more if the site had been owned or operated by the state or municipality). Before EPA could undertake a remedial action, the state was required to sign either a "cooperative agreement" (if the state was going to do most of the work) or a "contract" (if the agency had the lead at the site) and provide required "assurances" that it would be able to come up with its share of the cleanup cost. This cost-sharing requirement meant that no

176 Chapter 4

action was taken at many sites because a state was unable—or unwilling—to provide the necessary assurances.

During the first several years of Superfund implementation, Administrator Gorsuch consciously followed procedures that were designed to "conserve" the money in the fund. She announced at a mid-1982 press conference at which the National Priorities List (NPL) was updated (adding more sites) that it would not be necessary to reauthorize the Superfund tax when it expired in 1985. Career bureaucrats at EPA were appalled at this notion, and at the obvious political maneuvering of Gorsuch and other senior Reagan appointees. Partially in response to this, William N. Hedeman, Jr., whom Gorsuch has named director of OERR, initiated the methodological development and data collection required to complete the studies called for by Congress under Section 301 of CERCLA. This is a good example of the "incomplete control" of superiors over inferiors in a bureaucracy that we mentioned in the text. The studies, designed to demonstrate the need to reauthorize CERLCA, were initiated by a career bureaucrat without the knowledge of the administrator, who was publicly claiming that no such need existed. Work continued on the studies for the entire eight-month period after their initiation, completely unbeknownst to political appointees in EPA. When Gorsuch was forced to resign on March 9, 1983, she was still unaware that they had been started.

It was her management of Superfund that caused Gorsuch's resignation. For almost two years Congress had been faithfully performing its oversight function (as the case study at the end of chapter 2 makes clear), and its studies of the mismanagement and antienvironmental bias that had been developing within the agency were constantly in the nation's press. The Superfund is a "motherhood and apple pie" issue—one in which people's lives and health are at stake—and Congress pressed its investigators vigorously. When Anne M. Burford (she had married on February 20 and taken her new husband's name) resigned, her action precipitated a wave of resignations. The **Washington Post** aptly characterized the reactions of career EPA employees:

> At the EPA offices in Waterside Mall, dozens of career employees found cause for celebration. Staffers in (resigning General Counsel Robert) Perry's office were singing songs, drawing cartoons and performing skits. Downstairs in the shopping mall, Harry's Liquor, Wine and Cheeze sold eight cases of champagne and six ounces of Russian caviar to the general counsel's office. 'It's the most we've ever sold to the EPA,' the store manager said. 'They were jubilant.' In (another) office, former employees were said to be planning to come in from around the country for a party tonight.[8]

Reagan's choice to succeed Burford was viewed as beyond

---

[8] *Washington Post,* March 26, 1983, p. A2.

reproach by almost everyone. William D. Ruckelshaus had been named by Nixon as the first administrator of EPA when it was founded in 1970, and Reagan brought him back to head the now-embattled agency again. Ruckelshaus had the confidence of environmentalists, the business community, and Congress—as well as the support of the president. With Ruckelshaus came a team of senior-level managers that set about returning the agency to its traditional standards of professional administration of environmental laws.

Lee M. Thomas was named Assistant Administrator for Solid Waste and Emergency Response, taking the place of Rita Lavelle, who was later convicted of perjury for her role in the failure to enforce the Superfund law. Thomas not only "got Superfund moving" but, with the concurrence of the new administrator, ordered the Section 301 studies to be completed, thereby positioning the agency to be an active player in the reauthorization of Superfund.

Thomas established a CERCLA Reauthorization Task Force, chaired by his Special Assistant, Linda Fisher, to develop agency positions, assess the need for additional taxing mechanisms, work with congressional staff on a new Superfund bill, and consequently shape the hazardous waste response programs of the next decade. The task force worked through 1984, when Congress adjourned without reauthorizing CERCLA. When Ruckelshaus resigned as EPA administrator in December 1984, Thomas was named to replace him. Early in 1985, as Administrator of the Agency, Thomas proposed the administration bill that was based on the work of the task force and that ultimately resulted in the reauthorized Superfund.

What this demonstrates is that the bureaucracy does not exist in a vacuum. It exists within a political system, in which its actions face checks: direction from the president and his appointed senior management, oversight by Congress, intrabureaucracy squabbles, interest-group pressures, and requirements of the law. Considering the almost insurmountable odds, it may seem amazing that the bureaucracy is able to act at all. In sum, the politics of the situation may well determine the extent to which the structure is able to act effectively.

The Constitution of the United States

WE THE PEOPLE of the United States, in Order to form a more perfect Union, establish Justice, insure domestic Tranquility, provide for the common defense, promote the general Welfare, and secure the Blessings of Liberty to ourselves and our Posterity, do ordain and establish this Constitution for the United States of America.

Article I

Section 1. All legislative Powers herein granted shall be vested in a Congress of the United States, which shall consist of a Senate and House of Representatives.

Section 2. The House of Representatives shall be composed of Members chosen every second Year by the People of the several States, and Electors in each State shall have the Qualifications requisite for Electors of the most numerous Branch of the State Legislature.

No Person shall be a Representative who shall not have attained to the age of twenty five Years, and been seven Years a Citizen of the United States, and who shall not, when elected, be an Inhabitant of that State in which he shall be chosen.

Representatives and direct Taxes shall be apportioned among the several States which may be included within this Union, according to their respective Numbers, *which shall be determined by adding to the whole Number of free Persons, including those bound to Service for a Term of Years,* and excluding Indians not taxed, *three fifths of all other persons.*[1] The actual Enumeration shall be made within three years after the first Meeting of the Congress of the United States, and within every subsequent Term of ten Years, in such Manner as they shall by Law direct. The Number of Representatives shall not exceed one for every thirty Thousand, but each State shall have at Least one Representative; and until such enumeration shall be made, the State of New Hampshire shall be entitled to choose three, Massachusetts eight, Rhode-Island and Providence Plantations one, Connecticut five, New-York six, New Jersey four, Pennsylvania eight, Delaware one, Maryland six, Virginia ten, North Carolina five, South Carolina five, and Georgia three.

When vacancies happen in the Representation from any State, the Executive Authority thereof shall issue Writ of Election to fill such Vacancies.

The House of Representatives shall choose their Speaker and other Officers; and shall have the sole Power of Impeachment.

Section 3. The Senate of the United States shall be composed of two Senators from each State, *chosen by the legislature thereof*[2] for six Years; and each Senator shall have one Vote.

Immediately after they shall be assembled in Consequence of the first Election, they shall be divided as equally as may be into three Classes. The Seats of the Senators of the first Class shall be vacated at the Expiration of the second Year, of the second Class at the Expiration of the fourth Year, and of the third Class at the Expiration of the sixth Year, so that one third may be chosen every Second Year; *and if Vacancies happen by Resignation, or otherwise, during the Recess of the Legislature of any State, the Executive*

---

[1] See Fourteenth Amendment. Throughout, italics are used to indicate passages altered by subsequent amendments.

[2] See Seventeenth Amendment.

thereof may make temporary Appointments until the next Meeting of the Legislature, which shall then fill such Vacancies.[3]

No person shall be a Senator who shall not have attained to the Age of thirty Years, and been nine Years a Citizen of the United States, and who shall not, when elected, be an Inhabitant of the State for which he shall be chosen.

The Vice President of the United States shall be President of the Senate, but shall have no Vote, unless they be equally divided.

The Senate shall choose their other Officers, and also a President pro tempore, in the Absence of the Vice President, or when he shall exercise the Office of President of the United States.

The Senate shall have the sole Power to try all Impeachments. When sitting for that Purpose, they shall be on Oath or Affirmation. When the President of the United States is tried, the Chief Justice shall preside: And no Person shall be convicted without the Concurrence of two thirds of the Members present.

Judgment in Cases of Impeachment shall not extend further than to removal from Office, and disqualification to hold and enjoy any Office of honor, Trust or Profit under the United States: but the Party convicted shall nevertheless be liable and subject to Indictment, Trial, Judgment and Punishment, according to Law.

Section 4. The Times, Places and Manner of holding Elections for Senators and Representatives, shall be prescribed in each State by the Legislature thereof; but the Congress may at any time by Law make or alter such Regulations, except as to the Places of choosing Senators.

The Congress shall assemble at least once in every Year, and such Meeting shall be on the first Monday in December, unless they shall by Law appoint a different Day.[4]

Section 5. Each House shall be the Judge of the Elections, Returns and Qualifications of its own Members, and a Majority of each shall constitute a Quorum to do Business; but a smaller Number may adjourn from day to day, and may be authorized to compel the Attendance of absent Members, in such Manner, and under such Penalties as each House may provide.

Each House may determine the Rules of its Proceedings, punish its Members for disorderly Behaviour; and, with the Concurrence of two thirds, expel a Member.

Each House shall keep a Journal of its Proceedings, and from time to time publish the same, excepting such parts as may in their Judgment require Secrecy; and the Yeas and Nays of the Members of either House on any question shall, at the Desire of one fifth of those Present, be entered on the Journal.

Neither House, during the Session of Congress, shall, without the Consent of the other, adjourn for more than three days, nor to any other Place than that in which the two Houses shall be sitting.

Section 6. The Senators and Representatives shall receive a Compensation for their Services, to be ascertained by Law, and paid out of the Treasury of the United States. They shall in all Cases, except Treason, Felony and Breach of the Peace, be privileged from Arrest during their Attendance at the Session of their respective Houses, and in going to and returning from the same; and for any Speech or Debate in either House, they shall not be questioned in any other Place.

No Senator or Representative shall, during the Time for which he was elected, be appointed to any civil Office under the Authority of the United States, which shall have been created, or the Emoluments whereof shall have been encreased during such time; and no Person holding any Officer under the United States, shall be a Member of either House during his Continuance in Office.

Section 7. All bills for raising Revenue shall originate in the House of Representatives; but the Senate may propose or concur with Amendments as on other Bills.

Every Bill which shall have passed the House of Representatives and the Senate, shall, before it become a Law, be presented to the President of the United States; if he approve he shall sign it, but if not he shall return it, with his Objections to that House in which it shall have originated, who shall enter the Objections at large on their Journal, and proceed to reconsider it. If after such Reconsideration two thirds of that House shall agree to pass the Bill, it shall be sent, together with the Objections, to the other House,

---

[3]See Seventeenth Amendment.
[4]See Twentieth Amendment.

by which it shall likewise be reconsidered, and if approved by two thirds of that House, it shall become a Law. But in all such Cases the Votes of both Houses shall be determined by Yeas and Nays, and the Names of the Persons voting for and against the Bill shall be entered on the Journal of each House respectively. If any Bill shall not be returned by the President within ten Days (Sundays excepted) after it shall have been presented to him, the Same shall be a Law, in like Manner as if he had signed it, unless the Congress by their Adjournment prevent its Return, in which Case it shall not be a Law.

Every Order, Resolution, or Vote to which the Concurrence of the Senate and House of Representatives may be necessary (except on a question of Adjournment) shall be presented to the President of the United States; and before the Same shall take Effect, shall be approved by him, or, being disapproved by him, shall be repassed by two thirds of the Senate and House of Representatives, according to the Rules and Limitations prescribed in the Case of a Bill.

Section 8. The Congress shall have Power To lay and collect Taxes, Duties, Imposts and Excises, to pay the Debts and provide for the common Defence and general Welfare of the United States; but all Duties, Imposts and Excises shall be uniform throughout the United States.

To borrow Money on the credit of the United States;

To regulate Commerce with foreign Nations, and among the several States, and with the Indian Tribes;

To establish an uniform rule of Naturalization, and uniform Laws on the subject of Bankruptcies throughout the United States;

To coin Money, regulate the Value thereof, and of foreign Coin, and fix the Standard of Weights and Measures;

To provide for the Punishment of counterfeiting the Securities and current Coin of the United States;

To establish Post Offices and post Roads;

To promote the Progress of Science and useful Arts, by securing for limited Times to Authors and Inventors the exclusive Right to their respective Writings and Discoveries;

To constitute Tribunals inferior to the Supreme Court;

To define and punish Piracies and Felonies committed on the high Seas, and Offences against the Law of Nations;

To declare War, grant Letters of Marque and Reprisal, and make Rules concerning Captures on Land and Water;

To raise and support Armies, but no Appropriation of Money to that Use shall be for a longer Term than two Years;

To provide and maintain a Navy;

To make Rules for the Government and Regulation of the land and naval Forces;

To provide for calling forth the Militia to execute the Laws of the Union, suppress Insurrections and repel Invasions;

To provide for organizing, arming, and disciplining, the Militia, and for governing such Part of them as may be employed in the Service of the United States, reserving to the States respectively, the Appointment of the Officers, and the Authority of training the Militia according to the discipline prescribed by Congress;

To exercise exclusive Legislation in all Cases whatsoever, over such District (not exceeding ten Miles square) as may, by Cession of particular States, and the Acceptance of Congress, become the Seat of the Government of the United States, and to exercise like Authority over all Places purchased by the Consent of the Legislature of the State in which the Same shall be, for the Erection of Forts, Magazines, Arsenals, dock-Yards, and other needful Buildings;—And

To make all Laws which shall be necessary and proper for carrying into Execution the foregoing Powers, and all other Powers vested by this Constitution in the Government of the United States, or in any Department or Officer thereof.

Section 9. The Migration or Importation of such Persons as any of the States now existing shall think proper to admit, shall not be prohibited by the Congress prior to the Year one thousand eight hundred and eight, but a Tax or duty may be imposed on such Importation, not exceeding ten dollars for each Person.

The Privilege of the Writ of Habeas Corpus shall not be suspended, unless when in Cases of Rebellion or Invasion the public Safety may require it.

No Bill of Attainder or ex post facto Law shall be passed.

No Capitation, or other direct, Tax shall be laid, unless in Proportion to the Census or Enumeration herein before directed to be taken.

No Tax or Duty shall be laid on Articles exported from any State.

No Preference shall be given by any Regulation of Commerce or Revenue to the Ports of one State over those of another: nor shall Vessels bound to, or from, one State, be obliged to enter, clear, or pay Duties in another.

No Money shall be drawn from the Treasury, but in Consequence of Appropriations made by Law; and a regular Statement and Account of the Receipts and Expenditures of all public Money shall be published from time to time.

No title of Nobility shall be granted by the United States: And no Person holding any Office of Profit or Trust under them, shall, without the Consent of Congress, accept of any present, Emolument, Office, or Title, of any kind whatever, from any King, Prince, or foreign State.

Section 10. No State shall enter into any Treaty, Alliance, or Confederation; grant Letters of Marque and Reprisal; coin Money; emit bills of Credit; make any Thing but gold and silver coin a Tender in Payment of Debts; pass any Bill of Attainder, ex post facto Law, or Law impairing the Obligation of Contracts, or Grant any Title of Nobility.

No State shall, without the Consent of the Congress, lay any Imposts or Duties on Imports or Exports, except what may be absolutely necessary for executing its inspection Laws: and the net Produce of all Duties and Imposts, laid by any State on Imports or Exports, shall be for the Use of the Treasury of the United States; and all such Laws shall be subject to the Revision and Control of the Congress.

No State shall, without the Consent of Congress, lay any Duty of Tonnage, keep Troops, or Ships of War in time of Peace, enter into any Agreement or Compact with another State, or with a foreign Power, or engage in War, unless actually invaded, or in such imminent Danger as will not admit of delay.

Article II

Section 1. The executive Power shall be vested in a President of the United States of America. He shall hold his Office during the Term of four Years, and, together with the Vice President, chosen for the same Term be elected as follows:

Each State shall appoint, in such Manner as the Legislature thereof may direct, a Number of Electors, equal to the whole Number of Senators and Representatives to which the State may be entitled in the Congress but no Senator or Representative, or Person holding an Office of Trust or Profit under the United States, shall be appointed an Elector.

The Electors shall meet in their respective States, and vote by Ballot for two Persons, of whom one at least shall not be an Inhabitant of the same State with themselves. And they shall make a List of all the persons voted for, and of the Number of Votes for each; which List they shall sign and certify, and transmit sealed to the Seat of the Government of the United States, directed to the President of the Senate. The President of the Senate shall, in the Presence of the Senate and House of Representatives, open all the Certificates, and the Votes shall then be counted. The Person having the greatest Number of Votes shall be the President, if such Number be a Majority of the whole Number of Electors appointed; and if there be more than one who have such Majority, and have an equal Number of Votes, then the House of Representatives shall immediately choose by Ballot one of them for President; and if no Person have a Majority, then from the five highest on the List the said House shall in like Manner choose the President. But in choosing the President, the Votes shall be taken by States, the Representation from each State having one Vote; a quorum for this purpose shall consist of a Member or Members from two thirds of the States, and a Majority of all the States shall be necessary to a Choice. In every Case, after the Choice of the President, the Person having the greatest Number of Votes of the Electors shall be the Vice President. But if there should remain two or more who have equal Votes, the Senate shall choose from them by Ballot the Vice President.[5]

The Congress may determine the Time of choosing the Electors, and the Day on which they shall give their Votes; which Day shall be the same throughout the United States.

No person except a natural born Citizen, or a Citizen of the United States, at the time of the Adop-

---

[5]Superseded by the Twelfth Amendment.

tion of this Constitution, shall be eligible to the Office of President; neither shall any Person be eligible to that Office who shall not have attained to the Age of thirty five Years, and been fourteen Years a Resident within the United States.

In Case of the Removal of the President from Office, or of his Death, Resignation, or Inability to discharge the Powers and Duties of the said Office, the Same shall devolve on the Vice President, and the Congress may by Law provide for the Case of Removal, Death, Resignation or Inability, both of the President and Vice President, declaring what Officer shall then act as President, and such Officer shall act accordingly, until the Disability be removed, or a President shall be elected.[6]

The President shall, at stated Times, receive for his Services, a Compensation which shall neither be encreased nor diminished during the Period for which he shall have been elected, and he shall not receive within that period any other Emolument from the United States, or any of them.

Before he enter on the Execution of his Office, he shall take the following Oath or Affirmation:—"I do solemnly swear (or affirm) that I will faithfully execute the Office of President of the United States, and will to the best of my Ability, preserve, protect and defend the Constitution of the United States."

Section 2. The President shall be Commander in Chief of the Army and Navy of the United States, and of the Militia of the several States, when called into the actual service of the United States; he may require the Opinion, in writing, of the principal Officer in each of the executive Departments, upon any Subject relating to the Duties of their respective Offices, and he shall have Power to grant Reprieves and Pardons for Offences against the United States, except in Cases of Impeachment.

He shall have Power, by and with the Advice and Consent of the Senate, to make Treaties, provided two thirds of the Senators present concur; and he shall nominate, and by and with the Advice and Consent of the Senate, shall appoint Ambassadors, other public Ministers and Consuls, Judges of the Supreme Court, and all other Officers of the United States, whose Appointments are not herein otherwise provided for,

[6]See Twenty-fifth Amendment.

and which shall be established by Law: but the Congress may by Law vest the Appointment of such inferior officers, as they think proper, in the President alone, in the Courts of Law, or in the Heads of Departments.

The President shall have Power to fill up all Vacancies that may happen during the Recess of the Senate, by granting Commissions which shall expire at the End of their next Session.

Section 3. He shall from time to time give to the Congress Information of the State of the Union, and recommend to their Consideration such Measures as he shall judge necessary and expedient; he may, on extraordinary Occasions, convene both Houses, or either of them, and in Case of Disagreement between them, with Respect to the Time of Adjournment, he may adjourn them to such Time as he shall think proper; he shall receive Ambassadors and other public Ministers, he shall take Care that the Laws be faithfully executed, and shall Commission all the Officers of the United States.

Section 4. The President, Vice President, and all civil Officers of the United States, shall be removed from Office on Impeachment for, and Conviction of Treason, Bribery, or other high Crimes and Misdemeanors.

Article III

Section 1. The judicial Power of the United States, shall be vested in one Supreme Court and in such inferior Courts as the Congress may from time to time ordain and establish. The Judges, both of the Supreme and inferior Courts, shall hold their Offices during good Behaviour, and shall, at stated Times, receive for their Services, a Compensation, which shall not be diminished during their Continuance in Office.

Section 2. The judicial Power shall extend to all Cases, in Law and Equity, arising under this Constitution, the Laws of the United States, and Treaties made, or which shall be made, under their Authority;—to all Cases affecting Ambassadors, other public Ministers and Consuls;—to all Cases of admiralty and maritime Jurisdiction;—to Controversies to which the United States shall be a Party;—to

Controversies between two or more States;—*between a State and Citizens of another State*[7];—between Citizens of different States;—between Citizens of the same State claiming Lands under Grants of different States, *and between a State or the Citizens thereof, and foreign States, Citizens, or Subjects.*[8]

In all cases affecting Ambassadors, other public Ministers and Consuls, and those in which a State shall be Party, the Supreme Court shall have original Jurisdiction. In all the other Cases before mentioned, the Supreme Court shall have appellate Jurisdiction, both as to Law and Fact, with such Exceptions, and under such Regulations as the Congress shall make.

The Trial of all Crimes, except in Cases of Impeachment, shall be by Jury; and such Trial shall be held in the State where the said Crimes shall have been committed; but when not committed within any State, the Trial shall be at such Place or Places as the Congress may by Law have directed.

Section 3. Treason against the United States, shall consist only in levying War against them, or in adhering to their Enemies, giving them Aid and Comfort. No person shall be convicted of treason unless on the Testimony of two Witnesses to the same overt Act, or on Confession in open Court.

The Congress shall have Power to declare the Punishment of Treason, but no Attainder of Treason shall work Corruption of Blood, or Forfeiture except during the Life of the Person attainted.

Article IV

Section 1. Full Faith and Credit shall be given in each State to the public Acts, Records, and judicial Proceedings of every other State. And the Congress may by general laws prescribe the Manner in which such Acts, Records and Proceedings shall be proved, and the Effect thereof.

Section 2. The Citizens of each State shall be entitled to all Privileges and Immunities of Citizens in the several States.

A Person charged in any State with Treason, Felony, or other Crime, who shall flee from Justice, and be found in another State, shall on Demand of the executive Authority of the State from which he fled, be delivered up, to be removed to the State having Jurisdiction of the Crime.

No person held to Service or Labour in one State, under the Laws thereof, escaping into another, shall, in Consequence of any Law or Regulation therein, be discharged from such Service or Labour, but shall be delivered up on Claim of the Party to whom such Service or Labour may be due.[9]

Section 3. New States may be admitted by the Congress into this Union; but no new State shall be formed or erected within the Jurisdiction of any other State; nor any State be formed by the Jurisdiction of two or more States, or Parts of States, without the Consent of the Legislature of the States concerned as well as of the Congress.

The Congress shall have Power to dispose of and make all needful Rules and Regulations respecting the Territory or other Property belonging to the United States; and nothing in this Constitution shall be so construed as to Prejudice any claims of the United States, or of any particular State.

Section 4. The United States shall guarantee to every State in this Union a Republican Form of Government, and shall protect each of them against Invasion; and on Application of the Legislature, or of the Executive (when the Legislature cannot be convened) against domestic Violence.

Article V

The Congress, whenever two thirds of both Houses shall deem it necessary, shall propose Amendments to this Constitution, or, on the Application of the Legislatures of two thirds of the several States, shall call a Convention for proposing Amendments, which, in either Case, shall be valid to all Intents and Purposes, as Part of this Constitution, when ratified by the Legislatures of three fourths of the several States, or by Conventions in three fourths thereof, as the one or the other Mode of Ratification may be proposed by the Congress; Provided that no Amendment which may be made prior to the Year one thou-

---

[7] See Eleventh Amendment.
[8] See Eleventh Amendment.

[9] See Thirteenth Amendment.

sand eight hundred and eight shall in any Manner affect the first and fourth Clauses in the Ninth Section of the first Article; and that no State, without its Consent, shall be deprived of its equal Suffrage in the Senate.

Article VI

All Debts contracted and Engagements entered into, before the Adoption of this Constitution, shall be as valid against the United States under this Constitution, as under the Confederation.

This Constitution, and the laws of the United States which shall be made in Pursuance thereof; and all Treaties made, or which shall be made, under the Authority of the United States, shall be the supreme Law of the Land; and the Judges in every State shall be bound thereby, any Thing in the Constitution or Laws of any State to the Contrary notwithstanding.

The Senators and Representatives before mentioned, and the Members of the several State Legislatures, and all executive and judicial Officers, both of the United States and of the several States, shall be bound by Oath or Affirmation, to support this Constitution; but no religious Test shall ever be required as a Qualification to any Office or public Trust under the United States.

Article VII

The Ratification of the Conventions of nine States, shall be sufficient for the Establishment of this Constitution between the States so ratifying the Same.

Done in Convention by the Unanimous Consent of the States present the Seventeenth Day of September in the Year of our Lord one thousand seven hundred and eighty seven and of the Independence of the United States of America the twelfth. In witness whereof We have hereunto subscribed our Names.

ARTICLES IN ADDITION TO, AND AMENDMENT OF, THE CONSTITUTION OF THE UNITED STATES OF AMERICA, PROPOSED BY CONGRESS, AND RATIFIED BY THE SEVERAL STATES, PURSUANT TO THE FIFTH ARTICLE OF THE ORIGINAL CONSTITUTION.

Amendment I

[Ratification of the first ten amendments was completed December 15, 1791.]

Congress shall make no law respecting an establishment of religion, or prohibiting the free exercise thereof; or abridging the freedom of speech, or of the press; or the right of the people peaceably to assemble, and to petition the Government for a redress of grievances.

Amendment II

A well regulated Militia, being necessary to the security of a free State, the right of the people to keep and bear Arms, shall not be infringed.

Amendment III

No Soldier shall, in time of peace be quartered in any house, without the consent of the Owner, nor in time of war, but in a manner to be prescribed by law.

Amendment IV

The right of the people to be secure in their persons, houses, papers, and effects, against unreasonable searches and seizures, shall not be violated, and no Warrants shall issue, but upon probable cause, supported by Oath or affirmation, and particularly describing the place to be searched, and the persons or things to be seized.

Amendment V

No person shall be held to answer for capital, or otherwise infamous crime, unless on a presentment or indictment of a Grand Jury, except in cases arising in the land or naval forces, or in the Militia, when in actual service in time of War or public danger; nor shall any person be subject for the same offence to be twice put in jeopardy of life or limb; nor shall be compelled in any criminal case to be a witness against himself, nor be deprived of life, liberty, or property, without due process of law; nor shall private property be taken for public use, without just compensation.

Amendment VI

In all criminal prosecutions, the accused shall enjoy the right to a speedy and public trial, by an impartial jury of the State and district wherein the crime shall have been committed, which district shall have been previously ascertained by law, and to be informed of the nature and cause of the accusation; to be confronted with the witnesses agianst him; to have compulsory process for obtaining witnesses in his favor, and to have the Assistance of Counsel for his defence.

Amendment VII

In Suits at common law, where the value in controversy shall exceed twenty dollars, the right of trial by jury shall be preserved, and no fact tried by jury, shall be otherwise reexamined in any Court of the United States, than according to the rules of the common law.

Amendment VIII

Excessive bail shall not be required, nor excessive fines imposed, nor cruel and unusual punishments inflicted.

Amendment IX

The enumeration in the Constitution, of certain rights, shall not be construed to deny or disparage others retained by the people.

Amendment X

The powers not delegated to the United States by the Constitution, nor prohibited by it to the States, are reserved to the States respectively, or to the people.

Amendment XI (1798)

The judicial power of the United States shall not be construed to extend to any suit in law or equity, commenced or prosecuted against one of the United States by Citizens of another State, or by Citizens or Subjects of any Foreign States.

Amendment XII (1804)

The Electors shall meet in their respective states and vote by ballot for President and Vice President, one of whom, at least, shall not be an inhabitant of the same state with themselves; they shall name in their ballots the person voted for as President, and in distinct ballots the person voted for as Vice President, and they shall make distinct lists of all persons voted for as President, and of all persons voted for as Vice President, and of the number of votes for each, which lists they shall sign and certify, and transmit sealed to the seat of the government of the United State, directed to the President of the Senate;—The President of the Senate shall, in the presence of Senate and House of Representatives, open all the certificates and the votes shall then be counted;—The person having the greatest number of votes for President, shall be the President, if such number be a majority of the whole number of Electors appointed; and if no person have such majority, then from the persons having the highest numbers not exceeding three on the list of those voted for as President, the House of Representatives shall choose immediately, by ballot, the President. But in choosing the President, the votes shall be taken by states, the representation from each state having one vote; a quorum for this purpose shall consist of a member or members from two thirds of the states, and a majority of all the states shall be necessary to a choice. And if the House of Representatives shall not choose a President whenever the right of choice shall devolve upon them, *before the fourth day of March next following,*[10] then the Vice President shall act as President, as in the case of the death or other constitutional disability of the President.—The person having the greatest number of votes as Vice President shall be the Vice President, if such number be a majority of the whole number of Electors appointed, and if no person have a majority, then from the two highest numbers on the list, the Senate shall choose the Vice President; a quorum for the purpose shall consist of two-thirds of the whole number of Senators, and a majority of the whole number shall be necessary to a choice. But no person constitutionally ineligible to the office of President shall be eligible to that of Vice President of the United States.

[10] Altered by the Twentieth Amendment.

Amendment XIII (1865)

Section 1. Neither slavery nor involuntary servitude, except as a punishment for crime whereof the party shall have been duly convicted, shall exist within the United States, or any place subject to their jurisdiction.

Section 2. Congress shall have the power to enforce this article by appropriate legislation.

Amendment XIV (1869)

Section 1. All persons born or naturalized in the United States, and subject to the jurisdiction thereof, are citizens of the United States and of the State wherein they reside. No State shall make or enforce any law which shall abridge the privileges or immunities of citizens of the United States; nor shall any State deprive any person of life, liberty, or property, without due process of law; nor deny to any person within its jurisdiction the equal protection of the laws.

Section 2. Representatives shall be apportioned among the several States according to their respective numbers, counting the whole number of persons in each State, excluding Indians not taxed. But when the right to vote at any election for the choice of electors for President and Vice President of the United States, Representatives in Congress, the Executive and Judicial officers of a State, or the members of the Legislature thereof, is denied to any of the male inhabitants of such State, being twenty-one years of age, and citizens of the United States, or in any way abridged, except for participation in rebellion, or other crime, the basis of representation therein shall be reduced in the proportion which the number of such male citizens shall bear to the whole number of male citizens twenty-one years of age in such State.

Section 3. No person shall be a Senator or Representative in Congress, or elector of President or Vice President, or hold any office, civil or military, under the United States, or under any State, who, having previously taken an oath, as a member of Congress, or as an officer of the United States, or as a member of any State legislature, or as an executive or judicial officer of any State, to support the Constitution of the United States, shall have engaged in insurrection or rebellion against the same, or given aid or comfort to the enemies thereof. But Congress may by a vote of two thirds of each House, remove such disability.

Section 4. The validity of the public debt of the United States, authorized by law, including debts incurred for payment of pensions and bounties for services in suppressing insurrection or rebellion, shall not be questioned. But neither the United States nor any State shall assume or pay any debt or obligation incurred in aid of insurrection or rebellion against the United States, or any claim for the loss or emancipation of any slave; but all such debts, obligations, and claims shall be held illegal and void.

Section 5. The Congress shall have power to enforce, by appropriate legislation, the provisions of this article.

Amendment XV (1870)

Section 1. The right of citizens of the United States to vote shall not be denied or abridged by the United States or by any State on account of race, color, or previous condition of servitude.

Section 2. The Congress shall have power to enforce this article by appropriate legislation

Amendment XVI (1913)

The Congress shall have power to lay and collect taxes on incomes, from whatever source derived, without apportionment among the several States, and without regard to any census or enumeration.

Amendment XVII (1913)

The Senate of the United States shall be composed of two Senators from each State, elected by the People thereof for six years; and each Senator shall have one vote. The electors in each State shall have the qualifications requisite for electors of the most numerous branch of the State legislatures.

When vacancies happen in the representation of any State in the Senate, the executive authority of such State shall issue writs of election to fill such vacancies: *Provided,* That the legislature of any State may empower the executive thereof to make temporary appointments until the people fill the vacancies by election as the legislature may direct.

This amendment shall not be so construed as to affect the election or term of any Senator chosen before it becomes valid as part of the Constitution.

Amendment XVIII (1919)

Section 1. *After one year from the ratification of this article the manufacture, sale, or transportation of intoxicating liquors within, the importation thereof into, or the exportation thereof from the United States and all territory subject to the jurisdiction thereof for beverage purposes is hereby prohibited.*

Section 2. *The Congress and the several States shall have concurrent power to enforce this article by appropriate legislation.*

Section 3. *This article shall be inoperative unless it shall have been ratified as an amendment to the Constitution by the legislatures of the several States, as provided in the Constitution, within seven years from the date of the submission hereof to the States by the Congress.*[11]

Amendment XIX (1920)

The right of citizens of the United States to vote shall not be denied or abridged by the United States or by any state on account of sex.

Congress shall have power to enforce this article by appropriate legislation.

Amendment XX (1933)

Section 1. The terms of the President and Vice President shall end at noon on the 20th day of January, and the terms of Senators and Representatives at noon on the 3rd day of January, of the years in which such terms would have ended if this article had not been ratified; and the terms of their successors shall then begin.

Section 2. The Congress shall assemble at least once in every year, and such meeting shall begin at noon on the 3rd day of January, unless they shall by law appoint a different day.

Section 3. If, at the time fixed for the beginning of the term of the President, the President elect shall have died, the Vice President elect shall become President. If a President shall not have been chosen before the time fixed for the beginning of his term, or if the President elect shall have failed to qualify, then the Vice President elect shall act as President until a President shall have qualified; and the Congress may by law provide for the case wherein neither President elect nor a Vice President elect shall have qualified, declaring who shall then act as President, or the manner in which one who is to act shall be selected, and such person shall act accordingly until a President or Vice President shall have qualified.

Section 4. The Congress may by law provide for the case of the death of any of the persons from whom the House of Representatives may choose a President whenever the right of choice shall have devolved upon them, and for the case of the death of any of the persons from whom the Senate may choose a Vice President whenever the right of choice shall have devolved upon them.

Section 5. Section 1 and 2 shall take effect on the 15th day of October following the ratification of this article.

Amendment XXI (1933)

Section 1. The eighteenth article of amendment to the Constitution of the United States is hereby repealed.

Section 2. The transportation or importation into any State, Territory, or possession of the United States for delivery or use therein of intoxicating liquors, in violation of the laws thereof, is hereby prohibited.

Section 3. This article shall be inoperative unless it shall have been ratified as an amendment to the Constitution by conventions in the several States, as provided in the Constitution, within seven years from the date of the submission hereof to the States by the Congress.

---

[11] Repealed by the Twenty-first Amendment.

Amendment XXII (1951)

Section 1. No person shall be elected to the office of the President more than twice, and no person who has held the office of President, or acted as President, for more than two years of a term to which some other person was elected President shall be elected to the office of President more than once. But this Article shall not apply to any person holding the office of President when this Article was proposed by Congress, and shall not prevent any person who may be holding the office of President, or acting as President, during the term within which this Article becomes operative from holding the office of President or acting as President during the remainder of such term.

Section 2. This article shall be inoperative unless it shall have been ratified as an amendment to the Constitution by the legislatures of three fourths of the several States within seven years from the date of its submission to the States by Congress.

Amendment XXIII (1961)

Section 1. The District constituting the seat of Government of the United States shall appoint in such manner as the Congress may direct:

A number of electors of President and Vice President equal to the whole number of Senators and Representatives in Congress to which the District would be entitled if it were a State, but in no event more than the least populous State; they shall be in addition to those appointed by the States, but they shall be considered, for the purposes of the election of President and Vice President, to be electors appointed by a State; and they shall meet in the District and perform such duties as provided by the twelfth article of amendment.

Section 2. The Congress shall have power to enforce this article by appropriate legislation.

Amendment XXIV (1964)

Section 1. The right of citizens of the United States to vote in any primary or other election for President or Vice President, for electors for President or Vice President, or for Senator or Representative in Congress, shall not be denied or abridged by the United States or any state by reason of failure to pay any poll tax or other tax.

Section 2. The Congress shall have power to enforce this article by appropriate legislation.

Amendment XXV (1967)

Section 1. In case of the removal of the President from office or of his death or resignation, the Vice President shall become President.

Section 2. Whenever there is a vacancy in the office of the Vice President, the President shall nominate a Vice President who shall take office upon confirmation by a majority vote of both Houses of Congress.

Section 3. Whenever the President transmits to the President pro tempore of the Senate and the Speaker of the House of Representatives his written declaration that he is unable to discharge the powers and duties of his office, and until he transmits to them a written declaration to the contrary, such powers and duties shall be discharged by the Vice President as Acting President.

Section 4. Whenever the Vice President and a majority of either the principal officers of the executive departments or of such other body as Congress may by law provide, transmit to the President pro tempore of the Senate and the Speaker of the House of Representatives their written declaration that the President is unable to discharge the powers and duties of his office, the Vice President shall immediately assume the powers and duties of the office as Acting President.

Thereafter, when the president transmits to the President pro tempore of the Senate and the Speaker of the House of Representative his written declaration that no inability exists, he shall resume the powers and duties of his office unless the Vice President and a majority of either the principal officers of the executive departments or of such other body as Congress may by law provide, transmit within four days to the President pro tempore of the Senate and the Speaker of the House of Representatives their written declaration that the President is unable to discharge the powers and duties of his office. Thereupon Congress shall decide the issue, assembling within forty-eight hours for that purpose if not in session. If the Congress, within twenty-one days after receipt of the latter written declaration, or, if Congress is not in session, within twenty-one days after Congress is required to assemble, determines by two-thirds vote of both Houses that the President is unable to discharge the powers and duties of his office, the Vice President shall continue to discharge the same as Acting President; otherwise, the President shall resume the powers and duties of his office.

Amendment XXVI (1971)

Section 1. The right of citizens of the United States, who are 18 years of age or older, to vote shall not be denied or abridged by the United States or any state on account of age.

Section 2. The Congress shall have power to enforce this article by appropriate legislation.

Index

ABA, *see* American Bar Association
Abraham, Henry J., 134
ACLU, *see* American Civil Liberties Union
ACTION, 156
Adams, Brock, 17
Adams, John, 25, 30, 111, 147
Adams, John Quincy, 24
Adams, Sherman, 32
Adolph Coors Company, 174
Afghanistan, 4
Afroyin v. *Rusk*, 112
Agnew, Spiro, 29, 30
Agriculture, Department of, 36, 144
Albert, Carl, 69
Allen, Richard, 38
AMA, *see* American Medical Association
American Bar Association, 106, 122, 128
American Civil Liberties Union, 133
American Communist Party, 61
American Independence Party, 26
American Legion, 156, 168
American Medical Association, 168
American Paper Institute, 174
Amicus curiae briefs, 133
Annunzio, Frank, 74
Argersinger v. *Hamlin*, 115
Army of the Potomac, 2
Arthur, Chester, 159
Aspin, Les, 74, 76
Association of American Railroads v. *Costle*, 138

Baker, Howard, 71, 99, 100, 101
Baker, James, 147
Baker v. *Carr*, 121
Ball, Howard, 134
Barbary Wars, 3
Barron v. *Baltimore*, 114
Barser, Harold, 44
Baum, Lawrence, 134
Bill of Rights, 85, 114, 120, 132
Blackmun, Harry, 124, 126, 127
Blumenthal, W. Michael, 17
Bowsher, Charles, 60
Brademas, John, 70

Brandeis, Louis, 127
Breaux, John, 18
Brennan, William, 126-127, 128
Brewer v. *Williams*, 116
Brown v. *Board of Education of Topeka, Kansas*, 114-115, 118, 127
Brzezinski, Zbigniew, 38
Buchanan, James, 24
Buckley v. *Valeo*, 112
Budget and Accounting Act of 1921, 13
Budget and Impoundment Control Act of 1974, 10, 13, 91-92, 93, 96
Budgetary process, 90-93, 96
Bundy, McGeorge, 38
Burch, Dean, 152
Bureau of the Budget, *see* Office of Management and Budget
Bureaucracy:
   appointive policy-making positions, 160
   autonomy of units within departments, 148-149
   characteristics of, 142-143
   civil service, 159-160
   extragovernmental influences on, 168
   general schedule pay system, 161-162
   government influences on, 163-165
   institutional loyalty, 169-170
   internal influences on, 169-170
   leadership and limitations, 163-170
   organization, 143-159
   personnel, 160-161
   relations with Congress, 165-167
   relations with the judiciary, 167
   relations with the president, 163-165
   size, 1, 14-15
   specialization, 169
   spoils system, 159
   successes, 170
   tasks, 170-171
Burford, Anne, 136-138, 158, 173-174, 176
Burger, Warren, 124, 126, 127
Burger Court, 112, 116, 124
Burr, Aaron, 24-25
Bush, George, 31, 42, 68
Butterfield, Alexander, 33
Byrd, Robert, 68, 71, 82, 99, 101

192 Index

CAB, *see* Civil Aeronautics Board
Cabinet, 35–36, 143–149
  as advisory body, 36
  autonomous units within departments, 148–149
  characteristics of members, 146–148
  growth, 36, 144, 146
  line of presidential succession, 28
  origins, 35
Calendar Wednesday, 87
Califano, Joseph, 17
Cannon, Joe, 68
Carswell, G. Harrold, 124, 128
Carter, Jimmy, 26, 27, 44, 71, 125, 146, 148, 152, 165
  amnesty program, 165–166
  appointment of ambassadors, 8
  cabinet members, firing of, 17
  as commander in chief, 2
  elections, 27
  judicial appointments, 125
  merit appointments, 8
  national security adviser, use of, 38
  National Security Council, use of, 40
  organizational style, 34–35
  pocket vetoes by, 55
  power to pardon, use of, 15–16
  reorganization of the EOP, 41–42
  and Superfund law, 45–48, 94–100, 135–141, 172–175
  as treaty negotiator, 5
  vetoes by, 54
  vice-presidential role, expansion of, 31
  White House staff, use of, 34, 37
CBO, *see* Congressional Budget Office
Central Intelligence Agency:
  duties, 40
  role in Watergate affair, 33
  selection of director, 40
CEQ, *see* Council on Environmental Quality
CERCLA, *see* Superfund law
Chafee, John, 82
Chamber of Commerce, 168
Chase, Samuel, 108
Chemical Manufacturers' Association, 97, 174
China, 9, 43
Chisholm, Shirley, 82
CIA, *see* Central Intelligence Agency
Citizens for Kennedy, 127
Civil Aeronautics Board, 154
Civil Rights Act of 1964, 89
Civil service, 159–163
  creation, 159
  distribution of personnel, 161
  salaries, 162
  spoils system, 159
Civil Service Reform Act of 1883, 14, 160
Civil War, 109, 112
Clark, William, 38
Cleveland, Grover, 24, 54
Cloture, 89

CMA, *see* Chemical Manufacturers' Association
Coast Guard, 140
Commerce, Department of, 36, 144, 170
  Subcommittee on Transportation, 95
Commerce clause, 52–53
Commission on Drug Abuse, 42
Commission on Obscenity and Pornography, 42
Commissions within EOP, 41–42
Committee for the Reelection of the President, 33
Committee of the Whole House, 88
Comprehensive Environmental Response, Compensation and Liability Act, *see* Superfund law
Congress, *see also* House of Representatives; Senate
  activities of members, 66–67
  adjournment, 12
  appellate jurisdiction, right to limit, 109
  apportionment, 62–63
  appropriations, 90, 166
  authority to police itself, 55–57
  authorizing legislation, 90, 166
  bill, introduction of, 84
  bill becomes law, 84–90
  budgetary process, 90–93
  bureaucracy, relations with, 165–167
  cabinet departments, right to establish and abolish, 144, 146
  calendars, 87, 88
  campaign contributions, power to regulate, 57
  characteristics of members, 64–65
  committee actions on bills, 86
  committee chairpersons, 73–76
  committee meetings, 59, 66
  committees, 77–84
  conference committees, 89–90
  constituent service, 66–67
  constitutional amendments, 109
  constitutional prerogatives, 51–57
  court system, power to organize, 106
  dependence on president for implementation, 9–10
  electoral procedures, 56–57, 62–63
  executive agreements, concern with, 8
  government policy, legitimation of, 60
  hearings, 59
  House and Senate compared, 62–63, 72–73
  impeach and try, authority to, 55
  independent executive agencies, right to establish, 155, 156
  independent regulatory commissions, creation of, 149
  issue creation and clarification, 59
  joint committees, 83
  judiciary, control over size of, 109–110
  lawmaking, 61
  leaders, 67–76
  leadership roles, 57–61
  Legal Services Corporation preserved, 164, 166
  lobby registrations, requirements of, 56
  mark-up sessions, 59
  military affairs, role in, 3–4
  oversight of the executive branch, 59–60

Index

Congress *(continued)*
  party caucuses, 72–73
  presidential executive orders, right to object to, 41
  presidential power, role in expansion of, 13
  presidential vetoes, right to override, 53
  reforms of 1970s, 93
  rejection of initial Superfund proposal, 46–47, 95
  reorganizations of EOP, right to reject, 41
  representation, 57–59
  salaries, 55–56
  seniority system, 76–77
  session length, 1
  size, 63
  special committees, 83
  staff, 84
  subcommittee actions on bills, 86
  subpoena power, 83–84
  Superfund passage, 95–104
  veto overrides, 54, 90
Congressional Budget Office, 60, 93
Congressional-executive agreements, 5, 7
Congressional Quarterly, 94, 135
Congressional Record, 140
Consent Calendar, 87, 88
Conservatism, 58
Constitution, *see also* Amendments (listed by number)
  authority of the judicial system, 110–111
  commerce clause, 52–53
  elastic clause, 53
  framework of change, 1
  granting of specific powers, 52
  supremacy clause, 113
Constitutional Convention, 1, 3, 111, 159
Continental Congress, 25
Conventions, 26
Coolidge, Calvin, 19
Coors Co., Adolph, 174
Costle, Douglas, 46
Council of Economic Advisers, 39–40, 41, 93
Council on Environmental Quality, 48, 137
Council on Wage and Price Stability, 42
Courts:
  administrative courts, 106, 108, 131–132
  Court of Claims, 131
  Court of Customs and Patent Appeals, 131
  Court of International Trade, 108, 131
  Court of Military Appeals, 106, 108, 131–132
  courts of appeals, 108, 121–122, 124–125, 130
  district courts, 106, 121, 122, 124–125, 130–131
  special judicial courts, 131
  Tax Court, 108, 131
  territorial courts, 108, 131–132
COWPS, *see* Council on Wage and Price Stability
Cranston, Alan, 68, 72
CREEP, *see* Committee for the Reelection of the President
Crime Control Act of 1976, 148
Cuba, 9
Cuban Missile Crisis, 40

Culver, John, 98, 100

Danforth, John, 75
Daniel, John, 174
Darby, Fred, 52
Davis, John W., 25
Davis, Swep, 97
Deering, Christopher, 94
Defense, Department of, 155, 161, 163, 167, 169, 171
de la Garza, E. (Kika), 74
Dellums, Ronald, 74
Democratic National Committee, 33
Democratic Republicans, 159
Democratic Steering and Policy Committee, 69, 72, 81
DiClerico, Robert, 44
Dingell, John, 74
Discharge Calendar, 88
Dixiecrat Party, 26
Dixon, Julian, 74
Dodd, Lawrence, 94
Doe v. *Bolton,* 116
Dole, Elizabeth, 147
Dole, Robert, 65, 68, 71, 104
Domenici, Pete, 75
Douglas, William O., 128
Doyle v. *Ohio,* 116
Dred Scott case, 112

Eckart, Dennis, 50
Eckhardt, Bob, 103
EDF, *see* Environmental Defense Fund
Education, Department of, 146, 147
Edwards, George, 44
Ehrlichman, John, 40
1887 Act to Regulate Commerce, 151
Eisenhower, Dwight D., 169
  cabinet, use of, 31, 36
  as commander in chief, 3
  National Security Council, use of, 40
  Supreme Court appointments, 124, 126
  White House staff, use of, 34, 37
Elastic clause, 53
Electoral College, 24–27
Eleventh Amendment, 109
El Salvador, 60
Employment Act of 1946, 13, 39
Energy, Department of, 146, 147
Energy Research and Development Administration, 146
Engle v. *Vitale,* 119
Environmental Action, 97
Environmental Defense Fund, 138–139, 174
Environmental Protection Agency:
  environmental groups, relations with, 169
  National Contingency Plan, responsible for, 48–49, 173
  organization, 158
  regional headquarters, 155–156
  response to *Lesniak* case, 136
  size, 156

Environmental Protection Agency *(continued)*
  sued to force promulgation of regulations, 174
  Superfund law, implementation of, 49, 158, 173–177
  tasks, 156
EOP, *see* Executive Office of the President
EPA, *see* Environmental Protection Agency
ERDA, *see* Energy Research and Development Administration
Ethics in Government Act of 1978, 65
Executive agreements, 5–8
Executive Calendar, 87, 88
Executive Office of the President, 36–42
Exxon, 174

Fair Labor Standards Act of 1938, 52
Farm Credit Administration, 155
Fauntroy, Walter, 65
FBI, *see* Federal Bureau of Investigation
FCC, *see* Federal Communications Commission
FDIC, *see* Federal Deposit Insurance Corporation
FEA, *see* Federal Energy Administration
Federal Bureau of Investigation:
  agents pardoned by Reagan, 16
  background checks on judicial nominees, 123
  impeded by Nixon, 33
  independence in Justice Department, 148
Federal Communications Commission, 152–154
Federal Deposit Insurance Corporation, 158
Federal Election Campaign Act, 112
Federal Energy Administration, 146
Federalists, 111
Federal Power Commission, 146
Federal Register, 138–139, 174
Federal Reserve Board, 153, 154–155
Federal Reserve System, 154
Federal Trade Commission, 153–154, 170
Federal Water Pollution Control Act, 48, 154
Ferraro, Geraldine, 24, 30
Field, Thornton, 174
Fifth Amendment, 84, 115
Filibuster, 89
Fillmore, Millard, 24
First Amendment, 56
First Budget Resolution, 92
Fishbourne, Benjamin, 77
Fisher, Linda, 177
Florio, James, 95, 97, 102, 103, 140
Foley, Thomas, 68, 70
Food stamps, 60
Ford, Gerald:
  efforts at trucking deregulation, 151–152
  election, 27
  judicial appointments, 123, 125, 126
  pardoning of Nixon, 15
  as party leader, 21
  succession to presidency, 29
  as treaty negotiator, 5
  vetoes by, 54, 55
  White House staff, use of, 37

Ford, William, 74
Fortas, Abe, 124, 127
Founding Fathers, 14, 62
Fourteenth Amendment, 114–115, 121
Fourth Amendment, 109
FPC, *see* Federal Power Commission
Frankfurter, Felix, 129
Friends of Animals, 133
FTC, *see* Federal Trade Commission
Fuqua, Don, 74

Gallatin, Albert, 159
GAO, *see* General Accounting Office
Garfield, James A., 14, 24, 28, 159
Garn, Jake, 75
Garner, John Nance, 30
Gay Activist Alliance, 61
General Accounting Office, 60, 166
General Schedule Pay System, 161
General Services Administration, 155–156
Gideon v. Wainwright, 115
Gitlow v. New York, 115
Goldwater, Barry, 75, 128
Government Corporation Control Act of 1945, 158
Government corporations, 158–159
Government Printing Office, 83
Granada, 4
Grant, Ulysses S., 24, 147, 159
Gray, William, 74
GSA, *see* General Services Administration
GS rating, *see* General Schedule Pay System
Guiteau, Charles, 159

Haig, Alexander, 15, 30, 38
Haldeman, H.R., 33, 40
Hamilton, Alexander, 24, 36, 159
Hammer v. Dagenhart, 117
Harding, Warren G., 28
Harris, Patricia, 147
Harris v. New York, 116
Harrison, William Henry, 24
Hatch, Orrin, 75
Hatch Act of 1940, 56–57
Hatfield, Mark, 75
Hawaii, annexation of, 6
Hawkins, Augustus F., 74
Hayden, Carl, 29
Hayes, Rutherford, 25
Haynesworth, Clement, 124
Health, Education, and Welfare, Department of, 144
Health and Human Services, Department of, 144, 147
Hedeman, William, 176
Helms, Jesse, 75, 101
Hepburn Act of 1906, 151
Hernandez, John, 174
Herrington, John, 147
Hickel, Walter, 36

Index

Hodel, Donald, 147
Holmes, Oliver Wendell Jr., 121
Hooker Chemical Company, 45
Hoover, Herbert, 23
Hoover, J. Edgar, 148
House Committees:
    Agriculture, 60, 74, 76
    Appropriations, 60, 61, 74, 77, 79
    Armed Services, 59, 74, 76
    Banking, Finance and Urban Affairs, 74, 76
    Budget, 74, 79
    District of Columbia, 74
    Education and Labor, 74
    Energy and Commerce, 74, 95, 103
    Foreign Affairs, 60, 74
    Government Operations, 74, 174
    House Administration, 74
    Interior and Insular Affairs, 74
    Judiciary, 21, 74, 79
    Merchant Marine and Fisheries, 74, 94
    Post Office and Civil Service, 74
    Public Works and Transportation, 74, 94
    Rules, 69, 77, 78, 79, 80
    Science and Technology, 74
    Small Business, 74
    Standards of Official Conduct, 74, 79, 80
    Ways and Means, 69, 77, 78-79, 80, 96-97, 103
    Veterans Affairs, 74
House of Representatives:
    appointments to committees, 81-82
    apportionment, 61-62
    calendars, 87-88
    committees, 77-80, 81-82
    Committee of the Whole, 88-89
    discharge petitions, 86-87
    floor procedures, 88-89
    majority leader, 69
    majority whip, 69-70
    minority leader, 70
    minority whip, 70
    reforms of 1970s, 69, 72
    right to impeach, 55
    role in choosing president, 24, 26
    subcommittees, 79-80
    tenure of members, 64-65
    voting procedures, 88
House Speaker:
    authorization in Constitution, 68
    coordinator of budget process, 69
    line of presidential succession, 29
    selection, 67-68
    strengthened by Democrats, 68-69
    succession to, by majority leader, 69
Housing and Urban Development, Department of, 35, 146, 147
Howard, James, 74
Hughes Court, 112
Humphrey, Hubert, 19
Hunt, E. Howard, 149

ICC, *see* Interstate Commerce Commission
Immigration and Naturalization Service v. *Chadna*, 113
Impeachment, 32-33
Impoundment, 10
Incrementalism, 22
Independent Executive Agencies, 155-158
Independent Regulatory Commissions, 149-155
Indochina War, 3, 4, 16, 36, 43, 67, 133
    hearings on, 59
Interest groups, 168-169
Interior, Department of, 36, 144, 147
Internal Revenue Service, 108, 131, 170
International agreements other than treaties:
    congressional-executive, 5-6
    number of, 8
    presidential negotiation of, 5-7
    pure executive, 7-8
Interstate Commerce Commission:
    development of, 149
    organization of, 150
    regulation as protection, 151, 154
    regulatory commissions as decision makers, 152
Iran hostage crisis, 4, 9
IRS, *see* Internal Revenue Service
Item veto, 13

Jackson, Andrew, 18, 24-25, 159
Jacob, Herbert, 135
Japanese-Americans, internment of, 11
Jay Treaty of 1794, 6
Jefferson, Thomas, 10, 12, 24-25, 36, 159
Johnson, Andrew, 24, 32-33, 54
Johnson, Lyndon, 20, 37, 54
    cabinet, 35, 144
    failures in presidential leadership, 43-44
    Fortas nomination, 124
    and J. Edgar Hoover, 148
    judicial appointments, 125
    as majority leader, 82
    reaction to Kerner Commission report, 42
    Supreme Court appointments by, 126, 127
    vetoes by, 54
    White House staff, use of, 38
Joint committees:
    economic, 83
    library, 83
    printing, 83
    taxation, 83
Joint resolution, 85
Jones, Walter, 74
Judicial courts, *see* Judiciary
Judicial philosophies:
    activism, 119
    loose constructionism, 120
    myth of the law, 129-130
    restraint, 119
    strict constructionism, 120
Judicial review, *see* Judiciary

Judiciary:
    administrative courts, 131–132
    admiralty and maritime cases, 130
    and bureaucracy, 167
    civil cases, 110
    criminal cases, 110
    interdependent with other branches, 105
    judges, 106, 122–125
    judicial courts, 105–108
    jurisdiction, 110–111
    leadership, 111–119
    operation, 130–134
    route of appeal, 107, 108
    school prayer cases, 109
    size, 109–110
    special judicial courts, 131
Judiciary Act of 1789, 106, 111
Justice, Department of, 35, 128, 139, 143, 144, 148

Kennedy, John, 3, 18, 24, 28, 29, 34, 126, 127
    cabinet, 36
    civil rights concerns, 148
    and FBI, 148
    National Security Council, use of, 40
    vetoes by, 54
    White House staff, use of, 34, 37
Kissinger, Henry, 38, 40
Koenig, Louis, 44
Korean War, 3, 11, 113
Kreps, Juanita, 147
Ku Klux Klan, 61

Labor, Department of, 36, 169, 170
LaFalce, John, 103
Lavelle, Rita, 158, 177
League of Nations, 5, 18
Legal Services Corporation, 55, 164, 166
Lesniak et al. v. United States et al., 135
Liberalism, 58
Liberty Lobby, 133
Liddy, G. Gordon, 84
Lincoln, Abraham, 2, 11, 14, 18
Lobbying Disclosure Act of 1946, 56
Long, Russell, 99
Lott, Trent, 68
Louis Harris poll, 95
Love Canal, 45, 97, 103, 173
LSC, *see* Legal Services Corporation
Lugar, Richard, 75
Luther v. Borden, 121

Madigan, Edward, 102
Madison, James, 111
Maher v. Roe, 116
Marbury, William, 111
Marbury v. Madison, 111
Marcy, William Learned, 159
Marshall, John, 53, 111, 112, 114
Marshall, Thomas, 32

Marshall, Thurgood, 126, 127, 128
Mathias, Charles, 75
McClure, James, 75
McCormack, John, 29
McCulloch v. Maryland, 53
McKinley, William, 28, 148
Medicare, 171
Meese, Edwin, 15, 147
Meier, Kenneth, 171
Mexican-American War, 3
Michel, Robert, 68, 70
Michigan v. Tucker, 116
Military-industrial complex, 169
Miranda v. Arizona, 115–116
Mitchell, Parren, 79
Moffett, Toby, 174
Mondale, Walter, 19, 24, 30–31
Monroe, James, 14
Monsanto Co., 101
Montgomery, G.V. (Sonny), 74
Moore, Curtis, 101
Motor Carrier Act of 1980, 152
Mueller, John, 20
Murphy, Paul, 151
Muskie, Edmund, 98, 100
Myers, Michael, 56
Myers v. United States, 42

NAACP, *see* National Association for the Advancement of Colored People
Nakamura, Robert, 172
Nathan, Robert, 172
National Aeronautics and Space Administration, 155–156, 171
National Association for the Advancement of Colored People, 127, 133
National Contingency Plan, 48–49, 137–138, 173–174
National Football League, 127
National Foundation on the Arts and Humanities, 156
Nationality Act of 1940, 122
National Labor Relations Board, 153, 170
National Priorities List, 156
National Response Team, 137
National Science Foundation, 156
National Security Act of 1947, 39
National Security Council, 39–40, 41
Navy, Department of the, 144
NCP, *see* National Contingency Plan
Near v. Minnesota, 115
Neustadt, Richard, 16, 44, 51
New Deal, 110, 112–113, 121
Nixon, Richard:
    cabinet, use of, 36, 147
    judicial appointments, 125
    National Security Council, use of, 40
    organizational style, 34
    pardoned by Ford, 15
    partial recognition of China, 9
    regulation as harrassment, use of, 153

Index 197

Nixon, Richard *(continued)*
  relations with bureaucracy, 164
  reorganization of OMB, 38
  resignation, 33, 55
  Secret Service, misuse of, 148-149
  Supreme Court appointments, 124, 126
  as treaty negotiator, 5
  and Watergate, 21, 83, 130, 148
  White House staff, use of, 34, 37
Nixon v. *Sirica,* 130
NLRB, *see* National Labor Relations Board
Northern Pipeline Construction Co. v. *Marathon Pipe Line Co.,* 113
NRC, *see* Nuclear Regulatory Commission
NRT, *see* National Response Team
NSC, *see* National Security Council
Nuclear Regulatory Commission, 153-154

O'Callahan v. *Parker,* 132
O'Connor, Sandra Day, 126-127, 128
OERR, *see* Office of Hazardous Emergency Response
Oestereich v. *Selective Service Board,* 117
Office of Administration, 41
Office of the Comptroller General, 166
Office of Drug Abuse Policy, 41
Office of Emergency and Remedial Response, *see* Office of Hazardous Emergency Response
Office of Hazardous Emergency Response:
  implementation of Superfund law, 173-176
  renamed Office of Emergency and Remedial Response, 174
Office of Management and Budget, 38-39, 41, 93, 165
  role in Superfund implementation, 48-49
Office of Policy Development, 41
Office of Science and Technology Policy, 41
Office of U.S. Trade Representative, 41
OHER, *see* Office of Hazardous Emergency Response
Oleszek, Walter, 94
Olney, Richard, 151
OMB, *see* Office of Management and Budget
O'Neill, Thomas (Tip), 65, 68, 69, 96, 102
Oppenheimer, Bruce, 94
Oregon v. *Hass,* 116
Oregon v. *Mitchell,* 112

Packwood, Bob, 75
PACs, *see* Political Action Committees
Page, Benjamin, 1, 44
Panama Canal Commission, 156
Panama Canal Treaty, 5, 44
Parker, Alan, 140
Pendleton Act, *see* Civil Service Reform Act of 1883
Pepper, Claude, 74
Perry, Robert, 174
Petracca, Mark, 44
Pierce, Samuel, 147
Pocket veto, 13
Poff, William, 77
Political Action Committees, 57

Political parties:
  decentralization of, 21
  lack of patronage jobs, 21
  nomination of presidential candidates, 25-26
  origin, 24-25
Polk, James, 6, 24
Pollock v. *Farmers Loan and Trust Co.,* 109
Pork barrel, 58
Powell, Lewis, 124, 126, 127, 128
Powell v. *Alabama,* 115
Pratt, John, 138
President:
  as administrator of domestic affairs, 12-15
  appointive policy-making positions, 160
  appointment of agency heads, 149
  appointments of Senate Executive Calendar, 88
  as chief executor, 9-11
  combined constitutional prerogatives, use of, 10-11
  as commander in chief, 1-3
  and Congress, 17-18
  Current Services Budget, submission of, 91
  as director of foreign relations, 4-9
  eligibility for office, 23-24
  evolution of role of chief legislator, 12-13
  as head of state, 15-16
  impeachment, 32-33
  impoundment, use of, 10
  institutionalization, 34
  item vetoes, 55
  media, use of, 18-19
  as moral leader, 20
  as party leader, 21
  persuasion, use of, 16-20
  pocket vetoes, 54
  political nature of power, 21-23
  popularity, 18-20
  power to appoint ambassadors, 8-9
  power to appoint bureaucrats, 14-15
  power to convene and adjourn Congress, 12
  power to grant pardons, 15-16
  power to make the State of the Union address, 12
  power to negotiate international agreements, 5-8
  power to nominate judges, 13-14
  power to receive ambassadors, 9
  power to run the bureaucracy, 14
  power to veto bills, 13
  press conferences, 19
  prestige of office, 20-21
  as problem solver, 20, 21, 22
  reelection chances and leadership, 19-20
  relations with the bureaucracy, 163-165
  role in budgetary process, 91-92
  selection, 24-27
  succession, 28-29
  terms of office, 28
Price, Melvin, 76
Private Calendar, 87, 88

Randolph, Jennings, 100, 102

Index

Rayburn, Sam, 73
Reagan, Ronald:
  and air traffic controllers' strike, 152
  ambassodorial appointments policy, 8-9
  cabinet, 36, 146-148
  CIA, weakening controls on, 40
  elections, 19, 21, 27, 30-31
  environmental policies, 174-175, 177
  EOP, organization of, 41, 42
  impact on Superfund law passage, 100-102, 104
  implementation of Superfund law, 48-49, 173-177
  judicial philosophy and appointments, 119-120, 126
  legislative successes, 22-23
  military spending, support of, 4
  National Security Advisor, use of, 40
  organizational style, 34-35
  pardoning of FBI burglars, 16
  reconciliation, use of, 92
  strengthening of OMB, 39
  Supreme Court appointment by, 126, 128
  trucking regulations, support of, 152
  veto threat, use of, 55
  White House staff, use of, 37-38
Reciprocal Trade Agreement Act, 6
Reconciliation, 92
Reed, Thomas, 68
Reedy, George, 35
Regan, Donald, 148
Regulatory commissions, 152-154
Rehnquist, William, 126-128
Reorganization Act of 1939, 36
Reorganization Plan of 1953, 39
Republican National Convention, 103
Reynolds v. *Sims,* 115, 122
Rhodes, John, 70
Roberts, Owen, 110
Rockefeller, Nelson, 29
Rodino, Peter, 74
Roe v. *Wade,* 116
Romney, George, 23
Roosevelt, Franklin:
  breaking two-term tradition, 28
  Bureau of the Budget, control over, 38
  cabinet turnover, 147
  court-packing effort, 22, 110, 112
  Democratic party, rejuvenation of, 21
  fireside chats, 19
  Japanese-Americans, internment of, 11
  organizational style, 34
  vetoes by, 54
Roosevelt, Theodore, 12, 19, 144
Rostenkowski, Dan, 74
Rostow, Walter, 38
Roth, William, 75
Ruckelshaus, William, 158, 177

Saint Lawrence Seaway Development Corporation, 158
Santini, Jim, 97
Schattschneider, E., 168

Schultz, George, 147
Scott, William, 77
SEC, *see* Securities and Exchange Commission
Second Bank of the United States, 18
Second Budget Resolution, 92
Secret Service, 148
Securities and Exchange Commission, 153-154
Seidman, Harold, 169, 172
Selective Service Act, 16, 117, 118
Senate:
  apportionment, 62-63
  bills limiting courts' jurisdiction, 109
  calendars, 87-88
  cloture votes, 89
  committees, 80-83
  confirmation of appointments, 14-15, 122-125, 131, 148
  discharge motions, 86-87
  filibusters, 89
  floor procedures, 89
  as jury in impeachment trials, 55
  president, 70
  president pro tempore, 28, 32, 70-71
  reception of electoral votes, 24
  reforms of 1970s, 72
  senatorial courtesy, 77, 122-123
  subcommittees, 80
  tenure of members, 64
  treaty approval, 5
  voting procedures, 89
  Watergate committee, establishment of, 33
Senate committees:
  Agriculture, Nutrition, and Forestry, 75
  Appropriations, 75, 80
  Armed Services, 59, 80
  Banking, Housing, and Urban Affairs, 75
  Budget, 75, 92
  Commerce, Science, and Transportation, 75
    consideration of Superfund bill, 98, 101
  Democratic Policy, 72
  Democratic Steering, 72, 82
  Energy and Natural Resources, 75
  Environment and Public Works, 75, 103
    consideration of Superfund bill, 98, 99-100
  Finance, 75, 78, 80, 99, 101
  Foreign Relations, 5, 59, 75, 82
  Governmental Affairs, 75
  Judiciary, 75, 79, 123
  Labor and Human Resources, 75
  Republican Committee on Committees, 71, 82
  Republican Policy, 71
  Rules and Administration, 75, 80
  Select Committee on Presidential Campaign Activities, 83
  Select Small Business, 83
  Veterans Affairs, 75, 82
Senate majority leader, 71, 87
Senate minority leader, 71, 82, 87
Senate whips, 71-72
Senior Executive Service, 165
SES, *see* Senior Executive Service

Shell Oil Co., 99
Shepherd, Frank, 174
Simple resolution, 85
Simpson, Alan, 68, 72
Sirica, John, 33, 130
Sixteenth Amendment, 109
Small Business Administration, 156
Smallwood, Frank, 172
Smith, James, 151
Smith, Steven, 94
Smithsonian Institution, 156
Social Security Administration, 78, 171
Sorenson, Theodore, 34
Spanish-American War, 3
Special Assistant for National Security Affairs, 37-38
Spoils system, *see* Bureaucracy
Stafford, Robert, 75, 100, 101
Stalwart, 159-160
Stanford Law School, 128
Stanton, Edwin, 32
State, Department of, 5, 15, 28-29, 35, 142-143, 144
State of the Union address, *see* President
Stevens, John Paul, 126, 128
Stevens, Ted, 72
St. Germain, Fernand, 74
Stockman, David, 39
Strauss, Lewis, 15
Strict constructionism, *see* Judicial philosophies
Succession Act of 1947, 29
Succession Act of 1792, 28
Superfund law:
    congressional efforts at influencing implementation through publicity, 166
    development at EPA, 172-174
    disputes over committee jurisdiction, 95
    House floor debate, 97
    initial Carter proposals, 45-48
    lack of challenge to constitutionality, 135
    liability provisions, 139-140
    lobbying, 96-99
    public opinion on hazardous waste, 94-95
    Senate floor action, 100-103
Supremacy clause, *see* Constitution
Supreme Court:
    abortion issue, 116
    amicus curiae briefs, 133
    appellate jurisdiction, 108-109, 132
    appointment of judges, 123-124
    apportionment decisions, 115, 121-122
    authorized in Constitution, 106-107
    caseload, 130
    conservative bloc, 127-128
    disallowal of steel seizure, 11
    Friday conference, 126, 133-134
    impeachment threat, 108
    income tax case, 109
    interpretation of laws, 117
    issue creation and clarification, 118
    liberal bloc, 126-127

Supreme Court *(continued)*
    limitations and leadership potential, 134
    noncompliance with decisions, 118-119
    order to Nixon to surrender tapes, 33
    original jurisdiction, 108-109
    oversight function, 118
    as policy maker, 118-119
    political nature of decisions, 128-130
    political question doctrine, 121-122
    prestige, 110
    procedures, 132-134
    recess appointments, 126-127
    representation function, 117-118
    role of chief justice, 126
    selection of cases, 133
    size, 109-110
    voting order, 133-134
    writ of certiorari, 133

Taft Court, 121
Taney, Roger, 121
Teamsters Union, 152
Tennessee Valley Authority, 158
Tenth Amendment, 6, 120
Tenure of Office Act of 1867, 32, 42
Thomas, Lee, 177
Thurmond, Strom, 68, 71, 75
Train v. City of New York, 113
Transportation, Department of, 17, 35, 145, 147, 154
Treasury, Department of the, 17, 35, 144, 145, 148
Treaties, 5-8
    on Senate Executive Calendar, 88
Treaty of Versailles, 5
Truman, Harry, 10, 11, 28
    impoundment of funds, 10
    seizure of steel mills, 11, 113
Turner, David, 160
TVA, *see* Tennessee Valley Authority
Twentieth Amendment, 12
Twenty-fifth Amendment, 28, 29
Twenty-second Amendment, 28
Twenty-sixth Amendment, 109
Tyler, John, 6, 24, 28

Udall, Morris, 74
Ullman, Al, 96
Uniform Code of Military Justice, 132
Union Calendar, 87, 88
United Parcel Service, 158
United States Air Force, 144
United States Attorneys, 131
United States Government Manual, 143
United States Postal Act of 1971, 161
United States Postal Service, 155, 158, 161, 170
United States Treasury, 166
United States v. Darby, 52
United States v. Mitchell et al., 130
United States v. Tempia, 132

VA, *see* Veterans Administration
Vance, Cyrus, 38
Veterans Administration, 67, 155–156, 161, 168
Veterans of Foreign Wars, 157
Vice-President:
  authority, 29–31
  office in the EOP, 41
  role, 29–31
  selection by presidential candidate, 29
  succession to presidency, 29, 32–33
Vietnam War, *see* Indochina War
Vogler, David, 94
Voting Rights Act of 1965, 59, 89

Wabash, St. Louis, and Pacific Railroad v. *Illinois*, 151
Wallace, George, 26, 171
War, Department of, 144
War Powers Act, 4
Warren, Earl, 111, 122, 124
Warren Court, 112, 118–119, 127
Washington, George, 2, 4, 12
  cabinet appointments, 144
  vetoes, 53–54
Watergate, 21, 33, 124, 148, 149
  FBI improprieties, 148

Watergate *(continued)*
  role in Nixon's resignation, 33
  tapes, 124, 130
Waterside Mall, 176
Weber, Max, 142
Weberian model, 142–143, 148, 164
Webster, Daniel, 51
Webster, William, 148
Weinberger, Caspar, 147
Welsh v. *United States*, 117
Wentworth, Marchant (Lucky), 97
Whiskey Rebellion, 2
White, Byron, 126, 127
Whitehead, Clay, 153
White House Office, 37–38
White House Office of Telecommunications Policy, 153
Whitten, Jamie, 74
Wilson, James, 172
Wilson, Woodrow, 5, 11, 12, 18, 24, 31–32
Wood v. *Ohio*, 116
World War I, 11
World War II, 3, 9, 11, 44, 69, 127, 144
Wright, Jim, 68, 69

Youngstown Sheet and Tube Company v. *Sawyer*, 11, 113